Library of
Davidson College

Representation Rights and the Burger Years

Representation Rights
and
the Burger Years

Nancy Maveety

Ann Arbor
THE UNIVERSITY OF MICHIGAN PRESS

Copyright © by the University of Michigan 1991
All rights reserved
Published in the United States of America by
The University of Michigan Press
Manufactured in the United States of America

1994 1993 1992 1991   4 3 2 1

Distributed in the United Kingdom and Europe by
Manchester University Press, Oxford Road,
Manchester M13 9PL, UK

Library of Congress Cataloging-in-Publication Data

Maveety, Nancy.
    Representation rights and the Burger years / Nancy Maveety.
        p.   cm.
    Based on the author's thesis. Johns Hopkins University.
    Includes bibliographical references (p.) and index.
    ISBN 0-472-10227-3
    1. Apportionment (Election law)—United States. 2. Representative government and representation—United States. 3. United States. Supreme Court. 4. Burger, Warren, 1907–   . I. Title.
KF4905.M28   1991
342.73'07—dc20
[347.3027]   91-616
                                                                          CIP

British Library Cataloguing in Publication Data
Maveety, Nancy
    Representation rights and the Burger years.
    1. United States. Representation
    I. Title
    323.50973

    ISBN 0-472-10227-3

*For my father Donald
and my grandmother Theodosia*

Preface

My study of the U.S. Supreme Court's contemporary representation policy began as a doctoral thesis at the Johns Hopkins University. Fortuitously, the Burger years came to an end just as I completed my dissertation on the Burger Court's jurisprudence of political representation. Yet, somewhat disconcertingly, the first retrospective studies of the work of the Burger Court were fairly dismissive of its contributions. The Burger years were branded "rootlessly activist" and "directionless and confused"—clearly not a period of enduring jurisprudential significance. Indeed, the Burger era seemed quickly forgotten, sandwiched as it was between the liberal activism of the Warren Court and the conservative interventionism of the Rehnquist Court. If the Burger years had meant anything to constitutional law, it seemed to be only in terms of their uniquely indistinctive impact.

I began to despair that any documentation of the substantive contributions of the Burger Court would be dismissed as fanciful. However, because I was confident that the Court's work in the area of representation rights was distinctive and had been influential, I undertook the tortuous process of converting a Ph.D. thesis into a respectable book manuscript. Along the way, I profited greatly from the advice and critical commentary of certain "gerrymandering junkies"—especially Dan Lowenstein of the UCLA School of Law, who was a thoughtful and careful reader of the manuscript. In addition, I received valuable encouragement and support from my Ph.D. supervisor, Woody Howard, and my colleagues in political science at Tulane University. The final product is, of course, my responsibility.

Whatever its limitations, the study does communicate one important point: the constitutional discussions of representation rights occurring today are the direct result of developments initiated by the Burger Court. Specifically, the Burger Court's *group-balancing ap-*

proach to representation questions precipitated an ever-expanding judicial role of scrutinizing political institutions and processes, as well as inaugurated the concept of aggregate political rights in constitutional law. Thus, the Burger years were far from unimportant, at least in the area of political representation law.

Why, then, has this judicial era been largely ignored by many scholars? Clearly, the Burger Court lacked the drama of the Warren Courts or the tension of the emergent Rehnquist Court. The Burger Court's work was often typified by the introduction of "balancing tests" to govern individual rights questions. Balancing usually implied compromise between sets of group interests and accommodation between political viewpoints. Indeed, the Burger Court was a quintessentially pluralist court. As such, both its jurisprudential record and its institutional personality were subtle and understated. Yet, despite its self-effacing juridical presence, the Burger Court's balancing doctrines continue to inform current constitutional adjudication. This is nowhere more true than in the area of representation rights.

Representation is itself a perplexing issue in constitutional law. Until 1962, many issues of electoral participation were constitutionally off limits because of the Court's "political question doctrine." When the Warren Court finally began to scrutinize participation opportunities as equal protection and First Amendment issues, it announced that the Constitution's objective was, among other things, a system of "fair and effective representation." Yet the implications of this requirement were not fully understood until the Burger years. During the Burger era, the constitutional definition of "political representation" and the scope of actionable political access problems were substantially broadened. Because of these developments, representation rights are now more group-oriented and more concerned with the actual processes of effective political action. This legacy— even if ultimately repudiated—necessarily influences both the work of the Burger Court's successors and the polity's dialogue about meaningful representation and political equality.

It is perhaps unusual for an author to acknowledge indebtedness to particular scholarly works, but my own examination of representation rights during the Burger years was inspired by two works that deserve recognition. Although reflecting somewhat different political positions and disciplinary approaches, both Hanna Pitkin's *Concept of Representation* and Ward Elliott's *Rise of Guardian Democracy* enabled me to appreciate that constitutional questions are very much issues of democratic theory. While the latter seems a fairly pedestrian insight, it is sometimes forgotten by both scholars of judicial policymaking and specialists in representation law. A synthesis between the objectives of legal analysis, political theory, and political science is what I hope this study accomplishes; to the extent that it does, I am indebted to Colin Day, director of the University of Michigan Press, to Paul Betz, and to an anonymous reader.

Contents

Chapter

1. Supreme Court Endorsement of
   Group Representation 1

2. Malapportionment and Representation 19

3. The "Talisman" of Geography 39

4. Acres, Dollars, and Votes 69

5. Demographic Districting and Compensatory
   Majoritarianism 97

6. The Dualistic Conception of Partisan Representation ... 147

7. Administrative and Litigational Representation 189

8. Group Rights: Political Vigilance and
   Political Conflict 221

Appendixes

A. Table of Justices, the Warren and Burger Courts 233

B. Table of Cases, Listed Chronologically 235

Bibliography 241

Index 253

CHAPTER 1

Supreme Court Endorsement of Group Representation

For the past twenty-five years the U.S. Supreme Court has been struggling to provide a constitutional definition for political representation. For almost as long, legal commentators have been struggling to interpret the meaning and implications of the Court's decisions. Although the Warren Court's famous pronouncement of "one person, one vote" is part of our political vocabulary, its parallel goal of "fair and effective representation" remains more elusive. The numerically equal vote standard, announced in *Reynolds v. Sims* in 1964, was a radical reformulation of the American conception of *individual* political equality. But fair and effective representation was an even more dramatic assertion in that it called into question the constitutional foundation of political rights: it was a concept that, in the words of the Warren Court's successor, "necessarily applies to *groups*; [for] groups of voters elect representatives, individual voters do not."[1]

This question of group rights versus individual rights haunts the constitutional definition of political representation and threatens to dominate future post census electoral redistricting. Yet the question of "the focus of representation"—whether the need is to represent individual or group interests, localities, or the whole nation—is not new to the debate about representative institutions.[2] The Warren Court's "reapportionment revolution" merely initiated the constitutional version of a long-standing historical and theoretical discussion about representative government.

The Warren Court left a doctrinal legacy of support for both indi-

---

1. Davis v. Bandemer, 106 S. Ct. 2797, 2828 (1986) (Powell, J., dissenting in part) (emphasis added).
2. A. H. Birch, Representation 109 (1971); J. Wahlke, H. Eulau, et al., Legislative Behavior 270–72 (1962).

vidual voting rights and group political access,[3] which continues to complicate contemporary representation law. Given this legacy, how should the doctrinal record of the Burger years be evaluated: as simply that of a caretaker preserving the policies of its predecessor, or as that of an innovator transforming constitutional law on political representation? It is tempting to label the Burger years an atheoretical judicial interregnum between the progressive activism of the Warren Court and the emergent neoconservatism of the "Reaganized" Rehnquist Court.[4] Yet this characterization downplays the significance of the Burger Court's consideration of many new representation issues that required a balancing of plural interests.

The immediate political problems of the early 1960s compelled the Warren Court to concentrate on the reestablishment of majority rule in severely malapportioned legislatures. With the Burger Court's tenure, however, the questions regarding both districting and political access became increasingly more complex. In broadening the definition of activities involving the exercise of representation rights, the Burger Court adopted an overt group-balancing approach to questions of political representation. The complexities in the new questions about representation rights made the apparent absence of any underlying theory of representation seem an even more glaring omission. Indeed, the Burger Court and its commentators largely remained silent about the constitutional vision of representation implied by the Court's decisions.[5] Because of its imperspicuity, the doctrinal legacy of the Burger years has been branded insignificant.

Some scholars blame the theoretical paucity of recent decisions and

---

3. This is further illustrated by the fact that, in several decisions predating the reapportionment revolution, the Warren Court read the First Amendment freedom of association as protecting the collective political activities of groups. See Hadnott v. Amos, 394 U.S. 358 (1969); NAACP v. Alabama, 357 U.S. 449 (1958); Sweezy v. New Hampshire, 354 U.S. 234 (1957).

4. For two views of how President Reagan altered the ideological composition of the federal courts, see Goldman, Reaganizing the Judiciary: The First Term Appointments, 68 Judicature 313 (1985); Gottschall, Reagan's Appointments to the U.S. Courts of Appeal: The Continuation of a Judicial Revolution, 70 Judicature 50 (1986).

For a recent and representative discussion of the "nondevelopment of a distinctive Burger Court," see Kobylka, Leadership on the Supreme Court of the U.S.: Chief Justice Burger and the Establishment Clause, 42 W. Pol. Q. 545 (1989).

5. A recent exception to the unfortunate lack of theoretical commentary is Charles Beitz, Equal Opportunity in Political Representation, in Equal Opportunity (N. Bowie ed. 1988).

commentary on the early reapportionment decisions themselves. Indeed, one consequence of the Supreme Court's initial focus on electoral districting and "equally weighted votes" was the judicial and scholarly absorption in the technical criteria for districting—leaving the theory of popular government and democratic representation underlying the one person, one vote standard unexplained. Thus, the initial rhetoric of one person, one vote "diverted attention from the question of what constitutional objective it was designed to achieve."[6] It often seemed that for the purpose of justifying its one person, one vote doctrine, the Warren Court persuaded itself that the American system of government was organized on a populist principle.[7] Yet the efficacy and legitimacy of the one person, one vote standard for aggregating individual voter preferences hinged on whether voters saw themselves as autonomous individuals or as members of political groups.[8] Difficulties with the individual participation focus of one person, one vote inevitably arose when the Supreme Court began to consider the substantive—as opposed to the numerical—political influence of individuals. Clearly, the Court's original fixation on numerically equal votes misidentified the rights at stake for substantive political influence: the language of individual rights could not address either "fair and effective representation" or political competition in a pluralist system, because both concern group political action.[9]

In contrast, the Burger Court was reluctant to apply a nineteenth-century conception of atomistic liberalism to twentieth-century problems of group-biased gerrymanders.[10] Arguably, the Burger Court viewed representation in terms of a balancing of group interests; certainly, its decisions shifted the determination of that balance from state legislative institutions to the federal judiciary. "Popular control" was itself increasingly defined in terms of group political access. Yet it would be rash to conclude from these preliminary observations that the Burger Court made a definitive contribution to representation

---

6. Alfange, Gerrymandering and the Constitution: Into the Thorns of the Political Thicket at Last, 1986 Sup. Ct. Rev. 175, 177.

7. A. Bickel, The Supreme Court and the Idea of Progress 83 (1970).

8. Cain, Perspectives on *Davis v. Bandemer,* in Toward Fair and Effective Representation: Political Gerrymandering and the Courts (B. Grofman ed. 1990).

9. See Alfange, Gerrymandering and the Constitution, 1986 Sup. Ct. Rev. 175, 181.

10. Shapiro, Gerrymandering, Unfairness and the Supreme Court, 33 U.C.L.A. L. Rev. 227, 232 (1985).

law, for such a contribution depends on the articulation of a coherent theory of political representation.

The purpose of this study is to examine the Supreme Court's distinctive vision of political representation during the Burger years and to assess the impact of this vision on the contemporary debate about the representation of interests. The fifteen-odd years of Burger Court decisions appear to have shifted the emphasis of the debate from individual participation to the political access of group interests. The legacy of the Burger years, then, has been a broader constitutional discussion of the functions of representation. Popular control of governmental decision making is a critical function of representation and, arguably, was the key focus of the one person, one vote doctrine. Yet with judicial concern for group political access came attention to other important functions of representation: responsibility and recruitment of political leaders, legitimation and mobilization of consent, and relief of pressure by aggrieved citizens.[11] Thus, the Burger years were not a mere interregnum, but rather a time of unique and substantial contribution to modern representation law.

Before we can examine the nature of that contribution, we must address a preliminary question: can ideological coherence be attributed to the decisions of the series of eight justices whose service coincided with Chief Justice Burger's tenure from 1969 to 1986? Many political scientists who study political change in the Court employ the concept of "natural courts" to describe ideological coherence. Natural courts are the collegial bodies that exist with the appointments of new justices; their presence facilitates the identification of cohesive ideological voting blocs over the course of a chief justice's tenure.[12] This approach allows for greater precision in analyzing collective judicial behavior, but it is less helpful in summarizing the collective doctrinal legacy a Court leaves to its successor. The labels "Warren Court" and "Burger Court" do have meaning in common political parlance, and thus judicial scholars should attempt to assign doctrinal epitaphs to these entities. Unfortunately, judge-made representation policy does not necessarily fall within convenient temporal categories. While many important, formative decisions were made

---

11. A. H. Birch, Representation 107–8 (1971).
12. For an example of a study using such a methodological device, see Baum, Comparing the Policy Positions of Supreme Court Justices from Different Periods, 42 W. Pol. Q. 509 (1989).

by the Burger Court, an analysis of contemporary representation policy cannot be limited to that Court's tenure. Moreover, the purpose of this study is not to divine the true message of the Burger Court, as attributing hidden agendas to groups of justices risks misconstruing the judicial process. Given these methodological considerations, my compromise approach is to speak about the "Burger years," a categorization that stresses the doctrinal importance of a particular period on the Supreme Court without artificially confining the scope of analysis.

Even assuming the jurisprudential significance of the "Burger years," questions still remain about the utility and validity of characterizing this period as one of group-based policies of representation rights. Clearly, there is descriptive value to a study that documents a group theory of representation that left a lasting imprint on constitutional law. In addition, such an analysis of representation law lays the theoretical groundwork for empirical analysis of the actual functions performed by our representative institutions. Further, investigation of the jurisprudential contributions made during the Burger years facilitates judicial impact studies of intercourt communication of constitutional doctrine.

Of course, to be empirically useful, a study characterizing a particular judicial legacy must have presumptive validity; it cannot simply attribute a normative agenda to the judicial decision makers. Without trying to second-guess the Burger justices, one can still surmise that judge-made doctrines of political rights are necessarily influenced by prevailing conceptions of representative government.[13] Therefore, the validity of the claim that the Burger years occasioned a distinctive group approach to representation depends on the plausibility of the conceptual framework used to describe these theories of representation.

As a discipline, political science offers some fairly rigorous definitions of representation, which are useful to review at the outset of our examination of the Court's work on representation rights. While political scientists disagree about whether one can identify the actual nature of representation, most would concur that representation is a matter of both "standing for" and "acting for." The former usage,

---

13. Michaelman, Political Markets and Community Self-Determination, 53 Ind. L.J. 145, 147–48 (1977–78).

which we could term "descriptive" or "microcosmic" representation, indicates that a representative shares or typifies the characteristics of a larger class of persons. To be a representative in this sense, however, does not tell us anything about the individual's functions, intentions, or behavior.[14] The second usage of the concept relates more directly to the question of the representative's behavior or action. This view of representation, which we could term "substantive" or "delegated," designates a person who has an acknowledged duty to advance certain interests specified by his or her principal. The representative need not mirror the characteristics of the principal but is expected to be responsive to the latter's authorized instructions.

Because of its concern with accountable action, representation as "acting for" introduces what is called the mandate-independence controversy—the question of how closely a representative will be held to the instructions and preferences of his or her constituents.[15] This question arises in most contexts in which electoral representation is at issue, and tends to be complicated by the differences between representing a single or homogeneous principal and representing a large, diverse political constituency.[16] Indeed, representation as "acting for" reintroduces the problem of which interests are the focus of representation—specifically, whether the selection and retention of a representative are primarily a function of group pressures or individuals' input.

In an effort to address both the accountability and focus-of-interest problems inherent in modern elective representation, some political theorists posit that only the relation between electors and their political party has real political importance.[17] While the American experience has not been one of tightly disciplined and popularly responsive parties, electoral representation based on the party mechanism nevertheless entails a linkage between public opinion, partisan

---

14. A. H. Birch, Representation 15–16 (1971); H. Pitkin, The Concept of Representation 60–61 (1967); Diggs, Practical Representation, 10 NOMOS 28, 29–30 (1968).

15. A. H. Birch, Representation 15–16 (1971); H. Pitkin, The Concept of Representation 118ff. (1967); Pitkin, Commentary: The Paradox of Representation, 10 NOMOS 38, 39–40 (1968).

16. H. Pitkin, The Concept of Representation 145 (1967); Pennock, Political Representation: An Overview, 10 NOMOS 3, 15–16, 21–23 (1968).

17. Sobolewski, Electors and Representatives: A Contribution to the Theory of Representation, 10 NOMOS 95, 98–99 (1968).

affiliation, and electoral behavior.[18] In analyzing voting behavior and electoral representation, empirical political science has focused on the interaction between party preference and attitudes on political issues, while disciplines such as electoral geography have been more interested in the influence of spatial factors on interest cleavages and political behavior patterns.[19] For both groups of social scientists, however, electoral representation is a process whose outcome is the allocation of political power, or control over political decision making. From this perspective, representation rights concern the value of votes (or participatory actions generally) in terms of the power that they exert.[20]

It is evident that the American concept of representation—indeed, the concept generally—partakes of all of the above connotations.[21] If we reflect on the means through which representation has been effected in our political system (districting, parties, bureaucratic agencies) and the diverse and conflicting interests to be represented in society (racial groups, economic classes, ideological special interests), the inadequacy of the one person, one vote formula in accounting for such complex political phenomena is readily apparent. Clearly, a conceptual framework for describing the phenomenon of representation and for analyzing the constitutional law of representation must take into account both the theoretical and social complexity of the concept.

The articulation of a framework for understanding the concept's operative meaning within the American political context is the starting point for my evaluation of the representation policy associated with the Burger years. To test whether a coherent theory of group representation now influences Supreme Court policy-making, this

---

18. Sobolewski, Electors and Representatives, 10 NOMOS 95, 100–101 (1968); Stokes, Political Parties in the Normative Theory of Representation, 10 NOMOS 150, 152 (1968).

19. See, e.g., M. A. Busteed, Geography and Voting Behavior 40ff. (1975); A. Campbell, P. Converse, et al., The American Voter (1960); S. Kamieniecki, Party Identification, Political Behavior and the American Electorate (1985); P. J. Taylor and R. J. Johnston, The Geography of Elections 107ff. (1979); Miller, Party Preference and Attitudes on Political Issues, Am. Pol. Sci. Rev. 50 (1953); Schaffer, Partisan Loyalty and the Perceptions of Party, Candidates and Issues, 25 W. Pol. Q. 424 (1972).

20. P. J. Taylor and R. J. Johnston, The Geography of Elections 437, 458 (1979).

21. See A. H. Birch, Representation 124–25 (1971); Nordlinger, Representation, Stability and Decisional Effectiveness, 10 NOMOS 108, 110–11 (1968).

study presents five conceptual types of group representation that reflect enduring conceptions of political action. This typology of representation incorporates the definitions of the concept that were discussed above, while implicitly recognizing that institutional forms of representation are never pure manifestions of theoretical models of representation. Because it is a heuristic typology, I attempt to synthesize these theoretical interpretations of the concept with historical and legal examples of interest representation. The study's basic theoretical assumption is that judicial policy-making on representation rights is a product of the surrounding political context, and that such policy-making is best understood through consideration of the various American paradigms of group political action.

Studies of judicial politics have not tended to contain an explicitly identified, empirically based framework of analysis.[22] Legal doctrinal studies, as well as more quantitative forms of judicial data analysis, are each guilty of avoidance of theory—both a theory of their method of analysis and a theory of the judicial process itself. In the social sciences, the term "theory" is traditionally defined as a set of related propositions that attempt to explain or, sometimes, to predict a set of events. While a theory can be a systematic collection of hypotheses about relations among variables, the term usually connotes a degree of uncertainty about the validity of the understanding it offers; thus, a theory is best conceived as a guide to inquiry and as a way of organizing insights so as to isolate the significant.[23] A study's theoretical framework is frequently related to its research design. The latter defines the "domain of generalizability" of the study, that is, whether its findings and interpretations can be generalized to different situations. For a study whose primary objective is descriptive, this generalizability is a matter of how closely the theoretical framework links its conceptual categories with observed phenomena.

By presenting a heuristic taxonomy of group representation, this study supplies a theoretical framework for appreciating the coherence of constitutional doctrines of representation rights fashioned during the Burger years. The taxonomical classification relies on content analysis and data reduction of cases, rather than quantitative

---

22. Hensley and Rhoads, Studying the Studies: An Assessment of Judicial Politics Research in Four Major Political Science Journals: 1960–1987 (paper presented to the Southern Political Science Association, Atlanta, Ga.) (Nov. 3–5, 1988).

23. K. Hoover, The Elements of Social Scientific Thinking 27–28, 66–67 (1988).

or aggregated data analysis. Nor is it a pure doctrinal study of case law, for the typology's categories and method for measuring the case law's consistency with those categories attempt to systematically document a distinct and coherent approach to representation policy. To a certain extent, the study blends the objectives of hypothesis testing in social science research with the more descriptive focus characteristic of legal analysis of individual decisions. My approach perhaps is best summarized by an observation made in a recent judicial politics article:

> A more complete understanding of [legal] dynamics can be facilitated by combining analysis of empirical data with careful inferences from sources too long slighted by students of the judicial process—opinions and doctrinal development.[24]

A central theoretical assumption of the study concerns the process of conceptual change. When I argue that the constitutional understanding of representation underwent a change during the Burger years, I mean to suggest that the process of change was largely intellectual. While concepts may mirror the social or political world, their identity is not simply a reflection of changing social conditions or political circumstances (on or off the Court). Neither is a change in a court's own perception of its role a simple reflection of external conditions. Although the model of judicial behavior known as "political jurisprudence"[25] has plausibility for policy analysis, it cannot justifiably assert that change in any particular concept *must* result from change in something outside itself. As instruments of the legal system, courts need reflect only part of the social world—even if it is only a diminishing part.[26] Therefore, the judicial role in fashioning and/or revising the meaning of legal concepts may only be one part of a wider hermeneutic dialogue. Thus, my methodology is to examine the constitutional understanding of political representation using a

---

24. Koblyka, Leadership on the Supreme Court of the U.S., 42 W. Pol. Q. 545, 564 (1989).
25. See, e.g., M. Shapiro, Law and Politics in the Supreme Court (1964). The theory of political jurisprudence assumes that courts should be studied as policymakers and that judicial decisions should be analyzed as the products of political interaction and special interest bargaining.
26. The preceding discussion draws heavily from J. Vining, Legal Identity 49–50 (1978).

theoretical framework that, admittedly, may provide only a partial account of this interpretative process.

The study relies on the construction of "ideal types" of group representation, and then compares these types with the policies actually endorsed in the Burger decisions. To be heuristically useful, a taxonomy of political representation must reflect the ways that citizens—as well as judges—experience, interpret, or perceive political life.[27] Thus, our taxonomy of representation must be both analytically plausible and historically valid; it should reflect some consensus between the discipline of political science and the discourse of democratic theory about the central ways of thinking about the concept of representation. The taxonomy should also be appropriate to the subject matter actually considered by the Supreme Court. For example, the symbolic representation of a nation by its monarch is certainly an important historical form of representation, but it would hardly provide a useful model for describing and assessing any of the Court's decisions. Thus, a heuristic typology of representation policy during the Burger years should embrace the theories of representation both prominent in American history and political thought and relevant to the institutions and procedures affected by judicial scrutiny since the reapportionment revolution.

From consideration of these sources, I have inferred five conceptualizations of political representation that provide theoretical foundations for the Court's decisions. Each conceptualization of group representation refers to a category within a taxonomy, or classification. My objective is to operationalize this taxonomy by using each of its types to assess the extent of the Court's reliance on a group-oriented concept of representation. For purposes of convenience and consistency, I shall hereafter refer to each interchangeably as *conceptual types* or *conceptualizations* of group representation.[28] I emphasize that these conceptual types are not derived from the decisions themselves; the objective of this study is not to divine secret meanings in opinions, were such divination even possible. Certainly, it would be presumptuous to claim that judicial decision making was consciously

---

27. Michaelman, Political Markets and Community Self-Determination, 53 Ind. L.J. 145, 150 (1977–78).

28. On the operational definition of concepts in political science research, see J. Johnson and R. Josyln, Political Science Research Methods 60–61 (1986).

influenced by a particular paradigm of representation because judges, rather than imposing a theoretical agenda, more often work incrementally toward doctrines. In any event, such a claim would be difficult to verify without consulting judicial papers, letters, and other private (and often inaccessible) documents. Since my objective is more modest—to demonstrate the significance and lasting import of the representation policies of the Burger years—the purpose of the typology is to illustrate that the post-Warren Court's constitutional jurisprudence of political representation is more closely tied to the realities of modern pluralism.

The typology of collective access will be used to taxonomically classify the Court's body of decisions on representation, as well as to evaluate the policies implicit in the case outcomes. The goal of this method of analysis is to (1) evaluate the degree to which the Court's decisions conform to theoretical and historical conceptions of group representation, and (2) assess the coherence of contemporary representation law by analyzing the interplay of these conceptual types in the Court's decisions. Thus, the study will allow us to project the precedential impact of the Burger Court's decisions.

Before examining the state of current judicial representation policies, the decisions of the Warren and Burger Courts must first be compared and contrasted. Specifically, I must verify my earlier, impressionistic account of the doctrinal differences between the Courts, that is, that the early reapportionment cases focused on individual participation rights to the neglect of group factors in political representation. Accordingly, the first task of this study is to demonstrate that representation policy moved from an individualistic to a group-based doctrine of representation rights, and that this movement coincided with the transition from the Warren to the Burger Court.

Chapter 2 will illustrate that the Warren Court cases concerning malapportionment revived a historical debate in American politics between population-based apportionment and more corporatist, group-based notions. Essentially, the problems of articulating the one person, one vote rule were similar to the problems dividing the large and small states at the constitutional convention: how much attention should be paid to group entities in the apportionment of legislative representatives? The doctrinal differences between the Warren and Burger Courts can be viewed analytically as manifestations of this larger tension in the history of American political representation;

therefore, it is plausible to use an exogenous typology of representation to help explain recent representation decisions.

After verifying that attention to group factors was present in certain Burger Court representation decisions, I then present, in subsequent chapters, the five operative conceptualizations of group representation that test the decisions' theoretical coherence. After the origin and contemporary importance of each conceptualization is presented, case data relevant to these conceptualizations are reviewed. Cases are relevant to a particular conceptualization when they address the specific subject matter or set of questions that it describes. Subsequent chapters will evaluate Court decisions in terms of their (1) consistency with a conceptualization, (2) confirmation of a conceptualization, (3) contradiction of a conceptualization, or (4) irrelevance to a conceptualization. For a decision to confirm a conceptualization, it must reach a certain result or articulate a particular policy; thus, it is possible for a case to address the subject matter of a conceptual type without necessarily endorsing that conception of group representation. Using this approach, we can accurately describe and assess the importance of the opinions on political representation during the Burger years.

The typology itself reflects important and enduring conceptions of group representation in the American political context. Appropriately, the first conceptual type figured prominently at the Philadelphia convention in 1787. The large states were in favor of population-based apportionment for legislators; they were the defenders of an eighteenth-century version of one person, one vote. The small states, on the other hand, argued for a more communal definition of representation; these states defended spatial representation, that is, the apportioning of representatives by geographic communities regardless of population. In light of this dispute, we will term this first conceptualization *territorial representation.* To be accurate, the battle between the large and the small states—not to mention the debate among the Warren justices over one person, one vote—concerned the distribution of constituencies more than the actual process of legislative representation.[29] Constituencies of equal size did not necessarily guarantee each voter equal influence over the composition of the

---

29. G. Gudgin and P. J. Taylor, Seats, Votes and the Spatial Organisation of Elections 3 (1979).

legislature; voters' relative influence over electoral outcomes had more to do with the group demographics of electoral districts, with whether a district coincided with a territorially based community of interest.

The Warren Court never really relinquished the idea that an individual's membership in a particular geographic community was an important factor in aggregating voters into electoral constituencies. Indeed, the majority in *Reynolds* observed that following subdivision boundaries not only was a plausible method of aggregating interests, but also might deter manipulation of district lines. Of course, respecting township or county boundaries constricted equipopulous districting; *Reynolds* was, in a sense, an uneasy compromise between spatial and population-based representation. The decisions of the Burger era altered the terms of this compromise by permitting greater population variance among state districts drawn along subdivision lines.[30] But, arguably, the decisions that follow the paradigm of territorial representation most closely are those concerning the regulatory powers and legislative authority of *local* governments. A Burger Court dissenter thus credited one of these decisions with "ceding to geography a talismanic significance."[31] In chapter 3 we will investigate whether certain Burger Court decisions supported, if not expanded, the territorial conception of group representation.

The second conceptualization of group representation, lacking the historical familiarity of the previous geographic conception, responds to the prominence of interest group activity in American politics and to the prevalence of theories of interest group pluralism in the work of American political scientists. More specifically, this conceptualization is a product of changes in American politics resulting from modern economic policy-making. Comparative political studies have noted that in societies characterized by high social cleavage, an important unit of representation is the economic, or occupational, interest group. A conceptual type of representation attentive to the influence of such economic interests can be termed *corporatist representation*. Often associated with the consociational democracies of Scandinavia,[32] corporatism made a brief appearance in the United States, in

---

30. See the discussion of Mahan v. Howell, 410 U.S. 315 (1973), *infra* at 36ff.
31. See Holt Civic Club v. City of Tuscaloosa, 439 U.S. 60 (1978) (Brennan, J., dissenting).
32. See A. Lijphart, Democracies (1984).

the early 1930s, as part of Herbert Hoover's and, later, Franklin Roosevelt's governmental efforts toward economic and industrial recovery. But even in the traditional American system of district-based elections, corporatist representation has had an influence: the establishment of what are called special purpose governments. Their "special purpose" is to represent and to serve the interests of a particular economic or occupational constituency—often, the irrigation needs of agricultural producers. Though the Burger court dealt with only a small number of cases concerning electoral practices in special districts, the decisions are important because of the deviations from one person, one vote that the Court tolerated. The conceptual type of corporatist representation sheds light not only on these decisions, but also on the Court's receptivity to political activities by business corporations. This conceptualization raises the general issue of the balance between rights in a capitalist economy and rights in a democratic polity; these issues and related cases will be discussed in chapter 4.

While the first two conceptualizations of group representation are tangentially related to current districting practices, the third directly concerns practical problems of eliminating bias in districting. This conceptual type, which I call *demographic representation,* is drawn from political theorists' notions of "descriptive representation," the accurate correspondence between a delegate and the people he or she represents. This conceptualization captures the contemporary concern for demographic proportionality in the legislature—representatives must "stand for" their constituencies in order for the representatives' actions to be wholly legitimate.[33] The demographic conceptualization also has roots in the debate between large states and small states over legislative representation. The large states were in favor of congressional constituencies that reflected the diverse group interests within the state.[34] One of the group interests that the large states sought to represent through the districting process is still relevant to modern districting plans: the political party. Partisan-based (or -biased) districting is an enduring problem; the Burger Court's need to consider questions of partisan fairness in districting demonstrates the salience of the prototype of demographic representation.

---

33. H. Pitkin, The Concept of Representation 57–61 (1967).
34. R. Zagarri, The Politics of Size 36–37 (1987).

However, there is another group interest—outside the large state/small state debate—whose political fortunes in the districting process now consume even greater judicial attention: the racial minority. Chapter 5 applies the conceptualization of demographic representation to both partisan- and race-based districting, and examines whether these decisions are an example of a new theory of representation or simply an effort to secure electoral victories for a given political party or minority.

The fourth conceptual type of group representation is an attempt to articulate with precision the American conception of representation through political parties. Given that partisan interests are often the central focus of a districting plan, it is worth asking what representative functions parties perform in our system of government. The conceptualization of *partisan representation* is drawn from political scientists' conceptions of "responsible party government." However, there is a dualistic tradition of party government, both in American history and political studies. The dualism is between responsible yet centralized parties and responsible yet populist parties. The conceptualization of partisan representation is sensitive to this dualism and asks whether the Court's decisions, in part, were also. This conceptual type is applied to the Burger Court's scrutiny of specific party functions and operations—from primary elections to patronage appointments. The goal of chapter 6 is to see whether the decisions of the Burger years effectively endorsed a more centralized or a more populist version of responsible party government.

The final conceptualization of group representation that we will consider is relatively new to American political history and democratic theory, and thus the most difficult one to articulate. In substance, this conceptual type concerns the administrative branch of government and citizens' access to it. However, because the scope of administrative law is so broad, my survey of Burger Court decisions only covers citizens' access to judicial review of administrative decisions. Though the label is somewhat confining, I call this conceptualization *administrative representation*. Concern for the administrative branch's popular accountability had its statutory origins in the Administrative Procedures Act of 1942, in which Congress formalized public access to the administrative process. Although the conceptual type of administrative representation has not been a prominent conception of political representation, it does raise familiar issues of popular accountability and authorization for governmental actions.[35] Administrative agencies "act for" citizens in many policy areas; it is therefore worth inquiring in what sense the administrative branch is authorized by and accountable to those whose interests it allegedly represents.

Popular representation in the administrative process often entails litigation as a form of group political action. Administrative representation is in part a form of "litigational representation," in which judicial review of agency decision making serves as a popular check on bureaucratic action. Chapter 7 will describe more fully the origins of this conceptual type, and use it as a vehicle to examine the Burger Court's decisions on citizens' access to judicial proceedings for the purpose of challenging administrative actions. Although access to litigation is not the only form of administrative accountability, review of such case data will allow us to evaluate the extent to which the Court viewed the administrative branch as subject to representative procedures.

The above five conceptual types obviously do not exhaust the possible political, historical, or theoretical conceptions of representation, but they do incorporate most of the representation issues considered by the Supreme Court. An explanatory typology loses its descriptive ability to classify and organize case data as its categories proliferate; hopefully, these five conceptualizations integrate the dominant concerns of an interdisciplinary examination of representation. Their hermeneutic purpose lies in their presentation of the diverse accounts of plural representation that shape American politics and constitutional law. By illustrating the complexity of modern American pluralism, the typology helps to explain why recent Supreme Court jurisprudence on representation has seemed so inscrutable.

By exploring judicial policies on the group interests that merit constitutionally protected representational access, this study serves as a preliminary inquiry into the normative goals of representation in the American political system. The inquiry will be worthwhile, however, if it achieves even less:

> The most that we can hope to do ... is to be clear on what view of representation a particular writer [or Justice?] is using, and whether

---

35. See H. Pitkin, The Concept of Representation 55–59 (1967); J. Rohr, To Run a Constitution 181–86 (1986).

that view, its assumptions and implications fit the case to which he is trying to apply them.[36]

Ultimately, the question that this study addresses is whether the decisions of the Burger years on political representation altered the constitutional meaning of political influence. The answer is obviously of great moment, especially given recurring postcensus redistricting and its attendant political battles over relative group influence. In the concluding chapter, I will assess the current status of "fair and effective representation" in light of the representation case law of the Burger years and offer a prognosis for the future.

---

36. H. Pitkin, The Concept of Representation 228 (1967).

CHAPTER 2

Malapportionment and Representation

Before we can explore the Burger Court's "jurisprudence of group interests," we must first confirm this characterization. One way of illuminating the Burger Court's particular perspective is by contrasting it with the Warren Court's comparative lack of a group representation perspective.

In examining the Burger Court's decisions on political representation in light of those of its predecessor, two distinctions become apparent. First, in terms of the doctrinal rhetoric of the opinions, the issue of individual participation received more attention in the Warren Court's decisions. Conversely, the language of group political access had greater prominence in the Burger Court's decisions on representation. Second, the types of representation cases brought to the two Courts differed. The Warren Court's docket was dominated by cases concerning malapportioned districts and the resulting deprivation of individual voters' political influence. The cases brought to the Burger Court, on the other hand, concerned the more troublesome problem of aggregate-level fairness in otherwise equal districts. During the 1980s, litigants generally brought claims about the relative political influence of groups of voters under a particular districting plan. Thus, given the representation problems that the Burger Court faced, the language and directives of one *person,* one vote were not very helpful.

The purpose of this chapter is to verify that the Warren and Burger Courts should be distinguished in terms of their individualistic versus group-based views of representation rights. To do so, the chapter focuses on the Warren Court's development of the numerically equal vote standard and examines whether the standard conflated the individual right to participation and the process of representation.[1] As will become clear, the numerical vote remedy was at odds with the long-standing districting practice of balancing urban and rural group interests. Indeed, one of the first results of the Burger court's supervision of political representation was a reaffirmation of the relevance of geographic subdivision lines for state redistricting. The difference between the two Courts' interpretation of the requirements of one person, one vote is attributable, in my view, to the Warren Court's lack of a group-balancing approach to representation. Subsequent chapters explore further the Burger Court's own group-based analysis of representation.

Tensions in the Early Reapportionment Cases: Articulating Constituency Boundaries and Defining "Equal" Votes

In 1964, in *Reynolds v. Sims*,[2] the Warren Court held that equipopulous districting was the representational requirement of the equal protection clause. Only equally weighted votes could guarantee individual political equality—or so it seemed in cases of malapportionment. Contemporary commentators note that the one person, one vote doctrine ultimately ignores the problems of gerrymandering,[3] that is, discriminatory districting that operates unfairly to inflate the political strength of one group over another.[4] Gerrymandering has been part of electoral districting since the beginning of the republic; indeed, part of the small states' early objection to population-based districting that ignored town boundaries was the possibility of party manipulation of district lines.[5] The bane of the early reapportionment controversies, however, was the special protection of geographic group interests through districting—or, more often, through a failure to redistrict.

Geographic-based districts were not always flagrant gerrymanders; in theory, they had a representative purpose. Representation refers

---

1. Dixon, The Warren Court Crusade for the Holy Grail of One Man, One Vote, 1969 Sup. Ct. Rev. 219.
2. 377 U.S. 533 (1964).
3. Alfange, Gerrymandering and the Constitution: Into the Thorns of the Political Thicket at Last, 1986 Sup. Ct. Rev. 175, 177.
4. Dixon, The Court, the People and "One Man, One Vote," in Reapportionment in the 70s, at 7, 29 (Polsby ed. 1971).
5. R. Zagarri, The Politics of Size 119 (1987).

to the process of aggregating individual interests; such aggregation can be accomplished by districting that respects individuals' geographic proximity and commonality. Geographic and political boundaries have been recognized for their ability to reflect and mold political communities of interest.[6] As a matter of both democratic theory and practical convenience, states defended districting on a geographic basis, particularly as a means of balancing urban and rural interests. Such non-population-based apportionment was implicitly negatively sanctioned by the Supreme Court when it refused to intervene in redistricting issues in *Colegrove v. Green,* in 1946.[7]

Of course, citizens living under the same local jurisdiction may share no other attributes beyond their place of residence. If the geographic subdivision is not a substantive community of interest, then constituencies formed from subdivisions may have no greater claim to representativity than equipopulous electoral districts. This deficiency of geographic-based districting is compounded when concern for an urban-rural balance permits a numerical minority of citizens to control the legislature. Why, then, did the Warren Court tentatively admit in *Reynolds* that respect for subdivision lines might be an exception to the rigors of one person, one vote?

The Court in *Reynolds* seemed partially aware that considerations of group political power could not be expunged from electoral districting simply by asserting the equipopulous rule. For example, the majority noted that attention to subdivision lines in some districting situations might forestall the most egregious gerrymanders.[8] But the larger problem with which the Court was wrestling was how to draw boundaries that define meaningful constituencies.[9] A district system of elections is facilitated when a historically given geographic solution for boundaries is acceptable.[10] But when it is not acceptable—or worse, when it serves as a post hoc justification for legislators' delay

---

6. R. Kasperson, Participation, Decentralization and Advocacy Planning 37 (1974); Common Cause, Toward a System of Fair and Effective Representation 53 (1977).

7. 328 U.S. 549 (1946).

8. 377 U.S. at 581.

9. See Neighbor, Redistricting and Representation, 71 Natl. Civic Rev. 188, 190 (1982).

10. See Whelan, Democratic Theory and the Boundary Problem, 25 Nomos 3, 16 (1983).

or recalcitrance in responding to statewide population shifts[11]—alternative methods for defining constituency boundaries become necessary.

Baker v. Carr,[12] in 1962, initiated reexamination of the degree to which geographic boundaries could define electoral constituencies. The constitutional problem was whether a state's districting policy was a judicial or political question.[13] The Court decided that the formation of electoral constituencies was a justiciable matter, the Fourteenth Amendment's guarantee of equal protection under the law being the medium for judicial involvement. Sidestepped, of course, was the similarity of the case to a guaranty clause issue—specifically, its concern with questions of group balance of political power within a state.[14]

Baker did not ameliorate the boundary-drawing dilemmas in democratic theory or electoral politics. Since the composition of a political community legitimately concerns its prospective constituents, the drawing of district boundaries should be at least partially determined by popular consent.[15] Given the Warren Court's concern about the adverse impact of malapportionment on democratic participation, one might surmise that it would have looked favorably on geographic-based districting ratified by statewide majorities. But the Court did not emphasize the aggregate right of a majority to secure plural representation of groups; rather, it subordinated majority rule (as a composite representation of group interests) to numerical district equality.[16]

The Warren Court's focus on individual participation rather than

---

11. Alfange contends that the disputes in *Baker* and *Reynolds* were not about numerically equal votes at all, but about gerrymandering that consistently favored rural interests. He conjectures that had the unequally populated districts been random, i.e., not skewed in favor of certain group interests, there might have been no hue and cry for judicial relief. See Alfange, Gerrymandering and the Constitution, 1986 Sup. Ct. Rev. 175, 191.

12. 369 U.S. 186 (1962).

13. According to Luther v. Borden, 7 Howard 1 (1849), questions concerning the structure of governments fell under the guaranty clause of Article IV and were subject exclusively to the authority of the political branches.

14. But cf. Baker v. Carr, 369 U.S. 186, 301 (1962) (Frankfurter, J., dissenting).

15. See Whelan, Democratic Theory and the Boundary Problem, 25 Nomos 3, 15 (1983).

16. Alfange, Gerrymandering and the Constitution, 1986 Sup. Ct. Rev. 175, 182–83.

on representational outcomes is nowhere better illustrated than in *Lucas v. Colorado General Assembly*.[17] In this companion case to *Reynolds v. Sims,* the Court overturned a statewide referendum approving territorial, non-population-based districts for the upper house of the state legislature. In implementing the equipopulous standard in *Lucas,* the Court decided that state majorities were not entitled to arrive at a solution to the boundary problem for legislative districts.[18] In repudiating a state's majoritarian procedure for solving the district boundary problem, *Lucas* represented a dramatic departure from the federalist theory of representation. A popular mandate could not secure political influence for a geographic minority interest if the price was curtailing the equal weighting of individual votes.

The judiciary's authority to ratify the legitimacy of district boundaries gave it the power to implement judicial conceptions of electoral communities of interest. But the abandonment of geographic-based districts raised the question of what aggregative factor should replace geography. Would equipopulous districting fashion identifiable political communities out of numerical voting units, or was it constitutionally necessary to create "communal constituencies"?[19] Doubts about the fairness of purely numerical districting ultimately led the Court to reconsider the validity of using certain group factors in fashioning electoral constituencies. Specifically, while districting to protect regional group interests was tainted by an antimajoritarian past, districting to protect the interests of racial minorities was not. Further, such race-based districting might be necessary to make minority votes fully equal under conditions of racial bloc voting. Admitting this, of course, meant admitting that voters are not ciphers and that numerical formulas are insufficient to protect political rights. One person, one vote, which began as a remedy for the countermajoritarian maladies of geographical malapportionment, would eventually succumb to its own simplistic arithmetic conception of individual political influence.

Premonitions about the inadequacy of the numerically equal vote

---

17. 377 U.S. 713 (1964).
18. Cf. Whelan, Democratic Theory and the Boundary Problem, 25 Nomos 3, 22 (1983).
19. Wright v. Rockefeller, 376 U.S. 52 (1964). See R. Dixon, Democratic Representation 467 (1968).

standard were present in the Warren Court's earliest reapportionment cases. Although the 1962 case of *Baker v. Carr* concerned only the justiciability of apportionment, it occasioned a judicial debate about how to measure political influence and how to translate that measure into a constitutional right. Brennan's majority opinion had found only that the debasement of votes in the malapportioned Tennessee state legislature was a justiciable cause of action under the Fourteenth Amendment's equal protection clause. But Frankfurter reasoned, in his dissent, that a court could not determine the equal protection issue without first determining what constituted a republican form of government.[20] Frankfurter's point was that talk of vote debasement made no sense without a standard of representativity— "what a vote *should be* worth."[21]

Frankfurter further observed that to embroil the federal judiciary in apportionment battles changed the nature of the democratic contest. If the "discrimination" in *Baker* was that appellants were deprived of what they considered to be their proportional share of political influence, then, Frankfurter argued, "hardly any distribution of political authority that could be assailed . . . would fail similarly to operate to the prejudice of some groups, and to the advantage of others."[22] Majoritarian competition, by its very nature, ensured that some groups would be "disadvantaged": their candidate would lose.[23] Since Tennessee defended its method of apportionment as providing urban-rural balance in the state legislature, *Baker*'s dissenters specifically praised the system of representing local geographic interests. Both Frankfurter and Harlan argued that geographic representation was historically legitimate and no less rational than a distribution of electoral strength according to a population census.[24]

---

20. 369 U.S. at 297. The "republican form of government" question arguably fell under the guaranty clause of Article IV and was a nonjusticiable, political question.
21. 369 U.S. at 300–301 (emphasis added).
22. 369 U.S. at 299.
23. 369 U.S. at 299. The winner-take-all aspects of even equipopulous, single-member districts would later be challenged by complainants as depriving submerged political or racial minorities of their potential political influence. With respect to the numerically equal votes question, whether you win or lose depends on how you play the game.
24. 369 U.S. at 307 (Frankfurter, J., dissenting); 369 U.S. at 334 (Harlan, J., dissenting). Indeed, districts equal in population would not tend to be equal in voting-age population. The Court would later uphold a Hawaiian plan in which districts were apportioned by number of resident registered voters. See Burns v. Richardson, 384

The validity of separate representation for territorial subdivisions was formally tested in *Gray v. Sanders,* in 1963.[25] The case concerned Georgia's county-unit system of counting votes in the Democratic primary elections for federal and state representatives, which resembled the electoral college method by which the U.S. president is selected. County-unit votes were based on county population, but the winning candidate needed a majority of total county-unit votes, which might not equal the popular mandate of all voters. The Warren Court invalidated the state's system of county representation in candidate selection, analogizing the unequal weighting of votes by county residence to actual disenfranchisement practices. The majority rested this claim on the "idea that every voter is equal to every other voter in the state."[26] *Gray* was significant to the evolution of the one person, one vote doctrine because it weakened the geographic representation argument and suggested a numerical interpretation of the "worth" of votes. With the passage of time, it has been attributed an even greater significance; some commentators have even found it a foreshadowing of proportional political influence, or of the state duty to adopt electoral plans that minimize the "worthlessness" of votes.[27]

Gray was followed, in 1964, by two congressional reapportionment cases that broadened and clarified the numerically equal vote doctrine. In the first case, *Wesberry v. Sanders,*[28] the Court relied on Article I, section 2, of the Constitution to invalidate Georgia's malapportioned congressional districts. The majority argued that the article's requirement that representatives be selected by the electors of the states meant that each individual vote was to count as equally as practicable.[29] This time, the dissenting justices' strategy was not to

---

U.S. 73 (1966). The Hawaiian case was exceptional, however, because the total population did not equal the citizen population of the state. 384 U.S. at 76. A second dilemma of census-based apportionment is the very problem of vote dilution: to what extent is an individual's vote worth more in a district with a low proportion of voting-age persons than it would be in a district where total population more closely approximates voting population?

25. 372 U.S. 368 (1963).
26. 372 U.S. at 380.
27. Levinson, Gerrymandering and the Brooding Omnipresence of Proportional Representation, 33 U.C.L.A. L. Rev. 260, 265 (1985).
28. 376 U.S. 1 (1964).
29. 376 U.S. at 7–8.

defend geographic-based districting, but to point out the internal limitations of the Court's numerical approach. Harlan's dissent found the Court's exclusive focus on numerical equality—in disregard of the area, shape, and party affiliations of a district—to have little relevance to the realities of political life.[30] Harlan seemed to be alluding that if the Court wanted to prevent gerrymandering, as well as malapportionment, it had come up with the wrong rule.

This error was glaringly apparent in the second congressional case in 1964, *Wright v. Rockefeller*.[31] In *Wright* the Court dismissed a complaint concerning racial gerrymandering in New York's congressional redistricting for lack of evidence. Nevertheless, the case raised a problem that would come to fruition in the racial gerrymandering cases of the 1980s: if geographic subdivision lines were not legitimate bases for creating districts that represent communities of interest, should racial factors be considered in aggregating discrete individual's interests? The New York plan created racially homogeneous congressional constituencies, giving blacks and Hispanics their own delegates at the price of "packing" them into fewer districts.[32] The gerrymandering by race did not constitute numerical malapportionment, but it did "waste" the total statewide worth and influence of minority votes. The gerrymandering also divided the liberal bloc of the Warren Court; Douglas and Goldberg dissented from the Warren majority's dismissal of the complaint.

The position of Douglas in *Wright* exemplifies the problems that the Warren Court faced because of its individual participation approach to representation. Douglas interpreted one person, one vote as requiring that each individual voter be treated alike, without consideration of the relative political clout of different groups.[33] He saw race-based gerrymandering as "a divisive force in the community, emphasizing differences between candidates and votes that are irrelevant in the constitutional sense."[34] But it is unclear whether Douglas's objection in *Wright* was to the use of racial factors in drawing districts

---

30. 376 U.S. at 25.
31. 376 U.S. 52 (1964).
32. The goal of the packing was to waste black and Puerto Rican political strength in Manhattan and secure a safe white district for the Republican party. See Parker, Racial Gerrymandering and Legislative Reapportionment, in Minority Vote Dilution 85, 99 (C. Davidson ed. 1984).
33. M. Edelman, Democratic Theories and the Constitution 188 (1984).
34. 376 U.S. at 66.

per se, or to the uncorrected overconcentration of minority voters' political influence. Ironically, the *Wright* situation caused Douglas to retreat toward the safety of geographic-based representation. "No state," he declared, "may make an electoral district out of any racial bloc unless the electoral unit represent[s] an actual *neighborhood*."[35]

The formal articulation of the one person, one vote doctrine came in 1964, in *Reynolds v. Sims*,[36] and Warren's majority opinion made it clear that population was the controlling consideration in legislative redistricting. Douglas's comments in his *Wright* dissent notwithstanding, the *Reynolds* majority rejected any notion that regional group interests should be the dominant focus of representation: "Legislators are elected by voters, not farms or cities or economic interests."[37] States could attend to subdivision boundaries in their districting plans, but mainly because such districting was a legitimate means of deterring overt partisan gerrymandering.[38]

As noted at the outset of this study, *Reynolds* required both numerically equal votes and "fair and effective representation."[39] The latter was the ultimate aim of legislative apportionment, but the relationship between the two objectives was very imprecise. *Reynolds*, in fact, implied three goals: formal political equality, majority rule, and "effective" representation.[40] The decision also implied—at least to dissenting justice Harlan—the evolving judicial notion of a "guardian democracy" that would vitiate the participatory spirit of citizens and produce a complacent body politic.[41] Harlan was partially correct, for *Reynolds* seemed to replace citizens' accommodation of interests through political bargaining with reliance on the courts' numerical formulas of political influence. As long as an individual was a member of a frustrated majority, such an arithmetic option seemed attractive. It was a less attractive option in cases such as *Wright*, and in some of *Reynolds*'s companion cases.

For example, the companion case *Lucas v. Colorado General Assem-*

---

35. 376 U.S. at 67 (emphasis added).
36. 377 U.S. 533 (1964).
37. 377 U.S. at 562.
38. 377 U.S. at 580–81.
39. 377 U.S. at 565–66.
40. Levinson, Gerrymandering and the Brooding Omnipresence of Proportional Representation, 33 U.C.L.A. L. Rev. 260, 265 (1985).
41. 377 U.S. at 624. On this aspect of the *Reynolds* decision, see W. Elliott, The Rise of Guardian Democracy (1978).

bly[42] demonstrated that, "despite language to the contrary in *Reynolds,* [the Warren Court] perceived the [reapportionment] issue as a simple matter of protecting the individual's right to vote."[43] As mentioned earlier, the *Lucas* majority invalidated a "little federal plan"[44] for apportioning legislative seats that had been chosen by state referendum. The ruling seemed to compromise the Warren Court's own beliefs about populism, and inspired a dissent from Stewart that would be important in later judicial grapplings with gerrymandering.

Stewart was particularly disturbed by the holding in *Lucas* because it effectively disregarded the preponderant power of the majority while claiming to uphold it. Stewart observed that a majority of Colorado voters had consciously chosen by referendum a plan that protected the regional minority's interests; the popular majority then remained free to reverse its districting decision.[45] Stewart recast the objective of the *Reynolds* cases: the goal of any state apportionment plan, he argued, was the realistic accommodation of the diverse and often conflicting political forces operating within a state.[46] In contrast to the one person, one vote standard, Stewart proposed that a state's districting plan should not permit the systematic frustration of the will of the majority.[47] Stewart's test would have involved the Court in scrutinizing group power alignments in states in order to assess a plural majority's political influence.[48] But the implication of his dissent was that judicial review of districting plans involved the Court in choosing among different theories of representation—and any choice was bound to benefit certain group interests at the expense of others. Unfortunately, his point about the differing impact

---

42. 377 U.S. 713 (1964).
43. Alfange, Gerrymandering and the Constitution, 1986 Sup. Ct. Rev. 175, 194.
44. A "little federal plan" refers to a state representation system modeled on the federalism principles of the U.S. Congress. At the state level, this entails that the lower house of the legislature is apportioned by population while the upper house represents counties or towns as discrete units irrespective of population.
45. 377 U.S. at 759.
46. 377 U.S. at 744–45.
47. 377 U.S. at 753–54.
48. J. Ely, Democracy and Distrust 123–24 (1980). Interestingly, the Burger Court seemed to adopt Stewart's interest-balancing approach to districting and gerrymandering questions, without admitting it expressly. See, for example, Powell's reinterpretation of the meaning and directives of *Reynolds* in Davis v. Bandemer, 106 S. Ct. 2825, 2828 (1986) (Powell, J., dissenting in part).

of the equipopulous rule was seldom raised in the reapportionment rulings.

Clearly, certain members of the Warren Court were wary of the far-reaching ramifications of the one person, one vote doctrine, as evidenced by the decisions that immediately followed the *Reynolds* cases.[49] Court majorities intermittently permitted some local variety in representative government; for example, three cases decided in 1967 declined to extend the principle of equal voting influence to local government elections.[50] But by 1968, the Warren majority had expanded the doctrine's coverage, subjecting additional levels of government to equipopulous districting requirements. *Avery v. Midland County*,[51] for instance, considered the question of population disparity in the electoral districts for a Texas county commission. The state asserted that the commission's work disproportionately concerned rural areas, thus justifying apportionment based on non-population factors. Nevertheless, because of the general governmental powers of the county commission, the Court found an equal protection violation. *Avery* was an important ruling—the first decision to apply the

---

49. In Fortson v. Dorsey, 379 U.S. 433 (1965), the Court upheld Georgia's multimember districts for the election of state senators. Also, in Burns v. Richardson, 384 U.S. 73 (1966), the Court permitted Hawaii's use of registered voters as the basis for its state apportionment plan. In both cases, the Court found the resulting population variance to be tolerable and rationally related to legitimate state objectives of representation. However, in Kilgarlin v. Hill, 386 U.S. 120 (1967), a state apportionment plan that combined single-member, multimember, and floterial districts to preserve county lines was invalidated for impermissible population variance.

In Fortson v. Morris, 385 U.S. 231 (1966), the Court reconsidered the scope of its holding in *Gray v. Sanders*. A five-judge majority found that Georgia's requirement that run-off elections for governor receive a majority mandate by the state legislature did not violate the equal protection clause. The majority reversed the lower court's reliance on the vote dilution principle announced in *Gray* and upheld the state's right to choose any republican form of gubernatorial election. *Gray*'s reach had been qualified, but by a very slim majority.

50. In Moody v. Flowers, 387 U.S. 97 (1967), the Court upheld a districting system for New York's county board of supervisors that was based on the representation of towns, irrespective of their population. In Sailors v. Board of Education, 387 U.S. 105 (1967), the Court upheld election of the county school board by local school boards rather than by popular election. In Dusch v. Davis, 387 U.S. 112 (1967), a borough form of government was upheld, even though electoral influence was not in accordance with the population distribution of the member boroughs. Interestingly, all three decisions were authored by Justice Douglas.

51. 390 U.S. 474 (1968).

one person, one vote formula to local governments and to qualify, if not reject, the utility of local representative diversity.

This time, the predictable Harlan dissent found that the specialization of local governments, and the unequal impact of their special powers on different regional groups, were factors against extending one person, one vote to local governmental units.[52] Interestingly, Justice Fortas, a Warren ally, also introduced the special purpose argument in a dissent in *Avery*. His dissent—like that of Douglas in *Wright*—was another significant liberal split from the Warren-Brennan majority. And, like Douglas's earlier dissent, his was prompted by the majority's lack of attention to group factors in districting.

Fortas argued that there was good reason not to apportion county commission seats by population. The city of Midland, where most of the county population resided, already had a municipal government with jurisdiction over urban issues. If rural residents, residing in unincorporated areas, were denied a political forum devoted to their specific policy concerns, urban residents would dominate both the Midland city and county political agenda.[53] Fortas's opinion argued forcefully in favor of maintaining an urban-rural balance, a justification hitherto discredited by *Baker* and *Reynolds*. Fortas's dissent was evidence that, even among the Warren majority, geographic group interests had their proponents.

The one person, one vote bloc continued to erode as the Warren Court further strengthened the degree to which numerical equality *should* apply reapportionment plans. In *Kirkpatrick v. Preisler*,[54] decided in 1969, the Brennan majority held that congressional reapportionment should aim for equipopulous districts "as nearly as [is] practicable."[55] The Court rejected Missouri's concerns about representation of group interests, integrity of county lines, and compactness of districts, arguing that creating districts with specific interest orientations was "antithetical to equal representation for equal num-

---

52. 390 U.S. at 492. Harlan observed that only by classifying the governmental unit as other than "general" in power and responsibility could application of the *Reynolds* rule be avoided. This reasoning foreshadowed what was essentially the approach of the Burger Court toward special district elections. See the discussion of the conceptual type of corporatist representation in chapter 4.

53. 390 U.S. at 502–8.

54. 394 U.S. 526 (1969).

55. 394 U.S. at 528.

bers of people."⁵⁶ In *Wells v. Rockefeller*,⁵⁷ the Court championed the numerically equal vote rule just as strenuously for New York's congressional districts, over the dissents of Harlan, Stewart, and (surprisingly) White.

Harlan's *Wells* dissent reiterated his admonition in *Reynolds* that numerical equality would be perfectly compatible with political gerrymandering. The legislature, he felt, must do more than satisfy one person, one vote: "It must create a structure which will in fact as well as theory be responsive to the sentiments of the community."⁵⁸ Harlan's point was that the constraint of political subdivision lines prevented blatantly partisan legislative reapportionment. While his point about partisan gerrymandering would haunt future districting decisions, it was White's dissent in *Wells* that indicated the seriousness of the problems with the equipopulous districting standard. White objected to the Court's "unduly rigid and unwarranted application of the equal protection clause" in these new reapportionment rulings.⁵⁹ White seemed to be alluding to *Reynolds*'s neglected but parallel goal of securing fair and effective representation for groups of individuals.

The possibility of group representation, dismissed in the early reapportionment cases with respect to geographic interests, had rematerialized by 1969. In the same term as *Kirkpatrick* and *Wells*, the Court considered a local election procedure in *Allen v. State Board of Elections*.⁶⁰ *Allen* was a statutory construction case, involving the application of section 5 of the Voting Rights Act to a municipality's introduction of at-large election systems. Under section 5, "covered jurisdictions" with a history of racial disenfranchisement had to preclear all proposed electoral changes in federal court. At-large elections did not necessarily undermine the numerical equality of individ-

---

56. 394 U.S. at 533–34 (citing *Reynolds*, 377 U.S. at 579–80). Fortas concurred in *Kirkpatrick*. He argued that consideration of disparate local interests might be appropriate to local government units exercising limited governmental powers. However, he conceded that these same factors did not justify departures from one person, one vote in state or congressional electoral districts. 394 U.S. at 537 n.2. Fortas saw the need to carve out a realm of limited integrity for local government, echoing the concerns, but not the intensity, of Stewart's dissent in *Lucas*.

57. 394 U.S. 542 (1969) (New York's congressional reapportionment plan invalidated).

58. 394 U.S. at 551.

59. 394 U.S. at 553.

60. 393 U.S. 544 (1969).

ual votes, but they could dilute the influence of groups of votes, particularly the votes of racial minorities. Instead of invoking its numerical standard of political influence, the Warren majority in *Allen* suggested that inattention to group factors invalidated the proposed electoral system. In a sweeping statement the Court declared that the Voting Rights Act outlawed "the subtle as well as the obvious state regulations which *have the effect* of abridging the right to vote on the basis of race."[61] The problem of determining what effects actually constitute racial vote dilution was left for the future.

Not surprisingly, fear of further judicial supervision of the electoral process prompted a partial dissent from Harlan.[62] Harlan felt that the Court was now using section 5 of the Voting Rights Act to allow the federal judiciary to restructure state and local governments and, thus, to decide unilaterally what constituted a republican form of government.[63] He also raised the key question about aggregate voting influence for minority groups—a question for which the one person, one vote doctrine had no answer. Which best guarantees equal voting rights for minority citizens: some influence over the election of more officials, or more influence over the election of fewer officials?[64] Clearly, with the *Allen* problem, the Warren Court reached the limits of the logic of the one person, one vote doctrine. At-large systems did not undermine the numerical equality of voters, but such systems did affect the relative political influence of groups of voters. As such, at-large systems could not be attacked through the equipopulous district rule.

The early reapportionment cases show the Warren Court struggling to operationalize the concept of numerically equal votes. In fact, one person, one vote could never be absolute because of the existence of state boundaries, but regardless of this federalism factor, there was a practical point at which population variance between districts became *de minimis*. Mathematical variance between districts was not necessarily equivalent to practical consequences for individuals' elec-

---

61. 393 U.S. at 565 (emphasis added). The Court remanded the issue of the dilutionary effect of at-large elections to the lower court, noting only that the state had not demonstrated compliance with section 5. 393 U.S. at 569.

62. Black also dissented, arguing that section 5 of the act violated the federal principle of the U.S. constitution—its "conquered province" concept vitiated political decentralization. 393 U.S. at 595.

63. 393 U.S. at 585.

64. 393 U.S. at 586.

toral influence. Additionally, *Allen* highlighted the countervailing problem of how to guarantee equally effective votes. As the *Allen* majority recognized, group factors have to be taken into account if fair representation and majority political influence are to be evaluated.

The Warren Court's decisions on legislative districting could be described as the search for political equality through "quantitative fairness" in representation. But even when the requirement of numerically equal voting power was satisfied, the issue of "qualitative fairness"—the equality of voting power among groups, not discrete individuals[65]—remained unresolved. One person, one vote, as articulated by the Warren Court, was a doctrine unequipped to handle the problem of minority-group vote dilution.

By 1968, critics such as Robert Dixon were already questioning the wisdom of the Warren Court's reliance on the equipopulous rule and its blind faith in the rule's utility for fair districting. Dixon's famous observation that "all districting is gerrymandering" implied that, whatever criteria were used to construct a districting system, some interests would be disadvantaged and others advantaged relative to their prospects under another system using different criteria.[66] The greatest limitation of the numerically equal vote doctrine was not so much its individualized notion of political influence as its irrelevance to the real source of inequity in American district elections. Any geographic-based system of districting possesses a key infirmity: it must, of necessity, reflect a geographic distribution of individual political preferences. One person, one vote obscured this infirmity because it did not define district inequity as group-based. At the same time, the doctrine prompted the search for what Dixon called a "holy grail": the mathematically precise and penultimately fair districting plan.

Given the inherent limitations of the Warren Court's one person, one vote standard of representational fairness, it is not surprising that its successor gravitated toward a group-oriented approach to political representation. The Warren Court's racial vote dilution cases made clear that our district system of elections favors certain geo-

---

65. Beitz, Equal Opportunity in Political Representation, in Equal Opportunity 156–59 (N. Bowie ed. 1988).

66. R. Dixon, Democratic Representation 462 (1968); Beitz, Equal Opportunity in Political Representation, in Equal Opportunity 161 (N. Bowie ed. 1988).

graphic distributions of individual preferences. Because of this, the search for "fair and effective representation" must explicitly include consideration of group political influence. Arguably, once such group factors were introduced into the judicial dialogue on redistricting, the constitutional debate about political representation had to incorporate political actions beyond voting.

The Burger Court took this broader view of the meaning of political representation. And, as was evident in their initial scrutiny of the still unfinished reapportionment revolution, the Burger justices were conspicuously attentive to group factors in the districting process. The Burger Court's decisions on state redistricting suggest its receptivity to group-based conceptions of representational fairness, distinguishing it from its predecessor.

The Burger Court and State Redistricting

The 1970 term inaugurated the Burger Court, as well as the Supreme Court's evasion of a strict application of the equipopulous requirement. This evasion was especially dramatic with regard to state redistricting. Although the Warren Court majority on one person, one vote was already eroding by 1969, the Burger Court's new justices more forcefully and openly attacked the individualistic conception of representation, as well as the numerical standard of district fairness.

In the 1971 case of *Whitcomb v. Chavis*,[67] the Burger Court[68] reexamined the degree to which respect for political subdivision lines was compatible with equipopulous districting. To preserve the integrity of county boundaries, the Indiana districting plan created a multimember district for Marion County. One question was whether such plural representation unduly enhanced the influence of Marion County voters vis à vis other Indiana voters. Additionally, as in the 1969 at-large election case in *Allen*, a second question was whether the multimember district diluted the voting strength of racial minorities in the Indianapolis area.

The Burger Court's decision to uphold the multimember district

---

67. 403 U.S. 124 (1971).
68. At this point, the "Burger Court" had undergone a change of only two justices: Burger had replaced Warren as chief justice, and Blackmun had replaced Justice Fortas.

garnered only a plurality vote, hardly a decisive early precedent on districting. The most significant part of White's plurality opinion was his denial that the effects of racial bloc voting were exacerbated by the county-wide multimember district.[69] Some commentators have termed *Whitcomb*'s tolerance of multimember districts, in the face of a vote dilution challenge, the "scurrying back to the security and comfort of the one person, one vote standard."[70] Similarly, to Harlan, the line of cases from *Gray v. Sanders* through *Whitcomb* revealed a personal commitment on the part of some of the justices to the principles of "pure majoritarian democracy"—the equation of political equality with numerical voting equality.[71]

It is common to group *Whitcomb* with the Warren Court's one person, one vote decisions. Yet White's opinion was much more sophisticated in its assessment of the distribution of political influence within the state; indeed, he interpreted *Reynolds* as mandating that voters have an equally *effective* voice.[72] Quite clearly, White recognized that mathematical analysis was not the best gauge of the effectiveness of votes and, thus, of political equality. This observation predates future courts' reasoning: the infirmity of winner-take-all, at-large districts is not a matter of numerically unequal votes. Yet if White—a dissenter in 1969 against rigid equipopulism—recognized the complexities of assessing political influence, why did he not accept the group-based dilution charge? Perhaps he felt that while certain districting criteria—here, respect for subdivision lines—are not necessarily neutral in their effect on groups of voters, one can still advocate their use in order to avoid the greater evils of gerrymandering.[73] In other words, it was one thing to say that group factors such as race or party affiliation influence the effectiveness of votes; it was quite another thing to invalidate an otherwise impartial districting plan because of its failure to explicitly balance racial groups' electoral influence. Despite *Whitcomb*'s holding, White's opinion does not display the enthusiasm for one person, one vote that was so evident in the early reapportionment cases.

---

69. 402 U.S. at 141, 143–44.
70. Alfange, Gerrymandering and the Constitution, 1986 Sup. Ct. Rev. 175, 201.
71. 403 U.S. at 166.
72. 403 U.S. at 141, 146.
73. Beitz, Equal Opportunity in Political Representation, in Equal Opportunity 161 (N. Bowie ed. 1988).

While *Whitcomb* suggested a change of emphasis on districting questions, *Mahan v. Howell*,[74] a 1973 decision, was a clear example of stepping out of one political thicket into another. By permitting attention to subdivision lines in state redistricting, the Burger justices no doubt thought they were diminishing judicial supervision of the intricacies of state elections. However, by reexamining the legitimacy of geographic group factors in districting, the Burger Court opened the door to consideration of other group factors that might qualify the equipopulous standard.

Mahan involved Virginia's districting plan for its state legislature, which produced a 16 percent variance in population among districts but preserved political subdivision lines. The Burger Court faced the question of whether *Wesberry*'s standard for congressional electoral districts—strict numerical equality of votes—applied to state electoral districts as well. Without referring directly to the language of *Wesberry*, the Rehnquist majority upheld the Virginia plan's 16 percent variance and sanctioned the use of relaxed population standards for state redistricting. Rehnquist argued that ensuring a voice for political subdivisions, as such, was more important at the state level since much state legislation consists of enacting local policy directives.[75] His majority opinion went so far as to express doubts that a mathematical percentage could ever be the final standard of *any* reapportionment plan.[76]

Mahan did not address whether state districting objectives other than subdivision integrity could qualify the one person, one vote rule. But two other cases in 1973 showed that the Burger Court was not to be bound by equipopulous logic. In *Gaffney v. Cummings*,[77] the Court upheld a Connecticut redistricting plan—a so-called sweetheart deal—whose population variance resulted from intentional bipartisan gerrymandering of the districts. The Court emphasized that the plan followed town boundaries, and thus represented parties in their local

---

74. 410 U.S. 315 (1973).

75. 410 U.S. at 321 (citing *Reynolds*, 377 U.S. at 580–81).

76. 410 U.S. at 329. Three justices dissented in part, uneasy over the Court's creation of a dual standard for congressional and state electoral districts. The dissenters conceded that the integrity of political subdivisions is more pertinent in state than in federal districting, but objected to the Court's permitting a state "to reserve as the primary goal of apportionment the service of some state interest [other than equality]." 410 U.S. at 340–41.

77. 412 U.S. 735 (1973).

jurisdictions[78] *Gaffney*'s companion case, *White v. Regester*,[79] was an even clearer example of the Court's acceptance of the relevance of group factors in districting. In *White* the Court invalidated Texas's multimember districting plan because of racial vote dilution.[80] *White*'s particular importance lay in the fact that, for the first time, the Burger Court explicitly recognized that one person, one vote was not sufficient to guarantee fair representation to certain groups of voters. But the *White* majority opinion was cautious; outlawing invidious exclusion of minority voters "[was] not the same as declaring that every racial or political group has a right to be represented in the legislature."[81] Geographic-based district elections could not be made to guarantee proportional representation. Nevertheless, as the decisions of the Burger court were to show, a "community of interest" approach to districting was a possible route to the *Reynolds* goal of fair and effective representation.

At least in terms of articulating and accepting guidelines for districting, the above cases illustrate some of the differences between the Warren and Burger Courts. The equal participation and numerical influence of individuals were the basis of the Warren Court's representation theory; not surprisingly, the Warren justices emphasized population variance as crucial to fairness in the districting process. The Warren Court's focus on individual rights in reapportionment questions was most obvious in two areas: aggregating electoral constituencies and evaluating voters' political influence. Basically, both

---

78. 412 U.S. at 737.
79. 412 U.S. 755 (1973).
80. The *White* majority specifically addressed the problem of racial bloc voting from the earlier *Whitcomb* case. *White*'s majority opinion distinguished *Whitcomb*'s use of multimember districts to preserve county lines from *White*'s exclusion of racial groups from the electoral process. The use of multimember districts for two counties in Texas was invidious racial vote dilution, aimed at reducing the value of minority participation. 412 U.S. at 765.

The Court later restricted the use of multimember districts in judicially ordered reapportionment relief, in *Chapman v. Meier*. A unanimous Court found the judicial imposition of multimember districts for North Dakota's state legislature to be constitutionally impermissible. The Court held that a judicially ordered plan must be held to higher standards of equal representation than a state's own plan. 420 U.S. 1, 26 (1975). *Chapman* was, nevertheless, consistent with the Court's support for geographic representation concerns in state legislative districts; the decision merely provided that the state alone could judge that subdivision integrity dictated the use of multimember districts.

81. 412 U.S. at 769.

constituency formation and votes' worth were matters amenable to a numerical rule. However, the Warren Court—at least, certain of its members—was also sensitive to the thornier theoretical problem of how to aggregate voters into meaningful electoral constituencies. Faced with considering groups' political fortunes under particular districting systems, certain members of the Court began to realize that the numerical rule had limited utility.

Establishing the boundaries that define political units is recognized as a critical issue in democratic theory. The Warren Court's one person, one vote decisions made population equality of districts fundamental to the legitimacy of any particular district boundary. Indeed, for the Warren Court, numerical equality of votes was the first step in both defining political constituencies and assessing political influence. Without radically disturbing this foundation, the Burger Court decisions on districting pursued other aspects of the constituency boundary and political influence problems. As we have seen in this chapter, one aspect was the legitimacy of subdivision lines in districting—specifically, the use of subdivision lines to define constituencies with identifiable, if not common, interests. Arguably, the Burger Court's state redistricting decisions suggested a more group-based approach to representation issues. As we shall see, the parameters of this group-based approach would extend beyond the districting context to political forums not previously subjected to judicial scrutiny.

CHAPTER 3

The "Talisman" of Geography

In chapter 2, a prima facie case was made for viewing the Burger Court record as endorsing a group rights approach to political representation questions. In its state legislative redistricting decisions, the Burger Court showed some degree of concern for the integrity of at least one group interest—the geographically defined community. However, respect for subdivision lines in districting does not in itself demonstrate a substantive theory of group representation; it might only reflect an effort to minimize egregious political gerrymanders. Substate territorial boundaries, after all, do not necessarily coincide with identifiable or unitary communities of interest.

Nevertheless, a geographic conceptualization of political constituencies was defended by certain members of both the Warren and Burger Courts as a method of aggregating voters into "meaningful" electoral constituencies. In theory, districting respecting subdivision lines might protect the integrity of a geographic community of interest because, arguably, voters are less disoriented and more capable of collective political organization when they are not fractured among a variety of districts.[1] Indeed, empirical studies conducted after the *Mahan* redistricting suggest that when political communities are not fragmented, recognition of congressional candidates by voters is enhanced.[2]

In spite of the one person, one vote rulings, the spatial organization of American elections necessitates geographic as well as population-based constituencies.[3] Thus, a district-based system of elections

---
1. Alfange, Gerrymandering and the Constitution: Into the Thorns of the Political Thicket at Last, 1986 Sup. Ct. Rev. 175, 216.
2. Niemi, Powell, and Bicknell, The Effect of Community-Congressional Districting Congruity on Knowledge of Congressional Candidates, 11 Legis. Stud. Q. 187, 190–93 (1986).
3. See G. Gudgin and P. J. Taylor, Seats, Votes, and the Spatial Organisation of Elections 3 (1979).

presumes some degree of territorial representation. Such a concept of representation is strengthened by two further premises: (1) geographic political units are not merely random collections of individuals, but communities pursuing an objective "public interest,"[4] and (2) the political structure is responsive to such territorial group interests. Districting respecting subdivision lines would be one method of promoting elected officials' responsiveness to local geographic interests. Another equally effective mechanism for ensuring responsiveness would be by decentralizing policy-making authority. From this perspective, cases dealing with the governmental powers of political subdivisions would be more directly related to a fully developed conceptualization of territorial representation. Therefore, if the Burger Court's decisions defended or permitted the exercise of local governmental power, then it would be plausible to see these decisions as confirming the importance of territorial group representation.

In order to test this hypothesis, this chapter will first sketch the historical and theoretical bases of the conceptual type of territorial representation. The chapter will then compare the model with the local policy-making case data to determine if the latter are consistent with, confirm, contradict, or are irrelevant to the former. To focus the analysis on key elements of the territorial conception of representation, the case data are grouped according to two categories of local policy-making: legislation defining "stake in the community," and legislation defining "quality of community life." The first category comprises the Court's rulings on local suffrage restrictions that attempt to limit electoral participation to individuals who demonstrate commitment to the local community. The second category concerns the Court's attitude toward the local electorate's regulation of the conditions of community life. Regulating the quality of community life includes traditional zoning and referendum powers, as well as ordinances restricting pornography, commercial advertising, and nuisances. These two types of local prerogatives constitute the main ways through which local self-rule facilitates the territorial concept

---

4. See Michaelman, Political Markets and Community Self-Determination: Competing Judicial Models of Local Governmental Legitimacy, 53 Ind. L.J. 145, 149–50 (1977–78) (discussing the "community self-determination" model of local governmental legitimacy); D. Magleby, Direct Legislation 25 (1984) (discussing the "participationist" conception of popular government and the determination of "the public good").

of representation in the American federalist context. The final section of the chapter then assesses the relevance of the territorial conceptualization in evaluating the Burger Court's group-balancing approach to representation questions.

The Geographic Community: A Representable Interest

As a matter of both political theory and American constitutional history, size affects democracy. A community's physical size is one factor that determines whether direct or representative democracy is the more appropriate form of popular government. Political theorists who emphasize the importance of citizen participation in democratic government are frequently concerned with the optimal size of a political unit. Such theorists argue that meaningful popular government in the modern context depends on decentralized democracy—government composed of intermediary political institutions that give citizens control over quasi-open and quasi-autonomous agenda setting.[5] The issue of size in a representative democracy is also relevant to democratic accountability—that is, to ensuring that representatives are truly acting in their constituents' interest. Indeed, proponents of a spatial theory of elections argue that polity/district size can augment or diminish certain collective voting behavior patterns, such as the so-called neighborhood effect.[6]

Not surprisingly, the relationship between the size of political units and the accountability of representatives was central to the convention delegates' debates in 1787 over the composition of Congress[7]. Two of the fundamental battles about congressional representation inextricably coupled size with territorial integrity. The first dispute concerned the population size of each House district. Too large a district would destroy the bond of familiarity between delegate and constituency, a problem compounded by the rejection—by all but the

---

5. See B. Barber, Strong Democracy *passim* (1984); E. Spitz, Majority Rule 204–5 (1984); R. Dahl, Federalism and the Democratic Process, 25 NOMOS 11 (1983).

6. The "neighborhood effect" describes a higher-than-expected degree of support for the local party in a district or area, owing to community solidarity. See M. A. Busteed, Geography and Voting Behavior 46–47 (1975).

7. Malbin, Congress during the Convention and Ratification, in The Framing and Ratification of the Constitution 192 (L. Levy and D. Mahoney eds. 1987).

antifederalists—of instructed representatives.[8] Further, if district size was to be the divisor for determining the number of congressmen allotted to each state, a secondary question arose regarding how to avoid excessive discrepancies in congressional representation *between* the states.[9] The compromise was Article I, section 2, which specified a minimum size requirement for House districts, but presumed the existence of state constitutions to flesh out the incomplete representation.[10]

A second convention dispute about constitutional representation also linked constituency size with geographic interests. This dispute concerned whether House district lines should coincide with county or town boundaries within the states, thus requiring an at-large, general ticket system of structuring elections. This method of fashioning congressional constituencies was preferred by the small states, which were concerned with preserving representatives' loyalty to their state and its local communities.[11] Although the small-state and antifederalist rhetoric about the corporate interests of the local community was left out of the constitution, it was not left out of American politics. As one historian has commented, "The anti-federal interest in homogeneity and civic responsibility . . . bears some relation to the contemporary interest in referenda and in the 'communitarian' critique of our traditional emphasis on individual rights."[12] Thus, the contemporary concern for local self-rule finds its expression in advocating direct legislation through local initiatives and referenda.[13]

In the historical debate over the construction of House district constituencies, the link between size and democratic accountability

---

8. See J. R. Pennock, Democratic Political Theory 321ff. (1979); H. Pitkin, The Concept of Representation 145 (1967). Instructed representatives are directly and specifically accountable to the verbal instructions of their constituents. Such representatives' authorization extends only as far as these instructions specify. Clearly, small constituencies are more feasible for such instructed representatives than larger constituencies with more divergent opinions to be reconciled.

9. M. Balinsky and H. P. Young, Fair Representation 4 (1982).

10. Lutz, The First American Constitutions, in The Framing and Ratification of the Constitution 69 (L. Levy and D. Mahoney eds. 1987).

11. R. Zagarri, The Politics of Size 119 (1987).

12. Dry, The Case against Ratification: Anti-Federalist Constitutional Thought, in The Framing and Ratification of the Constitution 291 (L. Levy and D. Mahoney eds. 1987).

13. See D. Magleby, Direct Legislation (1984); B. Zisk, Money, Media and the Grass Roots (1987).

reflected a concern for the "collective territorial interest." Perhaps one reason for the enduring attractiveness of communitarian politics is that citizens would like to conceive of their political life in terms of geographic or localized interests. Whether such interests are defined as subjectively felt attitudes or observable group activities,[14] they are specifically protected by a representation scheme that includes territorial decentralization. Indeed, the one person, one vote doctrine itself reinforces the relevance of size to the cohesiveness of a political unit, but only within the framework of a geographically based district system of elections and only as an impediment to malapportionment's distortion of communities.[15]

Community cohesiveness may be expressed through community self-determination, which may include defining the quality of community life and determining who qualifies as a participating member. But community self-determination may not erode fundamental national rights, one of which is the individual right to a vote that counts equally with all others. At a certain point, then, a community's expression of its cohesiveness could conflict with the one person, one vote standard. The extent of the application of the one person, one vote doctrine was not fully delineated by the Warren Court, although the equal vote principle was applied to local elections in the 1968 ruling in *Avery v. Midland County*.[16] One of the Burger Court's first tasks was to determine whether the *Avery* ruling should be further extended to prohibit local suffrage restrictions, which were defended as guaranteeing voters' stake in the local community. To begin to see if the "cohesive community" finds protection in constitutional law, I shall first compare the Burger Court's decisions in these cases to the territorial conceptualization of representation.

Stake in the Community

Local suffrage regulations represent the clearest conflict between territorial representation and individuals' equal political influence. But

---

14. H. Pitkin, The Concept of Representation 160 (1967).
15. See G. Gudgin and P. J. Taylor, Seats, Votes and the Spatial Organization of Elections 3–5 (1979); Grofman and Handley, Why Are There So Few Black Congressmen from the South? (paper presented to the American Political Science Association, Chicago, Ill.) (Sept. 1987).
16. 390 U.S. 474 (1968).

such regulations also reflect the justifiable notion that the benefits and burdens of citizenship should be correlative. One way communities can protect their collective integrity is by requiring some stake in the community from prospective voters who wish to participate in collective community decision making.

Such regulations, although sensible on their face, were tainted by their association with racially exclusive political practices. The Warren Court, therefore, had long been circumspect in its review of local voting regulations. With the passage of the Twenty-fourth Amendment in 1964, poll taxes and other devices abridging the right to vote in federal elections were declared unconstitutional. The following year, the Warren Court upheld the application of the amendment to several cases involving discriminatory state practices. One of these cases, *Harman v. Forssenius*,[17] involved Virginia's practice of waiving the poll tax if the federal voter filed a certificate of residence six months before the election. The Court found that such a punitive use of a residency requirement violated the Twenty-fourth Amendment, and speculated that any attempt to define a voter's stake in the community, whether fiscally motivated or not, compromised the right to vote.[18] Similarly, *Harper v. Virginia Board of Elections*,[19] decided in 1966, invalidated a second Virginia poll tax requirement and its alleged stake-in-the-community rationale.[20] Rejecting the state's rationale for the poll tax, the Warren Court argued that wealth, like race, was not germane to a voter's ability to participate intelligently in the electoral process.[21]

As with the *Reynolds* cases, *Harper* prompted accusations that the Court was unilaterally imposing its conception of representative gov-

---

17. 380 U.S. 528 (1965).
18. Carrington v. Rash, 380 U.S. 89 (1965), concerned a provision in the Texas constitution prohibiting servicemen permanently stationed in the state from voting in state elections. The majority held that the restriction violated the equal protection clause because it *absolutely deprived* a segment of the population from exercising its suffrage right.
19. 383 U.S. 663 (1966).
20. *Harper* contained one of the first articulations of strict scrutiny standards for equal protection. Because the restriction abridged the fundamental right to vote, the Court examined whether the poll tax served a compelling state interest and was the least restrictive means of achieving that interest.
21. 383 U.S. at 668.

ernment on the special circumstances of the states.[22] For dissenters Black and Harlan, the poll tax was rationally related to the creation of an electorate committed enough to surrender a few dollars to the state's economy; the poll tax, they argued, legitimately apportioned the benefits of citizenship and its burdens.[23] This theme of the correlative benefits and burdens of citizenship, and the tenet that the community had the right to apportion them, would prove prominent in future local election cases.

Paradoxically, in two special purpose election cases decided in the Warren Court's last term, the majority used this benefits/burdens framework to extend the one person, one vote requirement. Both *Kramer v. Union School District*[24] and *Cipriano v. City of Houma*[25] concerned suffrage restrictions in specialized local elections. *Kramer* involved the use of real-property ownership and parental status as voting qualifications for state school district elections; *Cipriano* involved the use of real-property ownership as a condition for participation in municipal bond elections. In neither case did the Warren Court reject the concept of elections open only to "those primarily affected or interested";[26] rather, it invalidated these election provisions because they were insufficiently tailored to stake in the community. In each case, the Court maintained that the provision's infirmity was that the benefits and burdens of the electoral policies fell indiscriminately on enfranchised and disenfranchised community residents.[27] Interestingly, this benefits/burdens analysis—central to the Warren Court's last decisions on local suffrage restrictions—had been introduced in Harlan's and Fortas's dissents in the 1968 case of *Avery v. Midland County,* the first decision to apply one person, one vote to local elections. Indeed, both the *Avery* and *Kramer* majorities left open the possibility that the specialized character of some local elections might exclude them from the stringencies of the *Reynolds* voting requirement.

---

22. 383 U.S. at 676 (Black, J., dissenting); 383 U.S. at 682 (Harlan, J., dissenting).
23. 383 U.S. at 672 (Black, J., dissenting); 383 U.S. at 683 (Harlan, J., dissenting).
24. 395 U.S. 621 (1969).
25. 395 U.S. 701 (1969).
26. See *Kramer,* 395 U.S. at 632.
27. See *Kramer,* 395 U.S. at 630; *Cipriano,* 395 U.S. at 705. In the latter decision, the per curiam opinion employed the language of stake in the community: "The benefits and burdens of the bond issue fall indiscriminately on property owners and nonproperty owners."

In its first local suffrage case in 1970, *City of Phoenix v. Kolodzieski*,[28] the new Burger Court tested the limits of this hypothetical exception. *Phoenix* also concerned a municipal bond election that limited the franchise to real-property owners. The White majority invalidated the restriction, noting that the bond's tax base included non–property owners.[29] As in *Cipriano,* the financial burden of the general obligation bond was not correlative with the benefit of electoral choice. Although decided by nominally distinct courts, *Kramer, Cipriano,* and *Phoenix* are more similar than different. Arguably, their common analytic framework of the benefits and burdens of community membership implies an emerging recognition of territorial community interests.

Both the Warren and early Burger Court suffrage restriction decisions still maintained that if a local government service had a disproportionate impact on certain residents, modifications of the one person, one vote principle were justifiable. The Burger Court continued to grapple with the question of how specialized the functions of a local government must be to exclude it from the one person, one vote requirement. One year after the *Phoenix* case, *Abate v. Mundt*[30] demonstrated that apportioning the benefits and burdens of citizenship was indeed a valid framework for upholding suffrage restrictions. In *Abate* the Burger Court permitted the use of non-population-based, multimember districts for the election of the Rockland County Board. The average population deviation of 11.9 percent resulted from districting based on town boundaries—districting designed to reflect territorial communities of interest within the county. Marshall's majority opinion approved the system for a local government in which public services were provided by towns and the county working in close cooperation; Marshall denied, however, that the Court was suggesting "that certain geographic areas or political interests [were] entitled to disproportionate representation."[31] Without making too much of the result in *Abate,* we can still conclude that it is the first Burger decision that is clearly consistent with the conceptualization of territorial representation.

A vital difference between *Abate* and cases such as *Phoenix* was that

---

28. 399 U.S. 204 (1970).
29. 399 U.S. at 209.
30. 403 U.S. 182 (1971).
31. 403 U.S. at 185.

no resident was actually excluded from electoral participation. But if *Abate* was suggesting that stake in the community was related to geographic vicinity, then residency requirements for prospective voters might be a valid way to promote "intelligent use of the franchise." With *Dunn v. Blumstein*,[32] in 1972, the Burger Court began to examine the legitimacy of durational residency requirements for participation in state and local elections. In the *Dunn* case, Tennessee required one year of residence for eligibility to vote in state elections and three months for eligibility to vote in county elections. While the Court did not evaluate residency requirements per se, it noted that Tennessee's length of residency requirement was unrelated to the state's alleged purpose of guaranteeing a knowledgeable electorate. Long-term residence, in and of itself, did not necessarily indicate knowledge of local affairs.[33] In subsequent rulings in 1973, the Burger Court, citing administrative convenience and standardized consistency, settled on a fifty-day residency cutoff.[34] In upholding minimal residency requirements, the Court found uniform administration of local elections, rather than stake in the community, the controlling factor. Therefore, the voter residency cases are at best irrelevant to a territorial conceptualization of representation, and at worst contradictory to it.

In the wake of *Dunn* and its progeny, states and localities had to turn to other criteria to determine a prospective voter's stake in the community. *Hill v. Stone*,[35] a 1975 decision, concerned a renewed attempt to infer stake in the community from fiscal responsibility. Fort Worth, Texas, employed a rendering requirement for city bond elections, which limited the franchise to individuals who had listed real or personal property under voluntary tax assessment. The city argued that the rendering requirement was a self-enforced tax law, aiding the city in its collection of revenue. If an individual demonstrated modest civic-mindedness by rendering any amount of property, he demonstrated a sufficient level of municipal commitment to participate responsibly on questions of bond indebtedness. Neverthe-

---

32. 405 U.S. 330 (1972).
33. 405 U.S. at 354.
34. 410 U.S. at 680; 410 U.S. at 688. In Marston v. Lewis, 410 U.S. 679 (1973), and Burns v. Fortson, 410 U.S. 686 (1973), the Court upheld the validity of fifty-day voter residency and registration requirements for nonpresidential elections.
35. 420 U.S. 289 (1975).

less, relying on previous bond election decisions, the Marshall majority found this stake-in-the-community justification unconvincing and invalidated the suffrage restriction.

The result in *Hill* obviously contradicts the conceptual type of territorial representation; not surprisingly, the three-judge dissent strongly confirmed the principle of local self-rule. Rehnquist's dissenting opinion defended the restriction in terms of the correlative benefits and burdens of community membership.[36] In addition, the Court as a whole maintained that given a compelling interest, the community retains the right to restrict the franchise.

Two years later, in *Holt Civic Club v. Tuscaloosa*,[37] the Burger Court identified a condition that legitimated such community action: physical residence within territorial borders. Tuscaloosa excluded residents of unincorporated areas from voting in municipal elections, in spite of the fact that these outlying areas contributed some tax revenues for certain municipal services. The Rehnquist majority upheld the restriction, noting that community integrity included the right not to extend the suffrage beyond existing territorial boundaries.[38] This spatial boundary meant that the residents of Holt constituted a separate, geographically distinct community of interest.[39] Because of its attitude toward defining community membership, the *Holt* decision is a clear confirmation of the conceptualization of territorial representation.

The vehemence of the *Holt* dissenters further confirms this reading of the case; led by Justice Brennan, they explicitly rejected the theory of territorial representation. Brennan accused the Court of "ced[ing] to geography a talismanic significance contrary to the theory and meaning of past voting rights cases."[40] Central to the dissent-

---

36. Rehnquist found, first of all, that the alleged disenfranchised "class" consisted of individuals who had failed to render property out of carelessness and irresponsibility, or as a tax-avoidance method. 420 U.S. at 304. The regulation simply prevented citizens who violated their legal obligations "from influencing the process which results in the imposition of [bond] obligations." 420 U.S. at 307.

37. 439 U.S. 60 (1978).

38. 439 U.S. at 68.

39. Indeed, Stevens's concurrence emphasized that Holt residents were not "as interested in and connected with electoral decisions" as were Tuscaloosa residents. Tuscaloosa did not tax Holt residents directly, zone their property, or control their schools. 439 U.S. at 77.

40. 439 U.S. at 81.

ers' complaint was the Court's assumption that formal territorial boundaries delimit political communities. The purpose of residency requirements for the franchise, Brennan admitted, was to preserve the basic conception of a political community. But at the heart of the conception of community was "a reciprocal relationship between the process of government and those who subject themselves to that process by choosing to live within the area of its authoritative application."[41] This "area of authoritative application" was not, for Brennan, precisely geographical; rather, a community of interest with respect to a government's operations would consist of all those affected by its jurisdiction.[42] Brennan seemed to suggest that the geographic basis of representation was merely historical accident that should be overridden to foster the equal political influence of individuals. The only limitation on the extension of individuals' equal political influence would be constitutionally structural ones—the existence of the states.[43]

Talismanic or functional, geographic communities received some recognition from the Burger Court as entities that legitimately represent local interests. Although only two stake-in-the-community decisions confirmed or were consistent with the territorial concept of representation—*Abate* in 1971 and *Holt* in 1978—the Burger Court's careful scrutiny of different types of local suffrage restrictions produced local communities that more closely resembled plural communities of interest. By broadening the definition of who had a participatory stake in the community, the Burger Court's decisions strengthened the legitimacy of local governments as representative institutions. As a result, the *Mahan* policy of districting respecting subdivision lines gained validity.

The extent to which a local government may determine who has sufficient stake in the community to participate in its collective decisions is only one aspect of the territorial conceptualization. The second, and arguably more important, exercise of local self-rule is the

---

41. 439 U.S. at 82.
42. 439 U.S. at 85.
43. The logic of Brennan's argument in *Holt* had been foreseen by the dissenters in *Kramer*. If interest in the election was determinative of who should participate, Stewart mused in his *Kramer* dissent, then interest in election outcomes may often reach beyond the district in question—indeed, beyond state boundaries. 395 U.S. at 637. But was interest in an election really the same as material or personal stake in that election? If not, then geographic residence was surely a practical means of approximating stake in the election.

use of traditional local powers to define the conditions or quality of community life. The political role of local governments is not mentioned in the Constitution, but the Burger Court was supportive of such governments as structures for majoritarian self-determination and public participation, and as providers of public services.[44] In the following section, I will examine whether, during the Burger years, "community self-determination seemed to attain the status of a penumbral, quasi-constitutional principle that provided substantial protection for local governments against constitutional claims."[45] If the Burger Court did elevate local self-rule to a "higher law," were its decisions unambiguous confirmation of the conceptual type of territorial representation?

Quality of Community Life

The quality-of-community-life cases were a series of decisions recognizing the merit of local control in various substantive policy areas. Early on, education was an area in which a consistent policy of local self-rule was articulated by the Court. In three decisions in the early 1970s, the Burger Court considered the importance of permitting a local government the autonomous operation of its own school system.[46] In the wake of busing precedents such as *Swann v. Charlotte-Mecklenburg Board of Education*,[47] the "neighborhood school system" was still tainted by suspected de facto segregation. However, only one of the three Burger Court decisions restricted local control of schools,

---

44. Gelfand, The Burger Court and the New Federalism, 21 B.C.L. Rev. 763, 764–66 (1980).
45. Gelfand, The Constitutional Position of American Local Government, 14 Hastings Const. L.Q. 635, 636 (1987).
46. Wright v. Council of the City of Emporia, 407 U.S. 451 (1972) (establishment of a separate school system curtailed for its segregative effect); San Antonio Independent School District v. Rodriguez, 411 U.S. 1 (1973) (local tax system for financing education upheld); Milliken v. Bradley, 418 U.S. 717 (1974) (judicial relief of segregative effects invalid if it ignores school district lines). Both the language and the results of two of the cases, *San Antonio Independent School District v. Rodriguez* and *Milliken v. Bradley*, can be read as confirmation of the conceptualization of territorial representation.
47. 402 U.S. 1 (1971). This case, decided by the Burger Court, was the last unanimous ruling on school desegregation. It concerned the use of busing to relieve racial imbalances among schools within the same metropolitan school district.

and even in that case the Stewart majority recognized the value of local responsibility.[48]

The Burger Court's justification of decentralized control of education policy exhibits the foundation for its support of local initiative generally. The Court defended local control of schools as a benefit of pluralism, which "affords some opportunity for experimentation, innovation and a healthy competition for educational excellence."[49] To deny local initiative would be to deny the locality's existence as an independent governmental entity; to curtail local autonomy would adversely affect community investment in the quality of local policy.[50] These early education cases showed that the Burger Court would uphold local initiative at the expense of equal political influence for individuals. In fact, the quality-of-community-life decisions are an example of group representation concerns superseding an individual-based notion of politics.

Local Majorities as Legislators: The Referendum

In a particular subset of the quality-of-community-life cases, there was ostensible harmony rather than tension between local self-rule and equal opportunity to participate. These were the cases involving the use of the referendum as a local policy-making procedure. The Burger Court strongly supported these local legislative efforts, while approving the referendum's consistency with the one person, one vote directive. However, more important than the procedure's ostensible populism was its importance for community self-determination and for policy-making by local majorities. Examination of the referendum decisions reveals that the Burger Court clearly valued the latter, while paying lip-service to the former.

The Warren Court's doctrinal legacy on referenda was mixed. In its 1964 decision in *Lucas v. Colorado General Assembly*,[51] in which a

---

48. Wright v. Council of the City of Emporia, 407 U.S. at 469.
49. San Antonia Independent School District v. Rodriguez, 411 U.S. at 50. The *San Antonio* case was also significant to the development of equal protection law, for it found that education was not a fundamental right and wealth was not a suspect classification, so neither triggered strict scrutiny analysis. 411 U.S. at 16.
50. Wright v. Council of the City of Emporia, 407 U.S. at 478; Milliken v. Bradley, 418 U.S. at 742.
51. 377 U.S. 713 (1964).

"little federal" districting plan had been ratified by a popular majority, the Warren Court did not discredit the referendum procedure itself. However, in a referendum case decided in its last term, the Warren Court not only invalidated a specific use but also questioned the procedure's intrinsic fairness. *Hunter v. Erikson*,[52] in 1969, concerned a recently passed automatic referendum requirement in Akron, Ohio, for any proposed ordinance regulating real-estate transactions on the basis of race, religion, or national origin. While White's majority opinion argued that the referendum requirement was a substantial barrier to the enactment of fair-housing ordinances, he was also critical of the referendum procedure itself:

> [T]he reality is that the law's impact falls on the minority. The majority needs no protection against discrimination, and if it did, a referendum might be bothersome but no more than that. [The referendum procedure] places special burdens on racial minorities within the governmental process.[53]

Some political scientists also criticize the direct legislation process as significantly less representative than the candidate electoral process. Referenda are structured in such a way as to discourage participation by less educated and poorer voters, and ballot issues unaccompanied by candidate elections mobilize few citizens.[54] The image of the referendum as a device for encouraging broad participation is unrealistic; arguably then, the Burger Court's support for this procedure has more to do with local autonomy than individuals' political influence.

The Burger Court's first referendum case was a dramatic test of its commitment to local control, as it seemed to pit communitarian democracy against equal protection of the law. In *James v. Valtierra*,[55] in 1971, the Court examined California's constitutional requirement of mandatory referendum elections in communities proposing construction of low-income public housing projects. Black's majority opinion upheld the procedure, arguing that "provisions for referendums demonstrate devotion to democracy, not to bias, discrimination

---

52. 393 U.S. 385 (1969).
53. 393 U.S. 385, 391 (1969).
54. D. Magleby, Direct Legislation 197 (1984).
55. 402 U.S. 137 (1971).

or prejudice."[56] Black was unconvinced that a denial of equal protection existed simply because a referendum election disadvantaged certain individuals.[57] He defended the Court's position on the referendum in *James* with both an economic and a procedural argument. He first evoked the theme of collective economic burdens: because housing projects required a large expenditure of local funds for increased governmental services, despite a loss of tax revenue on the property designated for the project, it was appropriate that the entire community ratify such an undertaking.[58] Procedurally, he emphasized the referendum's adherence to one person, one vote: all those who were concerned cast a ballot, and the local electorate perceived that the burdens of the project outweighed its benefits.[59] The majority assumption clearly marks *James* as confirming the conceptual type of territorial representation.

In *Gordon v. Lance*,[60] decided that same term, the Burger Court considered West Virginia's constitutional requirement of a referendum to approve city bond indebtedness or tax increases beyond the constitutional limit. Like *James*, *Gordon* dealt with a question of state constitutional law and with the exercise of a traditional governmental power.[61] What distinguished the situation in *Gordon* was the fact that the referendum procedure included an extraordinary-majority requirement. The Burger majority upheld the procedure as reasonably related to the local community's decision to issue bonds; legalizing indebtedness was, after all, "committing the credit of infants and of generations yet unborn."[62] Interestingly, *Gordon* seemed to allude to the integrity of a territorial community beyond the current citizenry.

---

56. 402 U.S. at 141.
57. 402 U.S. at 142.
58. 402 U.S. at 143.
59. The dissenters—Marshall, Blackmun, and Brennan—did not criticize the referendum procedure per se, although they did challenge the majority's assumption that the referendum result represented the preference of a recognizable community of interest, or of the local "public interest." Marshall argued instead that low-income persons were made to bear the unfair burden of the mandatory referendum requirement for low-income housing projects. 402 U.S. at 144.
60. 403 U.S. 1 (1971).
61. *James* concerned a zoning decision, while *Gordon* concerned concurrent local taxing power and state budgetary autonomy as these affected a bond to finance county schools.
62. 403 U.S. at 6.

Its result, too, confirmed the conceptualization of territorial representation.

The *James* and *Gordon* holdings supported the referendum with respect to broad legislative acts. In *City of Eastlake v. Forest City Enterprises*,[63] in 1976, the Burger Court considered whether a referendum procedure was also appropriate for particular administrative decisions—specifically, whether majoritarian public administration was legitimate. *Eastlake* involved an Ohio constitutional provision reserving to the people of each municipality the power of referendum over all questions that the municipality was authorized to control. According to this provision, the city charter was amended by popular vote to require that changes in zoning law be passed by a 55 percent referendum vote. *Eastlake* is interesting because of the complaint of the appellees: they asserted that the zoning referendum requirement was an impermissible delegation of legislative power to the people, as voters were given no standards to guide their zoning decisions. The Court upheld the referendum, while correcting the appellee's designation of it as a delegation of power. It is the people, Burger argued for the Court, who reserve popular power to themselves and choose not to delegate it to their representatives.[64] As in *James* and *Gordon*, the collective actions of a geographic community in *Eastlake* were assumed to represent a community of interest.[65] *Eastlake*, then, must also be considered a confirmation of the conceptual type of territorial representation.

The Court moved a step closer to granting presumptive validity to referendum decisions in the 1977 case of *Lockport v. Citizens for Community Action*.[66] The *Lockport* opinion demonstrated even more decisively than the previous referendum decisions the Burger Court's apparent commitment to territorial representation. The case concerned a New York constitutional provision mandating that changes

---

63. 426 U.S. 668 (1976).

64. 426 U.S. at 672. He also found the procedural due process argument to be inapplicable, for the people of Ohio had specified this reservation of power in the state constitution. 426 U.S. at 673–75.

65. The justices who dissented from the populist implications of *Eastlake* were largely the same justices who most rigorously supported the one person, one vote doctrine in the reapportionment cases. Stevens's and Brennan's underlying concern was the equalization of political power. 426 U.S. at 688–89.

66. 430 U.S. 259 (1977).

in a county government charter be approved by referendum. The provision further required concurrent majority approval consisting of 50 percent of urban voters and 50 percent of nonurban voters within the county. *Lockport* raised the issue of whether the geographic representation in the referendum procedure was "residential vote dilution," or a means of apportioning the benefits and burdens of the ballot issue among the citizenry.

In upholding the procedure, the Stewart majority legitimated the aggregation of voters' interests by geographic residence.[67] City government had the greatest autonomy under state law, so changes serving to strengthen county government would have the most immediate impact on the power of the less autonomous town governments. The referendum issue dealt with county services that affected town residents to a greater degree than city residents; therefore, the concurrent regional majority provision appropriately recognized the unequal benefits and burdens of the issue on different constituencies.[68] The system certainly did not comport with a rigorous application of equal voting influence, but the importance of geographic representation outweighed concern for electoral equality. Because of this, the *Lockport* referendum decision confirms the conceptual type of territorial representation.[69]

---

67. 430 U.S. at 269.

68. 430 U.S. at 270–71.

69. The Burger Court supported the referendum procedure as representing the valid action of a geographic group interest. However, it was leery of direct regulation of group participation in referenda. In two referendum cases concerning municipal efforts to prevent electoral corruption, the Court invalidated local regulation of electoral competition in referendums. In First National Bank of Boston v. Bellotti, 435 U.S. 765 (1978), the Court struck down an ordinance restricting corporate political contributions to influence referendum outcomes. Similarly, in *Citizens Against Rent Control v. City of Berkeley*, 454 U.S. 290 (1981), the Court invalidated an ordinance limiting monetary contributions to political committees formed to support or oppose ballot measures at referendum. The Court dismissed the city's asserted interest in preventing corruption of the referendum process due to the influence of large expenditures for political advertising. Referendum procedures, while important for local control, received no special judicial deference when their conditions restricted certain groups' direct participation. Arguably, the Court was more solicitous of the rights of corporate associations than it was of community self-determination. I shall address this issue in the discussion of the conceptualization of corporatist representation in chapter 4.

Ironically, the last referendum case decided by the Burger Court resembled the Warren decision in *Hunter* and showed greater sensitivity to the political influence of racial minorities. In 1982, in *Washington v. Seattle School District No. One*,[70] the Court considered a state referendum procedure terminating mandatory busing. Blackmun's majority opinion held that the referendum requirement violated the equal protection clause by burdening future attempts to integrate schools.[71] Although it was a 5 to 4 ruling, *Seattle School District* firmly rejected local control as a justification for infringing federal rights.[72] While lack of minority representation was chiefly responsible for the Court's invalidation of the referendum procedure in *Seattle*,[73] the decision seemed to recall the *Lucas* principle that geographic representation must be sacrificed when minority groups or political interests are directly burdened by the referendum procedure.

While *Seattle School District* obviously contradicts the conceptualization of territorial representation, the referendum decisions as a whole reflect the Burger Court's concern for plural rather than equal representation. In effect, the referendum procedure allows a small number of voters to pass laws that bind the total community.[74] Yet the Burger Court conceded that a referendum's result in fact defined and represented a geographic community interest. Of course, the Burger Court could not always harmonize local control with the ostensible populism of the referendum procedure, as *Seattle School District* illustrates. Ultimately, the Court's support for geographic representation was qualified by judicial sensitivity to the political access of racial minorities. As we shall see, concern for racial groups' interests affected judicial scrutiny of other areas of local policy-making, particularly zoning.

---

70. 458 U.S. 457 (1982).

71. It did so by lodging decision-making authority at a "remote level of government." 458 U.S. at 483.

72. The four dissenters, led by Justice Powell, argued that the Court was intruding into state governmental structure. 458 U.S. at 492.

73. Under Washington v. Davis, 426 U.S. 229 (1976), and Arlington Heights v. Metropolitan Housing Corporation, 429 U.S. 252 (1977), a minority group must show that intent to discriminate was a motivating factor behind the referendum. See Gunn, Initiatives and Referendums, 22 Urb. L. Ann. 154–55 (1981).

74. W. Kelso, American Democratic Theory 67 (1978); Gunn, Initiatives and Referendums, 22 Urb. L. Ann. 137 (1981).

Zoning as Community Quality-Control

Land-use law is the primary method for local definition of the character of neighborhoods.[75] In the mid-1970s, the Burger Court sustained several commercial zoning regulations as valid efforts to define the quality of community life.[76] Generally, the Court exercised the same deference toward residential zoning ordinances. For example, in *Village of Belle Terre v. Boraas*,[77] in 1974, the Douglas majority upheld a local residential ordinance restricting land use to one-family dwellings. This ordinance applied the community's definition of a one-family household. Though there was disagreement about the result, both the majority and dissenting opinions evoked "quality of life" as a permissible subject of regulation by local governments.[78] As an example of both community self-determination and public participation, *Belle Terre* is a confirmation of the model of territorial representation.

---

75. Other methods include restriction of nuisance noise, door-to-door soliciting, and billboard placement. See City of Burbank v. Lockheed, 411 U.S. 624 (1973); Schaumburg v. Citizens for a Better Environment, 444 U.S. 620 (1980); and Metromedia Inc. v. City of San Diego, 453 U.S. 490 (1981). In all three cases, local attempts at regulation were struck down because of commerce clause or First Amendment conflicts.

76. The principle that localities should be permitted to preserve their community character was upheld in zoning for pornographic institutions, regulation to preserve the "local charm" of a tourist area, and local licensing for "head shops." See Miller v. California, 413 U.S. 15 (1973); Young v. American Mini Theaters, 427 U.S. 50 (1976); New Orleans v. Dukes, 427 U.S. 297 (1976); Hoffman Estates v. Flipside, 455 U.S. 487 (1982).

77. 416 U.S. 1 (1974).

78. 416 U.S. at 5, 13 (Marshall, J., dissenting). In sustaining the zoning ordinance, the majority supported both the power of municipal government and the participatory influence of local citizen groups. The fact that both local government and citizen lobbies favored the zoning explains the majority voting bloc of the "conservative" justices, the swingmen White and Blackmun, and the "liberal" justice Douglas. See R. Linowes and D. Allensworth, The Politics of Land Use Law 54 (1976).

Local control of the quality of community life was a prevalent defense in cases involving residential zoning restrictions. In Arlington Heights v. Metropolitan Housing Corporation, 429 U.S. 252 (1977), the petitioner village had denied the appellee permission to build a multiple-family dwelling on land already zoned for single-family residences. The housing corporation challenged the village zoning plan as motivated by racial discrimination. Arlington thus raised the issue of the representation of minority group interests in local decisions regulating neighborhood character. Despite the possibility of racial discrimination, the Court sustained the zoning ordinance because it reflected a consistent policy of using multiple-family residence zones as buffers between single-family neighborhoods and commercial areas.

If residential zoning regulations concern the quality of community life, a reasonable question would be what territorial subdivision boundary demarcates the community whose "life" is affected. *Warth v. Seldin*[79] linked stake in the community with residential zoning decisions. The key question in *Warth* was the petitioners' standing to bring the suit against the local zoning ordinance. The petitioners were residents and civic organizations from a neighboring township.[80] As they were not citizens of the appellee community and had no claim to be represented in that community's zoning decisions, the Powell majority denied them standing to sue. In an argument reminiscent of the suffrage restriction decision in *Holt*, the Court maintained that territorial subdivision boundaries constitute the local community of interest. The result of *Warth*—or, at least, the dicta of the majority opinion—should also be read as confirming the conceptual type of territorial representation.

Despite its commitment in decisions such as *Belle Terre* and *Warth* to local regulation of the composition of neighborhoods, the Burger Court drew the line at a residential zoning ordinance dictating the types of related individuals that could occupy single-family dwelling units. Thus, in 1977, in *Moore v. City of East Cleveland*,[81] a plurality overruled the ordinance because of its restrictive definition of what constituted a "family." The East Cleveland ordinance was directed against various permutations of the extended family in an overt attempt to prevent overcrowding; it had prohibited a woman from residing with her son, his son, and a grandchild by another son. The Powell plurality held that the ordinance's invasion of the private realm of the family was not adequately tailored to the city's stated purposes.[82] Brennan's concurrence broadly condemned the city's assumption that the zoning power was a license for local communities to encroach into private areas of family life in the name of regulating the quality of total community life.[83]

---

79. 422 U.S. 490 (1975).

80. They claimed that the zoning ordinance enacted by Penfield, New York, stipulating minimum size requirements for single-family dwellings, had forced their township to impose higher tax rates to subsidize the area's required low-income housing. 422 U.S. at 495–96.

81. 431 U.S. 494 (1977).

82. 431 U.S. at 499.

83. 431 U.S. at 507. A third separate, concurring opinion was filed by Stevens, whose vote was necessary for the 5–4 decision. His opinion emphasized property rights,

Moore pitted the local geographic community against a broader racial community of interest. The paradox of *Moore* was that the ordinance was not anti-black, but represented a dispute between two socioeconomic groups within East Cleveland's black community. The ordinance reflected the aspirations of middle-class blacks with respect to city-wide neighborhood planning and eradication of the "ghetto life-style."[84] As one scholar of family law commented, "seen from this perspective, victory for Mrs. Moore was total defeat for the other residents of East Cleveland, while victory for them was not total defeat for her, except insofar as she wished to remain in their community while transforming its membership to her taste."[85] Was the Court insensitive to the economic and emotional needs of the current majority of residents of East Cleveland? Perhaps, because it myopically viewed the case as a dispute between "a family" and "the state."[86] *Moore* was a repudiation of the concern for community attempts to preserve a common social identity; its result contradicts the territorial conceptualization of representation, but only because the plurality falsely construed the case as state-endorsed racial discrimination.

Moore proved an anomaly among the quality-of-community-life cases, for the Court continued to construe local zoning that furthered public welfare as a broad power serving spiritual, aesthetic, physical, and monetary values. In a series of land-use cases from the late 1970s to the early 1980s, the Court handed down decisions that clearly confirmed the conceptualization of territorial representation. In line

---

not the interest in family relations. 431 U.S. at 513. Four justices dissented in *Moore*. Stewart argued that the appellant's claim of a constitutionally protected right of association with respect to residence had been answered in *Belle Terre*. Of course, the Belle Terre ordinance had not discriminated between different groups of related persons in defining the family unit, excluding only nonrelated individuals from single-family dwellings. In contrast to Brennan (431 U.S. at 508) Stewart did not feel that the requirements of the ordinance represented an effort to force minority and ethnic groups to conform to white middle-class notions of family life, violating the integrity of community life in ethnic East Cleveland. He observed that both the city manager and city commission, not to mention the majority of the population, were black. The city government's values with respect to the quality of community and family life could thus not constitute the imposition of white suburbia's community values. 431 U.S. at 534–37.

84. Burt, The Constitution of the Family, 1979 S. Ct. Rev. 329.

85. Burt, The Burger Court and the Family, in The Burger Court 92, 111 (V. Blasi ed. 1983).

86. Id. at 110–11.

with its endorsement of the use of community standards to define obscenity, the Court continued to defer to local zoning that affected "adult" businesses.[87] The Court also deferred to local regulation of other types of property. In *Arlington County Board v. Richards*,[88] in 1977, a unanimous Court upheld a zoning ordinance prohibiting commuters from parking in certain residential neighborhoods, while allowing residents to park there. A year later, in *Penn Central Transportation Co. v. New York City*,[89] the Court upheld a city landmarks law requiring that properties declared to possess historic and artistic importance be maintained at the owner's expense. The Court dismissed the appellant's charge of a "taking" without due process, finding that an interference arising from a public program that adjusted the benefits and burdens of economic life to promote a greater community good was permissible.[90] In *Agins v. City of Tiburon*[91] in 1980, a unanimous Court upheld the city's authority to restrict the development of urban land according to residential specifications; Tiburon's use of zoning permits to protect city residents from the ill effects of urbanization was judged squarely within its power to regulate the quality of life[92] Lastly, in *City Council of Los Angeles v. Taxpayers for Vincent*,[93] in 1984, the Court sustained an ordinance restricting the placement and size of advertising billboards to preserve the aesthetic character of the community. In the above cases, the community's desire to use zoning power to enhance the quality of residential life was endorsed, often by a dramatic margin.

The Burger Court also assumed that local residents must expect to incur some burdens in the promotion of greater community values. The burdens an individual could be expected to assume in the name of public benefits had been a prominent theme in cases involving stake in the community, or local suffrage restrictions. What constituted one's fair share of a public burden was also significant in certain

---

87. On the Burger Court's standards for obscenity, see Miller v. California, 413 U.S. 5 (1973). On zoning to regulate pornographic businesses, see City of Renton v. Playtime Theatres, 472 U.S. 1006 (1986); Young v. American Mini Theatres, 427 U.S. 50 (1976).
88. 434 U.S. 5 (1977).
89. 438 U.S. 104 (1978).
90. 438 U.S. at 124.
91. 447 U.S. 255 (1980).
92. 447 U.S. at 261.
93. 104 S. Ct. 2118 (1984).

zoning cases, as exemplified by *City of Memphis v. Greene*,[94] in 1981. The city had closed off a public street through a predominantly white neighborhood at the residents' request, with the alleged purpose of preventing traffic pollution and interruption of community living in a residential area. Black residents of a neighboring housing development claimed they bore the burden of the street-closing, since the detour deprived them of the use of the property. Nevertheless, the Stevens majority found no evidence of negative effects on property values in the black neighborhood, nor of purposeful discrimination.[95] The Court labeled the traffic regulation's differential effect on the two neighborhoods merely a "routine burden of citizenship."[96]

Memphis illustrates two points about the zoning decisions. First, it shows the Court's strong support for zoning as an aspect of community self-determination, even in the face of disproportionate or discriminatory impact on minority group interests. Second, it shows that the benefits/burdens framework of analysis employed in the suffrage restriction cases was also important to the Court's justification of zoning restrictions. Like the quality-of-community-life decisions generally, these zoning cases confirm the conceptual type of territorial representation.

"Balkanization" of the Economy or Legitimate Protection of Local Markets?

The correlative benefits and burdens analysis was also invoked by the Court in its review of local economic protectionist legislation. State and local involvement in the local economy is another means of regulating the quality of community life. Like land-use controls, local protectionism is also an assertion that the community has a right to regulate private property in the public interest.

The Burger Court's defense of states as autonomous service providers is a well-known aspect of the brief resuscitation of the Tenth

---

94. 451 U.S. 100 (1981).
95. 451 U.S. at 114, 117.
96. 451 U.S. at 128. For the three dissenters, the regulation was far from a routine burden of citizenship. They stressed that legislating discriminatory racial separation, even if it might reflect community values, was beyond the absolute limit of local control of community character. 451 U.S. at 136.

Amendment.[97] The Tenth Amendment, which reserves to the states powers not delegated to the national government, had been central to the constitutional debate about states' legislative sovereignty. Though the reading of the Tenth Amendment as an "express prohibition" has played itself out, the notion that state and local governments should be protected from federal interference in their essential functions remains at the heart of the theory of federalism. Local protectionism numbers among these essential functions, the underlying theory being that local citizens merit certain economic benefits through protectionist legislation because of their greater contribution to the community.[98] However, in the local protectionism cases, as in the cases of local suffrage restriction, the Court was somewhat suspicious of regulations allocating rights in proportion to citizens' "commitment" to the community. For example, in *Zobel v. Williams*,[99] in 1982, the Court invalidated Alaska's preferential system of distributing its mineral income fund in proportion to citizens' years of residence since Alaskan statehood. Finding an equal protection violation, and echoing the reasoning of earlier stake-in-the-community decisions, the Burger majority argued that Alaska's rationale would "open the door to state apportionment of other rights, benefits and services according to length of residency."[100] One could argue that the reason

---

97. National League of Cities v. Usery, 426 U.S. 833 (1976). Cf. Garcia v. San Antonio Metropolitan Transit Authority, 469 U.S. 528 (1985). See generally Gelfand, The Constitutional Position of American Local Government, 14 Hastings Const. L.Q. 635 (1987).

98. Such "protectionism" is only legitimate when the state acts as a "market participant," not as a "market regulator." The latter role constitutes an impermissible burden on commerce. On this distinction, see Reeves v. Stake, 447 U.S. 429 (1980); Hughes v. Alexandria Scrap Corp., 426 U.S. 794 (1976). But cf. South-Central Timber Development v. Wunnicke, 467 U.S. 82 (1984).

A further bar to states' preference of residents over nonresidents for certain economic opportunities is the privileges and immunities clause of Article IV. See, e.g., Hicklin v. Orbeck, 437 U.S. 518 (1978) ("Alaska Hire" law invalidated).

Local protectionism, as an aspect of territorial representation, can also work against certain local efforts to bring revenue into the local economy. See Pennsylvania v. New Jersey, 426 U.S. 660 (1976); Austin v. New Hampshire, 420 U.S. 656 (1975) (both cases invalidated forms of state income tax for out-of-state commuters). The commuters' income tax cases nevertheless indicate support for the theory of territorial representation. The taxable community, like the voting community, is based on geographic residence, not degree of involvement in local affairs.

99. 457 U.S. 55 (1982).

100. 457 U.S. at 61. Compare the Court's concern over differential treatment of residents in *Zobel* with the argument in *Holt Civic Club v. Tuscaloosa* about municipal residence.

the Court found fault with the scheme in *Zobel* was that it discriminated between classes of permanent residents. There is no clear justification for such practices under a territorial conception of interest representation.

However *Zobel* is construed, the use of local protectionism to regulate the quality of community life figured prominently in subsequent cases. In 1983, in *White v. Massachusetts Council of Construction Employees*,[101] the Court upheld a Boston ordinance discriminating in favor of city residents in assigning contracts for municipally funded construction projects. The Rehnquist majority argued first that the city was acting as a market participant, not as a market regulator in violation of the commerce clause, because the city was expending its own funds in the construction of public projects. Second, the city's regulation merely encouraged local businesses to use federal funds for urban development, to directly benefit targeted urban economies.[102] Boston's involvement in the local construction trade, as well as its interpretation of the local involvement component of federal grants for local improvement, was a legitimate attempt to improve the quality of economic life of the community.

United Building and Construction Trades Council v. City of Camden,[103] decided the following year, also involved a municipal ordinance favoring city residents for city construction projects. What distinguished *Camden* from *White* was the constitutional challenge brought by the appellants. They argued that the ordinance violated the privileges and immunities clause of Article IV. The clause has served as a barrier against some discriminations by a state against citizens of other states; it prohibits state infringements on the privileges of national citizenship. Article IV challenges to protectionism had been brought before *Camden*, but only in such cases of discrimination on the basis of state citizenship—not on the basis of municipal citizenship. The Rehnquist majority upheld the clause's application but declined to address the question of whether Camden had any reason

---

O'Connor's concurrence argued that Alaska's dividend system abridged the federal interest in free interstate migration and violated the privileges and immunities clause of Article IV. 457 U.S. 73–74. But see cases cited *supra* note 98.

101. 103 S. Ct. 1042 (1983).

102. 103 S. Ct. at 1048. Two justices, dissenting in part, found that the ordinance impermissibly granted to city residents an exclusive right to business opportunities. 103 S. Ct. at 1049.

103. 104 S. Ct. 1020 (1984).

for discriminating in favor of city residents over other state residents like the appellants. Yet, paradoxically, the result of the majority's interpretation of the constitutional provision was an endorsement of local autonomy.

While ostensibly curtailing the possibility of local protectionism, the decision acknowledged a limited autonomy for local communities. By extending privileges and immunities restrictions to municipal action, *Camden* imposed on local governments a liability for their legislative acts as yet unrecognized by the Constitution. The Court reasoned that state residents excluded by the city's protectionism could be denied judicial redress, because they had a chance to remedy the discrimination through the state ballot box. However, out-of-state residents affected by the restrictive hiring had no such electoral avenue. Therefore, *Camden*'s ordinance should not be immune from a prospective constitutional challenge by out-of-state residents simply because some in-state residents were similarly disadvantaged.[104] Despite these legal acrobatics, constitutional liability did not necessarily imply legal responsibility, as the city's resident-preference ordinance was adopted pursuant to a statewide program.

It is rather difficult to square the results of *Zobel, White,* and *Camden.* Only one decision, *White,* permitted the local protectionism and could be interpreted as confirming the conceptual type of territorial representation. An essentially identical preference in *Camden* was invalidated under privileges and immunities protections,[105] although *Camden*'s expansive reading of that provision could confirm, or at least fail to contradict, the territorial conceptualization of representation. Of course, *Camden*'s interpretation of Article IV is hard to reconcile with that in *Zobel,* as Blackmun observed in his *Camden* dissent.[106] Although both the New Jersey and the Alaska regulations discriminated among state residents in a way that also disadvantaged nonresidents, no privileges and immunities violation was recognized in *Zobel.* The case itself seems to contradict the principle of the integrity of the territorial community. The mixed results of the local protectionism cases with respect to the territorial concept of representation are

---

104. 104 S. Ct. at 1028–29.

105. I am relying here on Gunther's interpretation of the relationship between *Camden* and *White.* See Gunther, Constitutional Law 308 n.3 (11th ed. 1985).

106. 104 S. Ct. at 1033–34 (Blackmun, J., dissenting). See the discussion of O'Connor's concurrence in *Zobel,* 457 U.S. at 71, in n.100.

probably due to the complex commerce clause and federalism issues that these cases raise. There are simply too many extraneous doctrinal factors present to make these decisions good evidence of anything. The safest conclusion, therefore, is that they are irrelevant to the conceptualization of territorial representation.

The Territorial Identity

To summarize the findings of this chapter, the conceptual type of territorial representation posits that political decentralization is important for democratic participation, since the opportunity to control the conditions of community life furthers citizens' political efficacy.[107] In the American political context, because of historical accident and proscription, geographic political units can serve the collective purposes of representation and foster citizen participation.[108] To test the importance of the territorial conceptualization to the Burger Court's group-based approach to representation, it was most appropriate to focus on cases dealing explicitly with the legislative autonomy of local governments. Those cases were subdivided into two categories: "stake in the community" and "quality of community life."

In cases concerning local definition of stake in the community, we find only weak consistency with the conceptualization of territorial representation. The integrity of the geographic group interest did not greatly modify the application of one person, one vote in cases of local suffrage restriction; judicial concern for the fundamental right to vote superseded concern for this aspect of local self-rule. The exception was *Holt Civic Club v. Tuscaloosa.* In that case, the Burger Court permitted the exclusion of some persons from local elections because they resided outside the subdivision's corporate boundaries. *Holt* made clear that residency defined a citizen's stake in the local community—a limited endorsement of the principle that the geographic community is a community of interest.

A more decisive result distinguishes the decisions on local definition of the quality of community life. The cases dealing with referenda and with zoning and land-use regulations strongly confirm the conceptual type of territorial representation, both in the language of

---

107. Richardson, Introduction, 6 Publius 5 (1976).
108. W. Elliot, The Rise of Guradian Democracy 197–98 (1974); E. Spitz, Majority Rule 71 (1984).

the opinions and in their rulings. These decisions of the Burger Court arguably accepted a key premise of traditional federalist theory: decentralization enhances responsive government. However, the results were less definitive in another type of quality-of-community-life case—those dealing with local economic protectionism. While at least one decision, *White,* could be interpreted as confirming the territorial model, the protectionism cases as a whole are irrelevant as evidence about political representation. Because they deal with commerce regulation, and because the regulatory powers of the modern Congress are plenary, the cases only treat local self-rule in conjunction with other factors. Thus, it is difficult to attribute the results of these cases to any particular perspective on territorial representation.

The overall conclusion we can draw about the results of the local government cases is that the Burger Court did alter the Warren Court's standard of equal political influence. The local policy-making decisions point out that an equally effective vote is not simply numerically equal; government's responsiveness to votes—the real measure of the effectiveness of those votes—depends on intermediate agencies for political communication and coordination.[109] Political subdivisions constitute one such intermediate agency. Thus, for the actions of discrete voters to effectively represent their interests, electoral participation requires a foundation of prior social cohesion. Of course, the geographic community is a community of interest mainly because of a shared jurisdiction and concomitant governmental powers. A geographic group interest is created because of preexisting subdivision boundaries, not necessarily demographic commonality.

The chief disputes among the justices in the local government decisions—for example, the disputes between the majority and dissent in *Holt* and in the referenda and zoning cases—concerned the definition and existence of a "local public interest." Often, the Burger Court seemed to assume that a preexisting community of interest animated local policy-making. But small communities can, by their very nature, suppress conflict because of their lack of formal avenues for redress.[110] Particularly when facilitated by the referendum procedure, community self-determination may simply restrict the segment of the citizenry to which a local government is responsive. Local ma-

---

109. W. Elliot, The Rise of Guardian Democracy 200 (1974).
110. W. Kelso, American Democratic Theory 199–200 (1978).

joritarian control is no more a panacea for the politically powerless than is one person, one vote.[111]

A comparison of the Burger Court's local government cases with the *Reynolds* line of precedents is instructive. The political impact of the reapportionment rulings has certainly been far-reaching.[112] But not everyone agrees on the substantive import of one person, one vote districting. One commentator argues that *Reynolds* had almost no measurable effect on public policy because "fair representation is itself so obscure . . . a goal that reapportionment can have only a superficial influence on achieving it."[113] In other words, the one person, one vote cases were long on political equality rhetoric, but short on practical implications for the representation of individuals' interests.

The local government rulings seem to promise the opposite. Despite the plausibility of subdivision integrity in certain policy-making and districting situations, the major shortcoming of the local government decisions was their inadequate theoretical justification of "the geographic community." The presumptive validity of the local government decisions is strengthened by reference to the historical and theoretical foundations of territorial representation. Nevertheless, an admonition about communitarian politics should not be forgotten:

> A territorial subdivision presents a visible threat to its participating members. Once a decision is made, members must choose to accept the decision, leave the association or face the consequences of being dissenters. Being tied to a geographic area is in this sense a restriction of freedom.[114]

---

111. On the dangers of pure majoritarianism in local governments, see A. Bickel, The Supreme Court and the Idea of Progress 166 (1970).

112. A selection of the literature on reapportionment should demonstrate the plausibility of this assertion. On the gains of minority candidates from redistricting, see B. Cain, The Reapportionment Puzzle 81ff. (1984). On the effects of redistricting on minorities and regional interests within the states, see L. Hardy and A. Heslop, Reapportionment Politics: The History of Redistricting in the States 24ff. (1981). On the general impact of reapportionment on party districting battles, see Scarrow, The Impact of Reapportionment on Party Representation, in Representation and Redistricting Issues of the 1980's, at 67 (B. Grofman and A. Lijphart eds. 1982).

113. Riker, Democracy and Representation: A Reconciliation of *Ball v. James* and *Reynolds v. Sims*, 1 Sup. Ct. Econ. Rev. 39, 44 (1982). Riker argues that in the absence of conscientious and fair-minded politician-redistrictors, equipopulous districting plans will probably be randomly unfair to certain electoral groups, which is precisely equivalent to the situation under malapportionment. Id. at 46–47.

114. Frug, The City as a Legal Concept, 93 Harv. L. Rev. 1059, 1145 (1980).

Although territorial representation as community self-determination has been an enduring part of American politics and political thought, it suffers from the same majoritarian excesses as one person, one vote's atomistic conception of electoral politics. As a group-balancing approach to representation, the territorial conceptualization is incomplete because it presumes too unitary an interest on the part of a geographic community. While the territorial conceptual type allows us to better evaluate some of the Burger Court's representation decisions, we must look beyond it to see if the Court recognized group interests other than those associated with geography.

CHAPTER 4

Acres, Dollars, and Votes

In the previous chapter, we examined cases in which the directive of one person, one vote conflicted with the collective authority of the local electorate. Many of the Burger Court's decisions treated political subdivisions as geographic communities with unique local interests rather than as mere administrative units of state government. Yet this concern for the representation of territorial group interests can explain only a small subset of the Burger Court's opinions. Before we can attribute a group-balancing approach to the Burger Court, we must verify its attention to group interests other than geographic ones. This chapter outlines the second conceptual type of group representation, which focuses on economic rather than geographic interests, and tests its explanatory power.

The second conceptualization posits that certain groups of individuals constitute communities of interest by virtue of the economic nature of their association and that these groups, in turn, constitute the units of political representation. When such groups consist of either corporate entities or economic special interests, their representation results in a political system often referred to as "corporatism." The label *corporatist representation* designates the conceptual type that I employ to assess the Burger Court's sensitivity to the representation of economic interests. While the sample of corporatist representation cases is small, it includes both districting and electoral participation issues. Both types of cases involve political structures or procedures that provide special access opportunities to certain economic or corporate interests. Like the geographic conceptualization, corporatist representation resolves the tension between individual participation and group representation in favor of the latter.

Corporatism, to clarify its definition, implies cooperation between the state, business organizations, and labor unions for the purpose of effective and efficient economic policy-making. Corporatism indicates a way of organizing representation, interest mediation, and social control.[1] Various forms of corporatist government have been employed in modern Western states, ranging from the syndicalist governments of Mussolini's Italy and Peron's Argentina to the "consociational" democracies of the Scandinavian nations.[2] In corporatist systems of government, the unit represented on governing boards is often an occupational or economic group and its corporate interests. The resulting governmental system fuses public and private authority and endorses social decision making of a cooperative rather than competitive nature.[3]

The representation of corporate entities in the political process or social order is not unique to modern forms of government. It has roots in medieval political thought and its conception of society as a composite or organic whole. One of the earliest political connotations of the word "representation"—as found in the writings of fourteenth-century jurists—implied the symbolic embodiment of the fictive person of the community, such as a king's embodiment of the realm as a single corporate entity.[4] The medieval polity was metaphorically conceived as a body "articulated into different ranks, professions and estates rather than into arithmetically equal units."[5] Thus, the beginnings of a corporatist conception of interests can be seen in the medieval organic conception of society.

The notion of representation as "standing for" static interest-components of society[6] is also found in the eighteenth-century political

---

1. R. Lustig, Corporate Liberalism 13 (1982).
2. A. Lijphart, Democracies xiv, 215ff. (1984).
3. W. Kelso, American Democratic Theory 20–21, 23 (1978). Kelso draws a distinction between "the corporativism of fascist Italy" and "corporate pluralism as practiced in the United States." He characterizes the difference as follows: "Corporate pluralism involves the private capture of public agencies and the establishment of semipublic monopolies, while corporativism involves public domination of private groups." Id. at 21. I am using the label "corporatist" in a more generic sense than is implied by either of Kelso's definitions, but the conceptual type articulated in this chapter probably bears more resemblance to what he calls corporate pluralism.
4. H. Pitkin, The Concept of Representation 242–45 (1967).
5. R. Lustig, Corporate Liberalism 217 (1982) (referring to Gierke's discussion of medieval political thought).
6. The goal of both modern corporatist representation and its medieval antecedents could be construed as "the welding of the nation into a unified whole." H. Pitkin, The Concept of Representation 106–7 (1967). Neither approach seems to view politics as a matter of conflict or competition, either between the individual and the collective or

writings of Edmund Burke, particularly in his theory of "virtual representation." Burke's view of interests was corporate because he conceived of them as broad, relatively fixed, largely economic, and unitary in any group or locality.[7] He identified occupational interests later common in corporatist systems of representation: a mercantile interest, an agricultural interest, a professional interest. But Burke also conceived of an interest as "unattached," as an objective reality apart from any individuals representing that interest. Clearly, for Burke, political representation did not mean aggregation of individuals' interests or opinions, but substantive articulation of fixed, identifiable corporate interests.[8] Thus, a township could be "virtually represented" by a delegate who spoke not for that particular township's inhabitants, but for the perceived interests of township dwellers generally.

The term "corporatist" distinguishes certain group-based forms of social organization from individualist political visions. If "individualism" in a political sense implies that the individual is distinct from his or her social group and not defined in terms of group qualities,[9] then neither modern nor more antiquated versions of corporatism treat representation as an individualistic process. In this sense, the concept of corporatist representation is the polar opposite of one person, one vote and of representation as the aggregation of discrete, individual political demands. Corporatist representation in a contemporary liberal context acknowledges the "fixed interests" identified in certain pluralistic theories of politics[10] and assumes that policy should be made through the mutual agreement of business and economic groups and government agencies, rather than through competition in the economic or political arenas.[11]

In the United States, experience with true corporatist government—as a national, functional structure—has been limited. Never-

---

among private interests. I do not mean to make too much of the superficial similarity between medieval political thought and modern corporatism; I only suggest that a case can be made for construing the model of "corporatist representation" as theoretically and politically significant.

7. H. Pitkin, The Concept of Representation 174 (1967).
8. H. Pitkin, The Concept of Representation 175–76 (1967).
9. Lane, Individualism and the Market Society, 25 NOMOS 374 (1983).
10. H. Pitkin, The Concept of Representation 174 (1967) (citing Beer, The Representation of Interests in British Government, 51 Am. Pol. Sci. Rev. 613, 617 (1957)).
11. W. Kelso, American Democratic Theory 21 (1978) (referring to Hugh Johnson's *Blue Eagle*).

theless, corporatist representation has several conceptual analogues in American politics. One of its earlier incarnations was the attempt at "industrial democracy" begun under Hoover and continued in the early New Deal policies of the Roosevelt administration. A second, more enduring, experiment in corporatist government involved states' endorsement of "special district governments" established to serve and represent the interests of a specialized occupational group, most often agricultural producers. A third manifestation of corporatist politics, and perhaps the most controversial, concerns the political role of the modern equivalent of the medieval "fictive person": the limited liability corporation.[12] Nineteenth-century European social theorists championed the idea that the corporation was a "social institution"—less a commercial association of natural persons than an *Anstalt*, or communitarian entity.[13] In twentieth-century America, the business corporation arguably enjoys a similar metaphysical status within society as exemplified by its First Amendment right of free speech.

Two of these examples of American corporatism, the special district government and corporate political rights, have been the objects of recent constitutional litigation. In decisions in these areas, the Burger Court seemed to endorse, or at least tolerate, special representational consideration for economic group interests. For example, in the special district election cases, the corporate "farmer" was presumed to be included under the one person, one vote doctrine. However, in order to assess the degree to which the Burger Court's decisions support the conceptual type of corporatist representation, we must first become familiar with the history of political representation of economic interests in the United States. Thus, the following section examines in more detail the corporatist analogues in American politics. Subsequent sections then discuss the relevant case materials and evaluate the Court's decisions in terms of how well they correlate with the conceptualization of corporatist representation.

Corporatist Structures and Corporate Entities

Corporatist influences in American government were largely, but not entirely, the product of European social thought and political experi-

---

12. Horwitz, Santa Clara Revisited: The Development of Corporate Theory, in Corporations and Society 17 (W. Samuels and A. Miller eds. 1987).

13. R. Lustig, Corporate Liberalism 255 (1982) (citing Franz Neumann's *Behemoth*).

mentation. European influences were apparent in the first corporatist analogue in American politics, the national economic planning of the Hoover and Roosevelt administrations.

Following World War I, turbulence in the world market economies, combined with an emerging group conception of politics, engendered reforms in representative government.[14] For example, the syndicalism of Mussolini's Italy in the early 1920s was one variant of the idea of "industrial democracy." In the early twentieth century, European corporatism looked toward more democratic economic planning and industrial management, and toward cooperative efforts between labor, capital, and state regulators. During the same era in the United States, corporatism as a form of political organization had widespread support from enlightened capitalists, left-wing Republicans, and nonsocialist intellectuals.[15] For thinkers such as John Dewey and Herbert Croly, American admirers of European guild socialism, true political representation could only be "representation of common purposes or functional representation."[16]

One political leader influenced by such corporatist ideas, Herbert Hoover, believed that the principal forces of political progress in the American system were voluntary organizations and state and local governments. As secretary of commerce, and later as president, he approached many problems of regulation by bringing together representatives of all interested economic groups in a conference or as a commission.[17] Hoover's version of industrial democracy entailed informal corporatism and voluntary cooperation among economic interest groups.

President Hoover's policy response to the Great Depression revealed his commitment to corporatist policy, as well as its perspective on the business corporation. Using the War Industries Board of World War I as a model, Hoover attempted to integrate private regulators—competitors acting in a market system—into an economic community of interest. He saw a great difference between "the social conception of capital combinations against public interest" and "coop-

---

14. See R. Lustig, Corporate Liberalism 34 (1982).
15. R. Johnson, Modern Times 243 (1983); Hawley, Herbert Hoover and American Corporatism, in The Hoover Presidency 102 (M. Fausold and G. Mazuzan eds. 1974).
16. R. Lustig, Corporate Liberalism 127 (1982).
17. Schwartz, Hoover and Congress, in The Hoover Presidency 89–90 (M. Fausold and G. Mazuzan eds. 1974).

erative action between individuals" producing "beneficial monopolies."[18] The goal of his policies was to "devise governmental machinery that could secure constructive private actions without creating new instruments of [economic] tyranny."[19] One such effort, the Agricultural Marketing Act, attempted to foster agricultural stability and progress by organizing farmers' cooperative associations. The act incorporated several corporatist ideals. For example, the concept of the functional representation of agricultural interests was implemented in the form of the quasi-public Farm Board.[20] Despite the lack of success of Hoover's "voluntary syndicalism," his administration resisted converting its informal corporatism into a formalized or compulsory system under federal supervision.

Industrial coordination through federal supervision had historical precedent in Theodore Roosevelt's New Nationalism policies and trust-busting efforts. The tentative economic interventionism of Hoover's programs were not the only policies, however, to reflect the early twentieth-century movement toward national economic regulation through trade associations. Although Franklin Roosevelt campaigned in 1932 against Hoover's recovery programs, he himself subscribed to cooperative competition through voluntary trade organizations, disagreeing with Hoover only on the scope of the federal government's role.[21] Thus, FDR's early New Deal legislation, in large part, built on or simply extended Hoover's reforms in banking, business, and labor operations.[22] FDR's Agricultural Adjustment Act and National Industrial Recovery Act of 1933 signaled the first real attempts at statist corporatism; the NIRA, in particular, instituted functional representation of industrial interests on economic councils.

The NIRA provided for national industrial planning through the use of local compliance boards and "voluntary codes" for production.[23] The corporatist policies of the NIRA were not entirely effective, however; once the acute phase of the Depression passed, so did the sense of emergency that gave the "public interest" much of its

---

18. See W. Kelso, American Democratic Theory 23–24 (1978).
19. Hawley, Herbert Hoover and American Corporatism, in The Hoover Presidency 103 (M. Fausold and G. Mazuzan eds. 1974).
20. Id. at 107.
21. Schwartz, Hoover and Congress, in The Hoover Presidency 100 (M. Fausold and G. Mazuzan eds. 1974).
22. R. Johnson, Modern Times 255 (1983).
23. A. Schlesinger, The Coming of the New Deal 120 (1957).

power over the self-interest of self-regulated industries. The NIRA, finally, fell victim to its own internal corruption and monopolistic tyranny.[24]

The Supreme Court also undermined FDR's efforts to establish a national system of American corporatism. In *Schechter Poultry Corp. v. U.S.*,[25] the Court found that legislative delegation of enforcement power for industrial code violations to local compliance boards was improper. But the *Schechter* ruling did not prevent the implementation of other forms of corporatist representation, particularly in local governmental units.

A more durable corporatist structure was established by the agricultural adjustment acts, which authorized locally chosen farm boards to implement federal directives on agricultural policy.[26] The AAA of 1933 provided for acreage allotments for different crops; allotments of commodities were to be apportioned by acre and accrued to the land, not the farmer who produced the crop. Additionally, transfer of crop land allotments from one farm to another required a referendum by commodity producers in the jurisdiction.[27] Although the Court struck down the processing tax of the AAA in *United States v. Butler*,[28] the acreage allotment system of the 1938 Act is retained in current agricultural management procedures, along with various price support and soil conservation measures consistent with a corporatist governmental system.[29]

Thus, although national corporatism was rather short-lived in American politics, the AAA's land-based form of representation of agricultural interests did survive. Indeed, this type of corporatist representation was already being used in a state-level fusion of public and private authority known as the special district government, the second corporatist analogue in American politics. A special district is a legally constituted governmental entity established by the state to perform specific functions within a defined jurisdiction; its original purpose was to provide specialized services such as flood control to

---

24. Id. at 172, 176.
25. 295 U.S. 495 (1935).
26. M. and R. Kweit, Implementing Citizen Participation in a Bureaucratic Society 5 (1981).
27. 7 U.S.C. §§ 1344(b), 1379. Specific procedures for adjusting quotas varied for different commodities.
28. 297 U.S. 1 (1936).
29. W. Kelso, American Democratic Theory 22 (1978).

economic or occupational groups. Although special districts derive their decision-making authority from state legislation, they are oriented toward local interest groups and the solution of local problems.[30] Special districts are created in various ways—sometimes by constitutionally authorized popular action, sometimes by state legislation repealable only by referendum.[31]

Special district government responded to certain historical exigencies, such as the failure of voluntary solutions to water-rights problems in the West, and the need for public services because of rapid industrialization.[32] State espousal of special governmental structures began with California's Wright Act of 1887.[33] At the urging of state farmers, the act was passed to establish a public irrigation district, with private contribution based on land ownership. After much litigation over organizational and electoral procedures within the district, the U.S. Supreme Court upheld the California law in 1896, thereby paving the way for increased use of special district government.[34]

Land-based voting was used in most of the special agricultural districts, since the importance of equal individual participation was lessened when the district focused on a particularized rural community of interest. Special district governments were viewed as offering specialized services to economic interest groups whose policy interests were outside the expertise of general government. Special districts differed from municipal governments in that the services provided by the latter—such as police, fire, and garbage services—serve the needs of the average citizen.[35] The distinct policy focus and service emphasis of special district governments suggest that they represent a different constituency; suffrage in special district elections was designed to maximize the voice of this specialized electorate. One could call such political representation corporatist, because it creates a governing structure in which private groups exercise regulatory powers that would otherwise be the exclusive responsibility of public officials.[36]

---

30. R. Hawkins, Self-Government by District 7–9 (1976).
31. J. Bollens, Special District Government in the United States 20 (1947).
32. R. Hawkins, Self-Government by District 14 (1976).
33. Id. at 15.
34. J. Bollens, Special District Government in the United States 144 (1957).
35. R. Hawkins, Self-Government by District 17 (1976).
36. W. Kelso, American Democratic Theory 20 (1978).

The special purpose, agricultural district actually serves a public interest: the collective interest in a productive agricultural economy. In suits involving actions of special districts, state courts presumed that the districts represented the statewide economic interest, rather than a narrow special interest.[37] But while a successful agricultural industry might be a concern shared by all state citizens, a citizen's stake in that industry and its operations depends on land ownership. Basing voting power within the district on land ownership, irrespective of the landowner's actual residence, emphasizes that the district's constituency is an economic or occupational group, not a community in the residential sense. In special district government, then, the public interest is collectivist and distinct from the simple aggregation of individual demands.[38]

Land-based voting, in conjunction with plural voting based on the amount of property owned, implies that the landowner casts a ballot as a functional rather than human entity. This suggests yet another aspect of corporatist representation: extension of an electoral or political role to the corporate landowner. Not only did special district elections accept corporate suffrage, but corporate political speech in the context of general elections received First Amendment protection. The concept of the corporate citizen, in effect, extended the fiction of the corporate person to the realm of politics.

Legal recognition of "corporate personality" is the third corporatist analogue in American politics. This nineteenth-century legal fiction granted corporations immunity from much state regulation, as well as the state-protected right to acquire and hold property.[39]

---

37. R. Hawkins, Self-Government by District 58–61 (1976); Levi, Application of Municipal Bond Ordinances to Special Purpose Districts, 12 Urb. L. Ann. 86–90 (1976).

Occasionally the authority of the special district and the municipal government conflict. A 1976 Supreme Court case, *Hill v. Gautreaux*, tangentially deals with such interlocal government conflict. *Hill* concerned a jurisdictional dispute between certain governmental units in the Chicago metropolitan area. The Court held that, while local governments retain the right to insist that housing programs adhere to local zoning laws, the relief granted to victims of discriminatory housing practices could extend beyond the boundaries of the affected housing district and into the metropolitan area. 425 U.S. 284, 304 (1976).

38. M. and R. Kweit, Implementing Citizen Participation in a Bureaucratic Society 44–45 (1981).

39. For the official beginning of the doctrine, see Santa Clara Co. v. Southern Pacific Railroad, 118 U.S. 394 (1886). *Santa Clara* was not so much an innovation as it was a

By the end of the nineteenth century, corporations were viewed not as entities chartered by and beholden to the state, but as private entities with many of the rights of natural persons. Indeed, by the early twentieth century, legal writers disputed whether the corporation was an artificial or a natural entity. In part, this dispute represented a conflict over whether the individual or the group was the appropriate unit of economic, political, and legal analysis.[40] The natural entity theory treated the corporation as separate and distinct from its members or shareholders, thereby increasing the power of corporate managers and establishing corporate associations as social and political entities just as "real" as individuals.[41]

When the Supreme Court affirmed the doctrine of corporate personhood, it made an important "normative 'ought' statement about the power structure of the economy" and the state's endorsement of it.[42] Recognition of corporate personhood led to a kind of corporatist representation in this sense: the doctrine obscured the transition from a society based on individualism to one based on powerful collective institutions.[43] Corporate personhood in the modern economic context of "the decline of individualist entrepreneurial capitalism and the rise of bureaucratized, corporate capitalism"[44] seemingly facilitates the worst sort of corporatism, where economic interest groups not only form the units of representation but also dominate the political machinery.[45]

The above characterization of corporatist influence in American politics contradicts the rosier picture of corporatist representation

---

logical consequence of a line of cases going back to Chief Justice Marshall's famous ruling in Dartmouth College v. Woodward, 4 Wheaton 518 (1819).

40. Horwitz, *Santa Clara* Revisited: The Development of Corporate Theory, in Corporations and Society 49–51 (W. Samuels and A. Miller eds. 1987).

41. Id. at 42–46, 49.

42. Samuels, The Idea of the Corporation as a Person: On the Normative Significance of Judicial Language, in Corporations and Society 117 (W. Samuels and A. Miller eds. 1987).

43. Flynn, The Jurisprudence of Corporate Personhood: The Misuse of a Legal Concept, in Corporations and Society 150–51 (W. Samuels and A. Miller eds. 1987); Horwitz, *Santa Clara* Revisited: The Development of Corporate Theory, in Corporations and Society 19 (W. Samuels and A. Miller eds. 1987).

44. Samuels, The Idea of the Corporation as a Person: On the Normative Significance of Judicial Language, in Corporations and Society 121 (W. Samuels and A. Miller eds. 1987).

45. W. Kelso, American Democratic Theory 21–24 (1978).

evoked by the theory of special district government. Indeed, the model of corporatist representation is itself Janus-faced, suggesting either special interest dominance of governmental apparatus or cooperative political engagement between private groups and governmental agencies. How, then, did the Burger Court's decisions view the political role of economic interests and of the business corporation? The Court's attitude toward corporatist representation structures hinged on its view of corporate personhood; arguably, its decisions treated the concept not as a functional doctrine but as a rigid definition as fixed as that of human personhood.[46] The Court yielded frequently to the fiction of the corporate "citizen" and, in so doing, tolerated a particular group-bias in representation procedures. We will address the nature of this group-bias by looking at the two corporatist analogues that have been subjects of constitutional adjudication: the special district election and political activity by corporations. As the special district decisions in many ways link the seemingly irreconcilable doctrines of one person, one vote and corporate free speech, we will examine the special district cases first, and then discuss how the decisions' particular view of "interest" justified application of the theory of corporatist representation.

One Acre, One Vote versus One Person, One Vote

In order to understand the Burger Court's approach in the special district decisions, we must return briefly to the local suffrage restriction cases discussed in chapter 3. The Court developed the so-called benefits/burdens analysis to determine whether the disenfranchisement of certain persons in certain types of elections was permissible. For example, in *City of Phoenix v. Kolodzieski,* a 1970 case involving a special purpose municipal bond election, the Burger Court found no justification for limiting the franchise to property owners.[47] However, the Court acknowledged that the legitimacy of a *Reynolds*-type election was conditional, depending on (1) the specialized responsibilities of the elected unit of government, and (2) the proportional benefits and burdens on persons within the government's jurisdiction. *Phoenix,* of course, concerned a special election within a general purpose

---
46. Flynn, The Jurisprudence of Corporate Personhood: The Misuse of a Legal Concept, in Corporations and Society 145, 151 (W. Samuels and A. Miller eds. 1987).
47. 399 U.S. 204 (1970).

local government, and it said little about the importance of correlative benefits and burdens in the context of special district elections.

The question that had originally divided the liberal bloc of the Warren Court in *Avery v. Midland County*, a case concerning districting for county commission elections, had been whether some specialized types of local governments were exempt from the one person, one vote requirement.[48] The Burger Court formally took up this question in the 1970 case of *Hadley v. Junior College District*.[49] *Hadley* applied one person, one vote guidelines to districts for the election of college trustees, because the trustees exercised general governmental powers equivalent to the county commissioners in *Avery*.[50] But the Black majority conceded that cases would arise "in which functionaries have duties that are so removed from normal governmental activities and so disproportionately affect different groups, that a *Reynolds* popular election might not be required."[51]

The *Hadley* dissent disagreed with the result but not the reasoning of the decision. Echoing the majority opinion, Harlan argued that local governments "vary in the magnitude of their impact upon various constituencies and in the manner in which benefits and burdens of their operations interact with elements of the local economic picture."[52] The language of *Hadley*, in essence, signified the beginnings of an "interest exception" to the right to vote, particularly in specialized governmental units. In other words, the Burger Court would examine whether plaintiffs' interest in the activities of the governmental unit were sufficient to justify equal, or even partial, participation.[53]

One difficulty in applying constitutional rights of political equality to the special district election lay in deciding whether the special district was a government or a private corporation. Until the Burger Court ruled on the legal identity of the special district, the constitutionality of its representative structure could not really be evaluated. The Court's first opportunity to classify the special district came in the 1971 case of *National Labor Relations Board v. Natural Gas and*

---

48. 390 U.S. 474 (1968).
49. 397 U.S. 50 (1970).
50. 397 U.S. at 53.
51. 397 U.S. at 56.
52. 397 U.S. at 61.
53. Durchslag, *Salyer, Ball* and *Holt:* Reappraising the Right to Vote in Terms of Political "Interest" and Vote Dilution, 33 Case W. Res. L. Rev. 1 (1982).

*Utility District.*⁵⁴ The case involved the statutory question whether, under the Labor-Management Relations Act, a utility district was a political subdivision and therefore exempt from unfair labor practice proceedings. Brennan's majority opinion held that under the statutory requirements of Tennessee's law concerning the formation and organization of special districts, the utility district was a political subdivision according to the act.⁵⁵ The Court's broad definition of political subdivisions easily included local corporatist structures, such as the semipublic, monopolistic utility corporation. The *NLRB* decision was the first to be consistent with the conceptual type of corporatist representation. However, the more important issue—namely, whether the one person, one vote standard applying to local governments now also applied to special purpose governments—was not part of the controversy in *NLRB*. Nevertheless, *NLRB* was a necessary foundation for corporatist representation in the special district context, because the special district was determined to be a public entity composed of and serving private economic interests.

The first major case on electoral procedures in special districts was *Salyer Land Co. v. Tulare Lake Basin Water District*,⁵⁶ in 1973. The question in *Salyer* was whether a special purpose government existing for acquiring, storing, and distributing water for agricultural purposes could restrict the suffrage in the election of the board of directors to landowners and apportion their votes according to the assessed acreage of their land. The weighted voting scheme assumed the benefits and burdens of the district's activities were in proportion to the amount of land owned.⁵⁷ Rehnquist's opinion for the majority agreed; not only did the actions of the district disproportionately affect landowners, but the burden of operating the district was legitimately assessed on a per acre basis.⁵⁸ Thus, the benefit of participation was proportional to an individual's financial involvement in the local agricultural economy.⁵⁹

---

54. 402 U.S. 600 (1971).
55. The Court defined political subdivisions rather broadly, as administrative arms created by the state and/or entities administered by persons responsible to public officials or to the general electorate. 402 U.S. at 604.
56. 410 U.S. 719 (1973).
57. Durchslag, *Salyer, Ball,* and *Holt:* Reappraising the Right to Vote in Terms of Political "Interest" and Vote Dilution, 33 Case W. Res. L. Rev. 1, 22 (1982).
58. 410 U.S. at 729.
59. 410 U.S. at 734.

Salyer is clearly a decision confirming the model of corporatist representation, so much so that the dissenters termed the doctrine it embodied "one acre, one vote." *Salyer* is an example of a functional approach to representation, as the Court evaluated both the functions performed by the district and the functional situation of those already voting relative to those excluded.[60] The dissent, authored by Douglas and joined by Brennan and Marshall, disagreed with both evaluations. Water decisions, Douglas argued, were not a matter of special interest, nor was the weighting of votes according to real-property wealth consistent with "our system of government."[61] As "our system" implied the liberal individualism of one person, one vote, Douglas objected most to the political dominance the electoral scheme allocated to a few landowning corporations. "It is grotesque," he concluded, "to think of corporations voting within the framework of political representation of people."[62] The essential disagreement between the majority and the dissent was whether "interest" was a legitimate basis for suffrage, and whether land should be the measure of such interest.

The special district situation in *Salyer* and its companion case, *Associated Enterprises v. Toltec Watershed Improvement District*,[63] presented the Burger Court with a fact pattern that raised unfamiliar legal issues. *Salyer* concerned a group-based representation system, yet the dissent discussed the case exclusively in terms of the representation of individuals. Even the majority did not say—in so many words—that the purpose of the district's political structure was to redefine representation as the apportionment of electoral influence according to degree of economic interest. Yet only in a representative structure based on group interests is it plausible that the interest of corporate landowners should be counted among other landowners' interests. The only way to reconcile *Salyer* with *Reynolds* and justify its "interest exception" to voting is to see it as a confirmation of the conceptualization of corporatist representation.[64]

---

60. Durchslag, *supra* note 53, at 13.
61. 410 U.S. at 738. Douglas likened the water district to the governmental entity in *Hadley*, and compared the public nature of the governmental decisions to that in *Phoenix*. 410 U.S. at 736, 740.
62. 410 U.S. at 741.
63. 410 U.S. 743 (1973).
64. Cf. Riker, Democracy and Representation: A Reconciliation of *Ball v. James* and

Other commentators have posited another possible explanation of the *Salyer* decision. In Fortas's dissent in *Avery*, Fortas analogized the special district government to a business corporation, in which stockholders vote on corporate affairs according to the type and amount of their capital stock.[65] Land-based plural voting could then be compared with stockholder voting, with acres as stock certificates and agricultural producers or other economic interest groups as investors. Such a defense of special district government downplays a corporatist conceptualization of political representation and its fusion of public and private power.

Some commentators draw the stockholder comparison to argue that the same liberal theory of democracy that justifies *Reynolds* also justifies the exclusivity of special district elections. Just what is meant by "liberal theory of democracy" is a matter of interpretation, but it presumably includes a clear separation between public and private rights. The special district, according to this view, facilitates the private right to run a profit-maximizing business enterprise.[66] Of course, the analogy between the special district and stockholder enterprise depends on a view of the corporation as an artificial entity in which stockholders are voting members, not as an institution of managerial capitalism as discussed by contemporary economists.

A more critical problem with the stockholder analogy as a defense of special district voting schemes is its incompatibility with the *NLRB* holding in 1971. *NLRB* had specifically defined the special district as a political subdivision, albeit for the purposes of statutory construction. Moreover, two decisions in 1977 that concerned administrative issues of special district governance, *Concerned Citizens v. Pine Creek*

Reynolds v. Sims, 1 Sup. Ct. Econ. Rev. 39 (1982). Riker argues that both types of decisions are consistent with the contemporary theory of democracy. *Reynolds*, he says, had almost no measurable effect on public policy, while *Salyer* and, especially, the subsequent case of Ball v. James (see *infra* note 69 and accompanying text) would have had a dramatic and detrimental effect had they been decided the other way. The reason is that a vindication of the suffrage claimants would have entailed a transfer of property on behalf of short-term consumer interests, not the long-term public interest.

65. 390 U.S. 474, 507 (1968). See also J. Bollens, Special District Government in the United States 146 (1957).

66. Riker, Democracy and Representation: A Reconciliation of *Ball v. James* and *Reynolds v. Sims*, 1 Sup. Ct. Econ. Rev. 39, 55–57 (1982).

District[67] and *Chappelle v. Greater Baton Rouge Airport District*,[68] clearly viewed the special district as a governmental entity. If the special district is legally considered a governmental entity, its representative procedures should be defended as such. A virtue of the conceptual type of corporatist representation is that it can explain the electoral procedures of special districts without creating internal inconsistency. Arguably, the conceptualization explains the Court's decisions on weighted voting more coherently than the opinions themselves.

The heuristic value of the conceptual type is further verified by the only case that tested the breadth of the *Salyer* ruling. *Ball v. James*,[69] decided in 1981, concerned the operations of the Salt River Project (SRP), a utility district that stored and delivered untreated water and sold the by-product, electricity, to much of metropolitan Phoenix. Although its elected officials had powers broader than those held by the board of directors in *Salyer,* the SRP board elections were limited to landowners, whose votes were apportioned according to the number of acres owned. Two factors seemed to distinguish *Ball* from the *Salyer* situation. First, the officials elected from the Arizona district exercised some general governmental powers, including condemning land, selling tax-exempt bonds, and levying taxes on real property. Second, the revenue from electricity consumers largely financed the SRP's general obligation bonds. The lower court held that, while the district's electricity-providing function substantially affected all persons, the actual financial burden of running the district did not fall primarily on landowners.[70] *Salyer*'s benefits/burdens rationale and specific "interest" requirement for participation seemingly should have guaranteed a verdict in favor of individual voting equality in *Ball.*

Nevertheless, a 5 to 4 majority, led by Stewart, upheld the land-based voting scheme in *Ball.* Stewart argued that the district was not a general purpose government because it did not enact laws govern-

---

67. 429 U.S. 651 (1977). Pine Creek was a flood control district in the state of Ohio formed and administered by conservancy court judges. In a per curiam opinion, the Court held that the appellant residents of the district could bring an equal protection challenge concerning the procedures for creating the district, but remanded disposition of the merits. Rehnquist, Powell, and Stevens dissented. They would have proceeded to the merits and found no one person, one vote violation.

68. 431 U.S. 159 (1977). The Court ruled, without issuing a formal opinion, that an airport district could not require parish (county) property ownership as a condition of eligibility for the post of airport commissioner. Rehnquist was the only dissenter.

69. 451 U.S. 355 (1981).

70. 451 U.S. at 360–62.

ing citizens' conduct; the "nominal public character" of the water district had been permitted by the state to enable SRP to obtain inexpensive bond financing.[71] To the majority, the special district remained essentially a business enterprise, "created by and chiefly benefiting a specific group of landowners."[72] Continuing the analogy, the Court likened the relationship between nonvoting residents and the district to that between consumers and a business operation from which they buy goods.[73] The *Ball* majority seemed to have returned to Fortas's inapposite stockholder voting example in his *Avery* dissent.

The four *Ball* dissenters stressed a different analogy. They likened the *Ball* situation to the special purpose elections of *Kramer* and *Cipriano,* decisions in which the *Reynolds* requirement had been applied.[74] Their view was that the majority had misapplied *Salyer*'s "one acre, one vote" principle, for "even if electricity revenues [were] being used to fund agriculture as a practice in the *public interest,* nonproperty owners still deserved input in designing the subsidy."[75] Ironically, it was the *Ball* dissenters who correctly viewed the case as raising the issue of the legitimacy of group-based conceptions of political action with respect to the public interest. The majority opinion accepted a corporatist structure without acknowledging or defending its rationale of fostering a collectivist public interest.

The result of the *Ball* decision was the acceptance of a system of representation whereby landowners and prominent agricultural interests would be represented as the major cooperatives in the local economy. From this perspective, the result certainly confirms the corporatist conceptualization. The argument of the majority, however, was disappointing theoretically and, at best, barely consistent with the conceptualization. One legal observer has argued that the special district cases have produced no law at all, good or bad, because "taken individually or together they establish neither a rationale for

---

71. 451 U.S. at 366. As an example of the sort of governmental powers that evoke the strict demands of *Reynolds,* Stewart noted that the SRP could not impose ad valorem property taxes or sales taxes.

72. 451 U.S. at 368. Stewart noted that voting landowners contributed to the district in the form of liens on their property, acreage taxes, and investment capital.

73. 451 U.S. at 370.

74. 451 U.S. at 380–81. White's dissenting opinion was joined by Brennan, Marshall, and Blackmun.

75. 451 U.S. at 384 (emphasis added).

their conclusions nor a principle of analysis."[76] *Ball* is woefully deficient in principled analysis,[77] but the special district cases as a whole do reveal a certain pattern. As a whole, they are consistent with the conceptual type of corporatist representation because, taken together, they directly challenge the individualist premise of one person, one vote. In other words, cases such as *Salyer* and *Ball* indicate that the Burger Court could relinquish the idea that political representation must be the aggregation of individual demands.

If the Burger Court seemed unready at times to explain the special representation of economic interests, this was perhaps due to unfamiliarity with the type of representation provided by the special district. Yet one aspect of the special district decisions was consistent and clear: the Court's acceptance (over several justices' objections, to be sure) of a political role for the "corporate citizen." If the specialized nature and limited applicability of the *Salyer* and *Ball* rulings confined the corporate political role to a circumscribed electoral context, the fiction of corporate personhood facilitated its extension beyond the special district election. As we shall see, the Burger Court justified an expanded corporate political role with another legal fiction—the fiction of a "marketplace" of ideas.

The Corporate War Chest and the Electoral Contest

In our introductory discussion of the concept of corporatist representation, we noted that one of the goals of a corporatist political system was to effect policy through cooperative, negotiated political settlements rather than through interest competition. One way to achieve this result was through a group-based approach to political representation that emphasized direct interaction among government officials and economic interest groups. Arguably, a drawback of corporatism's rejection of politics-as-conflict is the partitioning of public policy into a series of autonomous "fiefdoms," each controlled by a different

---

76. Durchslag, *Salyer, Ball,* and *Holt:* Reappraising the Right to Vote in Terms of Political "Interest" and Vote Dilution, 33 Case W. Res. L. Rev. 1, 49 (1982).

77. State courts have had much more experience with the legal issues involved in special district government, and have often construed the latter as representing a collective state interest as opposed to the more parochial interests of municipal governments. Levi, Application of Municipal Bond Ordinances to Special Purpose Districts, 12 Urb. L. Ann. 77, 86, 107 (1976).

special interest group and its captive agencies and officials.[78] Political science literature is replete with criticism of such interest group hegemony because it prevents equal competition among all social groups.[79] Not surprisingly, corporate and business interests often figure prominently in discussions of "captive" governmental agencies and special interest dominance of the political process.

In the modern political context, much of this special interest dominance and destruction of group competition is achieved through money. Money is a tool for political persuasion, and large business corporations usually have a lot of it; the legal status of the corporation, in fact, provides various incentives for the accumulation of capital assets and reserves. The fiction of corporate personhood was part of the protective legal umbrella under which business enterprises could and did flourish during the late nineteenth century,[80] and the protection of corporate economic enterprise facilitated corporate application of economic power in the national political arena.[81] By the turn of the century, with suspicion of corporate power now prevalent, the first in a series of corporate anticorruption laws began to emerge, challenging corporate political activity and influence in the electoral process.

Beginning in 1907, with the passage of the Tillman Act, the government abandoned its role as sponsor of corporate influence and took on the role of regulator. The Tillman Act prohibited monetary contributions by corporations to federal elections; the Federal Corrupt Practices Act of 1925 expanded the Tillman prohibition to ban political contributions, including property or in-kind services, by national banks or nationally chartered corporations. The two provisions clearly were intended to protect the political process from the undue

---

78. W. Kelso, American Democratic Theory 19–20 (1978).
79. For general critiques of the imperfect pluralism of interest group liberalism, see T. Lowi, The End of Liberalism (1969); G. McConnell, Private Power and American Democracy (1966).
80. A. Miller, The Supreme Court and American Capitalism 24–26 (1968).
81. Miller, Corporations and Our Two Constitutions, in Corporations and Society 241–42 (W. Samuels and A. Miller eds. 1987). Miller argues that the economic and political rise of large business corporations during the past century has resulted in a "secret constitution," under which there is no separation between public and private authority, but rather a fusion between political and economic power and a symbiotic relationship between government and corporations. The "secret constitution" provides for corporate politics. See also A. Miller, The Supreme Court and American Capitalism 160–63 (1968).

influence of economic interests and the resultant loss of integrity.[82] Later legislation, fueled by post–World War II suspicion of the power and influence of labor-oriented economic associations, made the prohibition applicable to political contributions by labor unions.[83] Finally, after a brief but unsuccessful attempt to ban direct corporate or union political expenditures,[84] Congress passed the Federal Election Campaign Act of 1971 (FECA), which imposed both disclosure and spending limitations. This measure marked the culmination of the anticorruption legislation.

Although prohibiting direct corporate financial involvement in federal election campaigns, FECA allowed the establishment of separate segregated funds for political sponsorship by political action committees, or PACs. In 1972, in *Pipefitters Local v. United States*, the Burger Court granted constitutional imprimatur to political contributions by union- and corporate-sponsored PACs.[85] *Pipefitters*, along with the 1974 amendments to FECA,[86] signaled a new era in corporate political activity: corporate political fund-raising became the euphemism for what was once recognized as political bribery. By undermining federal and state campaign finance regulations designed to prevent the buying of elective offices and officials, the decisions of the Burger Court on corporate political spending seemed to favor "corporate statism."[87]

---

82. A Matasar, Corporate PACs and Federal Campaign Finance Laws 7–8 (1986). It should be noted that shortly after the passage of the Federal Corrupt Practices Act, the federal government began experimenting with corporatist representation and cooperation among economic interests. Yet part of the controversy surrounding the NIRA, for instance, was that its attempt to legitimate cooperative activity among businessmen was activity otherwise afoul of the antitrust laws at that time. See A. Miller, The Supreme Court and American Capitalism 165–66 (1968).

83. E. Rome and W. Roberts, Corporate and Commercial Free Speech 208–9 (1985).

84. The Supreme Court held in United States v. C.I.O., 335 U.S. 106 (1948), that the government could not prohibit corporate expenditures from segregated funds earmarked to support political candidates and positions. See A. Matasar, Corporate PACs and Federal Campaign Finance Laws 8–9 (1986).

85. 407 U.S. 385 (1972).

86. The 1974 amendments to FECA established limitations on political contributions and expenditures, strict reporting requirements for federal candidates, and public financing for major-party presidential candidates. The limitation on independent expenditures was invalidated on First Amendment grounds in *Buckley v. Vales*, 424 U.S. 1 (1976).

87. Flynn, The Jurisprudence of Corporate Personhood: The Misuse of a Legal Concept, in Corporations and Society 157 n.67 (W. Samuels and A. Miller eds. 1987).

In terms of the conceptualization of corporatist representation, corporate exercise of economic power in the political arena bears little resemblance to the cooperative policy-making envisioned by corporatism. But the PAC mechanism is not restricted to corporate political influence; in fact, various studies indicate that many PACs are ideological organizations through which individuals of modest means can pool their resources for more effective political action and financial sponsorship of candidates.[88] The decisions supporting the PAC mechanism could be read as consistent with the conceptualization of corporatist representation, since PACs promote the direct interaction of public officials with economic, occupational, and ideological special interest groups. Nevertheless, our main concern is not the PAC phenomenon generally, but the Burger Court's treatment of political involvement by economic interests—specifically, corporate entities.

The preceding summary of federal regulation of corporate political involvement served two purposes. First, it showed that the Burger Court's protection of corporate political speech, including that of PACs, broke with the established pattern of restricting corporate political activity. Second, the summary prepared the way for discussion of the Court's doctrinal basis for protecting corporate political expenditures as First Amendment speech. This doctrine consisted of two assumptions: first, that monetary political expenditures are speech, or simply amplify political speech protected by the First Amendment;[89] and, second, that the listeners' right to hear and receive information justifies the protection of corporate-sponsored communi-

---

88. See, e.g., Eismeier and Pollock, Political Action Committees: Varieties of Organization and Strategy, in Money and Politics in the United States 122 (M. Malbin ed. 1984); Latus, Assessing Ideological PACs: From Outrage to Understanding, in Money and Politics in the United States 142 (M. Malbin ed. 1984). Indeed, in the two major cases in which the Burger Court invalidated restrictions on political expenditures by PACs, the Court defined PACs as populist organizations serving individuals' freedom of association. See Buckley v. Valeo, 424 U.S. 1 (1976) (ceiling on independent political expenditures by individuals and PACs declared invalid; limitations on contributions by individuals and PACs, and disclosure requirements in federal campaigns, upheld); Federal Election Commission v. National Conservative Political Action Committee, 105 S. Ct. 1459 (1985) (ceiling on independent expenditures by PACs in Presidential Election Campaign Fund Act declared invalid).

89. See Federal Election Commission v. National Conservative Political Action Committee, 105 S. Ct. 1459, 1469 (1985); Buckley v. Valeo, 424 U.S. 1, 64–66 (1976).

cation.[90] In order to protect corporate political involvement, the Burger Court endorsed a new legal fiction, analogous to and coextensive with that of corporate personhood—namely, that corporate political speech can be protected by the First Amendment without granting free speech rights to the corporate person.

It is important to recognize that the "listeners' right to hear" argument was not unique to the corporate political speech context, but was also critical to the Burger Court's protection of commercial advertising.[91] Because of the difficulty of fitting protection for corporate speakers of commercial speech into a theoretical framework of free speech, the Court clearly relied on the presumed interest of the audience to justify First Amendment protection.[92] Rather than critiquing the listeners' rights defense as First Amendment doctrine, we will examine the corporate political speech cases that employ the legal fiction of protecting corporate speech but not the corporate speaker.

Most of the corporate political speech issues examined by the Court concerned state efforts to prevent electoral corruption. Many states enacted statutes parallel to the Federal Corrupt Practices Act, limiting campaign contributions, campaign fraud, and corporate political action.[93] The first of these regulations to be examined by the Burger Court was a Massachusetts statute prohibiting banks and business corporations from making expenditures intended to influence the vote on referendum proposals unless the proposal materially af-

---

90. E. Rome and W. Roberts, Corporate and Commercial Free Speech 229 (1985); Lee, The Supreme Court and the Right to Receive Expression, 1987 Sup. Ct. Rev. 303, 327–28.

91. See Central Hudson Gas v. Public Service Commission, 447 U.S. 557, 561–62 (1980); Virginia Board of Pharmacy v. Virginia Citizens Consumers Council, 425 U.S. 748, 765 (1976). Some commentators locate the origin of the "public right to know" in the libel case of *New York Times v. Sullivan,* 376 U.S. 254 (1964). See Denniston, The Burger Court and the Press, in The Burger Years 23 (H. Schwartz ed. 1987).

92. Lee, The Supreme Court and the Right to Receive Expression, 1987 Sup. Ct. Rev. 303, 316. The literature on the constitutional value of commercial expression is vast for so recent a subject. For a general review of doctrinal problems, see Farber, Commercial Speech and First Amendment Theory, 74 Nw. U.L. Rev. 372 (1979); Simon, Defining Commercial Speech, 20 New Eng. L. Rev. 215 (1984–85).

93. See F. Sorauf, Money and Elections in the United States 260–74, 284–90 (1988); Note, Campaign Hyperbole: The Advisability of Legislating False Statements out of Politics, 2 J.L. Pol. 405 (1985); Note, Corporate Speech on Political Issues, 1985 U. Ill. L. Rev. 445, 470–72 (appendix of state statutes regulating corporate political involvement).

fected the corporation's business, property, or assets. The statute prevented the appellant corporation in the 1978 case of *First National Bank of Boston v. Bellotti* from spending funds to express its view on a proposed tax on individuals' incomes. While the state supreme court had viewed the case in terms of corporate *speakers'* rights, Powell's majority opinion argued that "the proper question was not whether corporations 'have' First Amendment rights ... coextensive with natural persons," but rather, whether the statute abridged *speech* protected by the First Amendment.[94] Noting that political expression was the heart of First Amendment speech, Powell held that the corporate identity of the speaker was irrelevant to the citizens' right to receive information from various political viewpoints.[95] Thus, what was at stake for the *Bellotti* majority was the "marketplace of ideas." Any analysis of the effect of the decision on the meaning of corporate personhood was notably absent.[96]

There were four dissenters in *Bellotti*. White's was the major dissent, emphasizing that corporate participation in elections through political expenditures would destroy a true marketplace of ideas. White saw the decision as granting powerful economic interests disproportionate political access and influence, as "the special status of corporations has placed them in a position to control vast amounts of economic power which may, if not regulated, dominate not only the economy but also the very heart of our democracy, the electoral process."[97] White's dissent seems to reject the possibility of cooperative decision making through interaction between business and other

---

94. 435 U.S. 765, 776 (1978) (emphasis added).

95. 435 U.S. at 777, 782–83.

96. Flynn, The Jurisprudence of Corporate Personhood: The Misuse of a Legal Concept, in Corporations and Society 147–48 (W. Samuels and A. Miller eds. 1987); Lee, The Right to Receive Expression, 1987 Sup. Ct. Rev. 303, 328; O'Kelley, The Constitutional Rights of Corporations Revisited, 67 Geo. L.J. 1347, 1369 (1979).

97. 435 U.S. at 807–8. White was joined in dissent by Brennan and Marshall. White was also critical of Powell's dismissive attitude toward the rights of dissenting shareholders, should corporations attain speech rights. Because of the reality of shareholders' lack of a private right of action against a corporation or its directors, Cort v. Ash, 422 U.S. 66 (1975), he argued that the decision allowed managers to expend corporate funds to promote their personal views. On the rights of shareholders in the modern corporation, see Flynn, The Jurisprudence of Corporate Personhood: The Misuse of a Legal Concept, in Corporations and Society 148–49 (W. Samuels and A. Miller eds. 1987); Schneider, Free Speech and Corporate Freedom, 59 S. Cal. L. Rev. 1227, 1253, 1260–63 (1986).

group interests in political debate. More pointed criticism of corporatist electoral participation came in Rehnquist's dissent, which focused on the "proper aim" of the business corporation and its status as an "artificial entity" created by the state and enjoying only those rights necessary to its commercial functions under its state-granted charter.[98]

It seems curious that the dissenters would spend so much time refuting the idea of corporate political rights if such rights were not, in fact, the net result of the majority's opinion. For all intents and purposes, the listeners' rights theory for protecting corporate speech functioned equivalently to granting political rights to corporate persons. The *Bellotti* decision should be interpreted as confirming the conceptual type of corporatist representation for two reasons. The first is that the decision revives and extends the nineteenth-century doctrine of corporate personality, using that doctrine to protect the political access of economic special interests. The second is that the decision implicitly affirms that deliberative government involves interaction between public institutions and private economic organizations.[99]

A question that remains about *Bellotti* is whether the Burger Court was captive to the fiction of the corporate person, or whether the Court was legitimately preventing state interference with the operating freedom of *all* corporations—commercial businesses as well as churches and citizens' organizations.[100] A partial answer came in the second case to address the protection of a business corporation's political speech. *Consolidated Edison v. Public Service Commission,* a 1980 decision, concerned New York's ban on a utility company's use of bill inserts to discuss controversial issues of public policy. *Con Ed* directly raised the question of whether the charter of a commercial corporation included the right to advocate particular social policies. With Powell again writing for the Court, the *Con Ed* decision invalidated

---

98. 435 U.S. at 826.

99. Corporations and Society 7 (W. Samuels and A. Miller eds. 1987).

100. Evidence for the assertion that the Court was indeed protecting the rights of all corporate entities, and not simply the rights of business corporations, is found in *Citizens against Rent Control v. City of Berkeley,* 454 U.S. 290 (1981). The Court struck down a city ordinance limiting personal contributions to committees formed to support or oppose ballot measures. Burger's opinion for the majority argued that the ordinance abridged the freedom of association because some of the committees were corporate entities formed with an explicitly expressive purpose.

the New York Public Service Commission's ban on such political advocacy by the utility.

The corporation "speaking" in *Con Ed* was a regulated public monopoly; the political speech endorsed and elicited public support for the development of nuclear power. As in *Bellotti,* Powell focused on the fact that, regardless of who "spoke," the government could not restrict particular viewpoints or choose permissible subjects for public debate.[101] Again, the countervailing right to receive information was the legal device that supported the corporation's right to political advocacy. Though Powell adroitly avoided the issue of corporation personhood, Stevens's concurrence came dangerously close to endorsing the rights of corporate "citizens." Stevens described the issue in *Con Ed* as concerning "the right of one group of persons... to address a selected audience on [political] issues."[102]

Con Ed should also be seen as confirming the conceptualization of corporatist representation, because it permitted a publicly regulated utility to discuss political matters with its consumer-citizens directly, without the state government as an intermediary. *Con Ed* allows a corporation to operate almost as a state within a state—especially when one considers that certain utility districts are accountable to a separate, special electorate. By enjoying the right of political advocacy, the utility in *Con Ed* exercised a blend of public and private authority over policy. The situation is a far cry from corporatism proper, but the decision suggests the Burger Court's sympathy for political access of corporate and economic interests.

Con Ed also exemplifies the general problem with the Burger Court's doctrine of corporate political speech. Powell's majority opinion failed to investigate whether the utility's "free" speech was contingent on the forced subsidy by ratepayers or stockholders.[103] But the Court's inattention to the economic inequalities present in the corporate speech context was not unique to *Con Ed*. In addressing corporate political speech generally, the Burger Court never considered that the "marketplace of ideas" might be a legitimating myth for

---

101. 447 U.S. 530 at 538.
102. 447 U.S. at 538.
103. This problem of the ratepayers' "forced aid" for the monopolistic utility's speech was the heart of Blackmun's dissenting opinion.

public debate dominated by the economically powerful.[104] Ironically, the "equal" access to political debate that the Court granted to corporations in *Bellotti* overshadowed the "special" representation of corporate and economic interests that the Court tolerated in *Salyer* and *Ball*.

American Corporatism and Economic Interests

The American version of corporatism transcends any single political system or tradition; therefore, the case data on the conceptualization of corporatist representation are necessarily nonhomogeneous. The corporatist case data can be divided into two subject areas: the special district election and the political rights of corporations. For both sets of cases, the Burger Court's decisions were strongly consistent with the conceptual type of corporatist representation. Though the number of decisions is small, the pattern of support is unequivocal.

The special district decisions, particularly *Salyer* and *Ball*, upheld electoral systems not premised on individual representation. The corporate political speech decisions, specifically *Bellotti* and *Con Ed*, required that political advocacy by corporate "citizens" receive First Amendment protection. Taken together, the decisions seem to alter the nature of political competition in the electoral process, tilting the balance in favor of collectives and against the individual.[105] The corporatist representation cases thus illustrate a second facet of the Burger Court's group-based approach to representation.

The corporatist decisions do not seem to effectuate a *group balance* in the process of political representation, so much as they privilege the special representational access of certain economic interests. One commentator has termed this stance toward the model of corporatist representation "the *Buckley* manifesto." The label refers to the first Supreme Court decision to forbid limitations on political expenditures by PACs; it designates the judicially created barrier against legislative adjustment of the "relative voices" of various "elements of

---

104. Fiss, Free Speech and Social Structure, in Equal Opportunity 183 (N. Bowie ed. 1988); Tushnet, Corporations and Free Speech, in The Politics of Law 253, 260 (D. Kairys ed. 1982).
105. Flynn, The Jurisprudence of Corporate Personhood: The Misuse of a Legal Concept, in Corporations and Society 157 n.67 (W. Samuels and A. Miller eds. 1987).

our society."[106] Thus, the *Buckley* manifesto adopts a protective stance toward the political use of personal wealth or corporate funds legally channeled through PACs. The Court tolerated such political use of economic power in both the corporate political speech cases and the land-based voting schemes of *Salyer* and *Ball*.

Arguably, then, there are two possible ways to interpret the corporatist representation cases. One is to see them as endorsing a form of group representation—here, the corporate, economic, or occupational interest. A second is to view the cases as legitimating the political manipulation of concentrations of wealth, whether individually or collectively held. Both interpretations are consistent with the concept of corporatism. The latter interpretation merely assumes that plutocratic politics would be the *result* of special representation for economic interests in the United States, with the wealthy, as a group, the economic interest benefited by corporatist representation. Rather than evaluating the viability of corporatist politics or the political impact of the corporatist representation cases, my purpose has been to demonstrate that the decisions show some solicitude for the political fortunes of economic interests.

Whether the Burger Court's decisions on special district government and on corporate political speech constitute an unfortunate doctrinal and political legacy is a question best left for subsequent investigation. The key question for this study is how the decisions balance individual, one person/one vote participation with the representation of group interests—specifically, economic interests. The corporatist representation cases discussed plainly favor group-based economic concerns; the decisions also tended to favor the political access of the economically prosperous, particularly that of corporate entities. The special role of business corporations in American politics has probably been the most significant manifestation of corporatism in our history and in constitutional law. The conceptual type of corporatist representation not only explicates a particular group-ori-

---

106. Michaelman, Political Truth and the Rule of Law 16 (1987) (unpublished manuscript). Michaelman identifies an apparent shift in attitude on the Rehnquist Court reflecting the Court's increasing recognition of the negative impact of corporate wealth on the political process. See, e.g., Federal Election Commission v. Massachusetts Citizens for Life, 479 U.S. 238 (1986). See Michaelman's discussion of the selective enfranchisement cases generally, in Conceptions of Democracy in American Constitutional Argument: Voting Rights, 41 Fla. L. Rev. 443 (1989).

ented approach to representation rights, but also helps to describe a very important aspect of American political development.

Whatever one's view of its fairness as a system of representation, the corporatist conceptualization was not the only judicial statement on group political access. Nor was it the most blatant example of judicial solicitude for the political fortunes of a particular group; that distinction belongs to the next conceptual type that we will discuss.

CHAPTER 5

Demographic Districting and Compensatory Majoritarianism

The previous chapter discussed a series of cases in which the Burger Court considered certain economic aspects of political competition. The conceptualization that best explained the Court's decisions, that of corporatist representation, legitimates the competitive edge of economic interest groups. In general, the corporatist representation cases recognized the group nature of political action, as does modern pluralist theory. Yet pluralists disagree about the fairness of the distribution of political resources in American society and the resultant competitive advantage of various interest groups. The question of what kind of remedy would rectify imperfect political competition among social groups is the focus of this chapter and the conceptual type it will discuss. Our third conceptualization of group representation returns our attention to the districting process and its corollary, "fairness" of elections; like the two previous conceptual types, it addresses the political access of particular group interests.

The conceptualization I term *demographic representation* is a set of criteria for reform of geographic-based electoral districting. This conceptualization attempts to offer a more sophisticated account of electoral competition than the one person, one vote doctrine can provide. "One person, one vote" offers an individualistic account of the forces of electoral competition, despite modern pluralism's recognition of groups as the basic unit of politics.[1] The immediate origins of the demographic conceptualization are the writings of political scientists and legal scholars interested in electoral procedures. Collectively, such studies of the problems of reapportionment have influenced both the justices of the Supreme Court and other analysts

---

1. Shapiro, Gerrymandering, Unfairness, and the Supreme Court, 33 U.C.L.A. L. Rev. 227, 232 (1985).

of districting and representation. The conceptual type cannot be attributed to any particular reapportionment scholar; it is instead an "ideal type" drawn from various, and sometimes divergent, works. The conceptual type has two parts: first, a theory of demographic districting, and, second, the premise that modern pluralism requires compensatory majoritarianism for certain electoral groups under certain circumstances.[2] The general thrust of the demographic conceptualization of representation is to resolve the tension in the American electoral system between majoritarian government and plural representation.

Before examining the historical and theoretical foundations of the conceptual type, let us discuss the relevance of this alleged tension. One scholar of comparative politics identified the American system of government as a hybrid of "majoritarian" and "consensus" models of democracy.[3] This fusion is most apparent in the American electoral system, which represents locally segmented majorities. Arguably, the tension between majoritarian government and plural representation originates from a dualism in the American vision of politics, between an individualistic, competitive vision of politics and a group-oriented, interactive vision of politics. The former vision can be called results-oriented, in that its concern is protecting individual rights in order to satisfy certain interests. The latter vision is means-oriented, in that it focuses on meaningful participation and cooperative public action.[4] It does not take much imagination to see how these visions might conflict; a good example is the now familiar special district election. Arguably, the land-based voting cases illustrated that a long-term majority interest—preservation of property rights and values—can be overrepresented to maintain political stability.[5] Here, the goal of political stability necessarily limits political competition among plu-

---

2. Inspiration for this conceptual type came from Cain's notion of a "group compensating" approach to districting. See Cain, Perspectives on *Davis v. Bandemer:* Views of the Practitioner, Theorist and Reformer, in Toward Fair and Effective Representation: Political Gerrymandering and the Courts (B. Grofman ed. 1990).

3. A. Lijphart, Democracies 32–36 (1984).

4. Althoff and Greig, The U.S. Supreme Court on Rights and Participation: The Deviant Voting and Redistricting Cases, 13 J. Contemp. L. 31, 42–44 (1987); Michaelman, Political Markets and Community Self-Determination: Competing Judicial Models of Local Government Legitimacy, 53 Ind. L.J. 145, 149–50 (1977–78).

5. Althoff and Greig, The Deviant Voting and Redistricting Cases, 13 J. Contemp. L. 31, 60 (1987); Riker, Democracy and Representation: A Reconciliation of *Ball v. James* and *Reynolds v. Sims,* 1 Sup. Ct. Econ. Rev. 39, 60–61 (1982).

ral interests. Translating the point to a broader electoral context, winner-take-all district elections also sacrifice proportional representation of various demographic interests to stabilize political competition among them.

The tension between a majoritarian and a plural vision of representation is fundamentally between two conceptions of political competition. Districting thus becomes an important issue for representation theory because of the need to balance majoritarian and plural conceptions of political competition. Historically, the American district system of elections has been attempting to strike this balance since the constitutional convention debates about the size of congressional districts. What unites modern and historical discussions of political competition is the dispute over homogeneous versus heterogeneous districts. The convention delegates saw an inverse relationship between district size and district homogeneity; those who favored small districts were essentially attracted to the kind of representation that homogeneous districts allowed.[6] Demographically homogeneous districts would be more likely to return representatives who would faithfully embody the characteristics and spectrum of interests of the general population. Demographically homogeneous constituencies would make competitive district elections unlikely; a delegate was expected to be the agent of his constituents, both descriptively and formally.[7] Since a delegate "made present" the people who had elected him, groups and interests within the electorate competed via proxy delegates in the legislature.

Such "descriptive" representation, and the political competition it implied, was at odds with the Madisonian argument for the filtering effect of representation.[8] The filtering effect referred to the process whereby a representative refined his constituents' express views into his own conception of wise public policy. Convention advocates of larger, more heterogeneous districts wished to avoid divisive political competition—the kind produced by the excessive local pluralism of the representation scheme under the Articles of Confederation.

---

6. R. Zagarri, The Politics of Size 71 (1987).
7. Malbin, Congress during the Convention and Ratification, in The Framing and Ratification of the Constitution 192–93 (L. Levy and D. Mahoney eds. 1987). Because, ideally, a representative would mirror his constituents' attributes, he would also transmit their wishes as his own. See H. Pitkin, The Concept of Representation 63ff. (1967).
8. The Federalist No. 10.

Their proposed alternative, demographically heterogeneous districts, would provide stable competition since representatives would be responsive to the moderating influence of a "median preference coalition."[9] As we know, this historical debate resulted in a compromise. The single-member, geographic-based district system—an English import—allowed for local diversity without compromising stability.[10] Although plural interests competed at the intradistrict level, the plurality-winner system ensured a delegate chosen by a coalition of interests in a geographic area. The goal of legislative districting, at least at the national level, was to create a working legislative majority of delegates who were themselves the products of majoritarian consensus.

Historically, then, the districting process has been used to induce balanced political competition. The criteria used for districting would determine whether competition was weighted in favor of majoritarian government or plural representation. The foundation of the conceptual type of demographic representation was the recognition that the demographics of districts could or should be manipulated to effect a certain competitive balance among particular groups in the electorate.

Gerrymandered Competition: History and Theory

The first formal criteria for electoral districts were requisite size and some degree of compactness. The latter was important because of the difficulties of communication and the need for access between constituents and delegate.[11] Districting following political boundaries also responded to a traditional sense of the community as the appropriate basis for representation.[12] The representational goal of these criteria was both the filtering of regional factions and the selection of representatives from a certain "esteemed" class of men.

The political advantages of more demographic districting were apparent to legislators unenamored of Madison's "clash of interests" approach to political representation. If that clash occurred in one's

---

9. B. Cain, The Reapportionment Puzzle 65–66 (1984).
10. E. Morgan, Inventing the People 246, 274–75 (1988).
11. B. Cain, The Reapportionment Puzzle 32–33 (1984).
12. Dixon, Fair Criteria and Procedures for Establishing Legislative Districts, in Representation and Redistricting Issues 17 (B. Grofman, A. Lijphart, et al. eds. 1982).

own district, political competition could have an unfortunate personal outcome. The most obvious political advantage gained by the purposeful use of demographic criteria for districting was a "safe seat," a district composed of persons or interests favorable to a certain incumbent or partisan persuasion. The first documented use of such districting was Elbridge Gerry's famous Massachusetts "salamander" district of 1812.[13]

The Gerry case illustrates that *gerry*mandering is almost as old as the American district system of elections itself. But more important, it shows that in a district system of elections, political competition is easily altered by manipulating district boundaries. Thus, as long as boundaries are susceptible to gerrymandering, there is nothing inherently stable about single-member, spatially organized electoral districts. Gerrymandering has been defined as "the drawing of district boundaries in a discriminatory fashion... to inflate the political strength of one group and deflate that of another."[14] It is destabilizing when it operates unfairly to deny majority rule or suppress a particular group in the electorate. Historical examples of districting that manipulated political competition include the "silent gerrymanders" of the *Baker* and *Reynolds* cases. Although the discriminatory district boundaries in these cases were the result of neglect rather than conscious political design, they produced population discrepancies uniformly disadvantaging the majority interest of urban voters.[15]

Gerrymandering is also historically associated with deprivation or dilution of the right to vote on the basis of race. Initially, strategies for depriving racial minorities of political access were blatantly exclusionary, including devices such as literacy tests, grandfather clauses, poll taxes, and all-white primary elections. Indeed, such devices prompted judicial scrutiny of the state electoral process even before the reapportionment revolution.[16] But, until *Baker*, no remedy for gerrymandered electoral competition existed beyond the political process itself; matters of state electoral redistricting were assumed to

---

13. R. Dixon, Democratic Representation 1–2 (1968).
14. Dixon, The Court, the People and "One Man, One Vote," in Reapportionment in the 1970's, at 29 (N. Polsby ed. 1971).
15. Alfange, Gerrymandering and the Constitution, 1986 Sup. Ct. Rev. 175, 191.
16. See, e.g., Smith v. Allwright 321 U.S. 649 (1944). See also Kousser, The Undermining of the First Reconstruction: Lessons for the Second, in Minority Vote Dilution 27 (C. Davidson ed. 1984).

be nonjusticiable political questions.[17] An isolated exception to this hands-off attitude was the 1960 decision of *Gomillion v. Lightfoot*,[18] in which the Warren Court invalidated, under the Fifteenth Amendment, a districting plan drawn to exclude black voters as a group. The city boundaries of Tuskeegee, Alabama, had been redrawn to prevent blacks, who made up the majority of the citizenry, from voting in municipal elections.[19]

Gomillion's absolute deprivation of minority voting rights through exclusionary gerrymandering was comparatively rare; geography did not always cooperate. More prevalent were the manipulation of district lines and the use of at-large electoral systems to water down racial minorities' political strength. The replacement of small geographic wards with at-large city elections formed part of the Progressive municipal reform movement at the turn of the century. This otherwise laudable movement was associated with a desire to "de-ethnicize" city politics, as well as to further disenfranchise blacks in the South.[20] The choice of an at-large system, essentially an affirmative decision not to district at all,[21] favors a certain kind of political competition. The at-large election of representatives generally results in the district majority being "overrepresented," in that the majority controls or dominates the selection of all delegates.[22] Clearly, the at-large system favors majoritarian, not pluralistic, political competition. For this reason, local white majorities deployed it to dilute the potential political influence of black voters.

This brief history of gerrymandering is intended only to show that political competitiveness within the American electoral system hinges on the criteria for determining what makes a districting plan fair. Equipopulous districting was, of course, one of the first standards articulated by the Supreme Court. Yet, while population equality is

---

17. See Colegrove v. Green, 328 U.S. 549 (1946).

18. 364 U.S. 339 (1960).

19. See Davidson, Minority Vote Dilution: An Overview, in Minority Vote Dilution 8–9 (C. Davidson ed. 1984).

20. Kousser, The Undermining of the First Reconstruction, in Minority Vote Dilution 31–37 (C. Davidson ed. 1984).

21. See Blacksher and Menefee, At-Large Elections and One Person, One Vote, in Minority Vote Dilution 203, 230 (C. Davidson ed. 1984).

22. Certain modifications of the at-large electoral system, such as numbered slots for delegates from multimember districts, lessen the majority's predominance because they allow minority group voters to engage in "single shot" voting and elect a minimal number of candidates of their choice.

an accepted criteria for fair districting, its acceptance has not prevented disagreement among contemporary reapportionment theorists over what counts as a competitive electoral structure. One commentator locates the roots of this disagreement in the rivalry between "public interest" and "pluralist" approaches to districting.[23] The former approach argues that districts should be internally competitive—not deliberately homogeneous and therefore safe for a particular party's or interest's candidate. The alternative approach offers a less precise verdict on the relationship between demographic districting and political competition; rather than dictating the specific nature of a reapportionment plan, redistricting should "encourage groups to come together."[24] We can take this to mean that both political competition and representation should be more pluralistic than majoritarian.

Despite the ongoing dispute over the relative competitiveness of given districting systems, modern reapportionment theorists do agree on the list of criteria relevant to fair districting. Although there is less agreement on their ordering and implementation, these criteria constitute an acknowledgment that demographic districting should be employed to produce a certain sort of competitive environment. In other words, demographic criteria must be consciously considered in creating electoral constituencies, to avoid gerrymandered political competition. As one commentator put it, for single-member districts, random is not equal.[25]

Modern reapportionment theory is the crucial foundation for the conceptual type of demographic representation. In addition to recognizing the importance of demographic criteria to districting, it is receptive to group-based remedies for individual voters' lack of political influence. In other words, the purpose of considering demographic factors in districting is to minimize what one scholar called the "con-

---

23. B. Cain, The Reapportionment Puzzle 179–80 (1984).
24. Id. at 180.
25. Grofman, For Singlemember Districts Random Is Not Equal, in Representation and Redistricting Issues 55 (B. Grofman and A. Lijphart eds. 1982). Grofman takes issue with the widely held view that "for singlemember districts, 'a chance pattern will, over the long haul, operate in such a way as to make the percentage of the population and the percentage of representation more or less equal.'" Id. at 55 (quoting David Wells, Testimony at the Hearings before the Committee on Governmental Affairs of the U.S. Senate on S. 596, 96th Congress, First session, 529 (1979)).

textual worthlessness of votes."[26] Concern for the contextual worth of an individual's or a group's vote calls for a particular vision of the competitive political environment. Modern reapportionment theory's concern for fair electoral results lends credence to the assertion that it embraces the goal of compensatory majoritarian representation. To demonstrate, let us look at the districting criteria commonly accepted by most commentators and at the theoretical assumptions about political competition underlying them.

Criteria for Competitive Fairness

The historical background on electoral districting, discussed in the preceding section, prefaces an examination of the theoretical foundations of the conceptualization of demographic representation. This section sketches the criteria for "fair districting" and shows that two, in particular, have been central to the Supreme Court's redistricting decisions.

In discussing the history of electoral districting, three criteria were mentioned that are still relevant in modern debates: population size and variance, the integrity of political subdivision boundaries, and compactness. Although the historical impetus for the compactness criterion—mitigating the difficulties of communication over long distances—has diminished in importance, compactness remains significant as a negative requirement: its violation may signal a gerrymander, although a noncompact district can just as easily result from following a natural community of interest.[27]

"Respecting communities of interest" is itself an acknowledged criterion for districting that occasionally overlaps with respecting subdivision boundaries. Although it is difficult to implement, this criterion usually implies that a district should unite persons of similar interests—for example, farmers living in a river valley or commuters living in middle-class suburbs. However, the community of interest crite-

---

26. Levinson, Gerrymandering and the Brooding Omnipresence of Proportional Representation, 33 U.C.L.A. L. Rev. 260, 265 (1985).
27. Backstrom, Problems of Implementing Redistricting, in Representation and Redistricting Issues 49–50 (B. Grofman ed. 1982). Compactness means that the boundaries of districts should be as short as possible—approaching perfect squares. Some commentators feel there exists a "myth of compactness," because compact districts can easily be used to disguise the submergence of groups of voters.

rion does not necessarily imply homogeneous districts; it can just as easily suggest that districts should be microcosms of the plural interests of the people in the state.[28] Thus, community of interest districting does not mandate a particular electoral outcome—for example, the election of representatives who are spokesmen for particular interests—nor does it require that interest groups in the electorate have a particular degree of influence over a limited number of representatives. Because the protection of communities of interest is a somewhat imprecise goal, an additional districting criterion, contiguity, is sometimes employed as a substitute. Contiguity means that no part of one district may be completely separated from another part, presumably because proximity implies interest commonality.[29] Of course, creating constituencies with shared interests is not necessarily the appeal of contiguous districts; contiguity, like compactness, is often thought of as a formal deterrent to gerrymandering.

The five criteria above—population variance, subdivision integrity, compactness, community of interest protection, and contiguity—are sometimes referred to as formal criteria,[30] because they transcend any particular interpretation of political competition. For example, as noted, the community of interest criterion can be applied to either homogeneous or heterogeneous districting and, thus, can further either pluralist or majoritarian political competition. However, two further criteria for districting are not formal, but results-oriented. These two criteria are the nondilution of racial minority voting strength and partisan fairness. The result these demographic districting criteria seek is compensatory majoritarianism. In other words, according to these two criteria, districting fairness must be viewed as a question of the relative political influence of *groups* of voters. While the objective of demographic districting is obviously not true propor-

---

28. Id. at 47–48.
29. One study observes that geographic contiguity is an "uneasy compromise" between interest-based and random electoral constituencies. Lowenstein and Steinberg, Districting in the Public Interest, 33 U.C.L.A. L. Rev. 16, 20 (1985).

An ancillary problem is how much contiguity is enough. Most modern commentators agree that areas that touch only on their corners do not satisfy the contiguity criterion for districting. See Backstrom, Problems of Implementing Redistricting, in Representation and Redistricting Issues 49 (B. Grofman, A. Lijphart, et al. eds. 1982).

30. Lowenstein and Steinberg, Districting in the Public Interest, 33 U.C.L.A. L. Rev. 16, 35 (1985); Grofman, Criteria for Districting, 33 U.C.L.A. Rev. 77, 78 (1985).

tional representation,[31] electoral constituencies can still be designed to compensate certain minority groups that are disadvantaged in majoritarian elections. Political competition as compensatory majoritarianism, then, treats "the majority" as just another group interest to be balanced in the electoral districting process.[32]

Let us examine these two results-oriented, demographic districting criteria to see how they contribute to compensatory majoritarian competition. The first criterion commands that districting plans may not dilute the voting strength of racial minorities, whether by "cracking," "stacking," or "packing"[33] concentrations of minority voters into particular districts. This criterion for districting emerged as a corrective measure responding to decades of racial discrimination in voting practices. The nondilution criterion has been interpreted to mean that a districting plan should approximate the potential[34] political influence of racial groups in the state population. Whether or not this is its primary goal, the nondilution criterion has often entailed a

---

31. One must be careful with this label. Proportional representation does not imply a specific electoral structure, but simply an ideal or principle of proportional influence to which different electoral systems seek to conform. See V. Bogdanor, What Is Proportional Representation? 46 (1984). For a commentator who sees a legacy of proportional representation in the reapportionment decisions, see Levinson, Gerrymandering and the Brooding Omnipresence of Proportional Representation, 33 U.C.L.A. L. Rev. 260 (1985).

32. This observation has been made by commentators who are no fans of the "false distinction" between malapportionment and gerrymandering as a distinction between individual and group voting claims. See, e.g., Jacobs and O'Rourke, Racial Polarization in Vote Dilution Cases under Section 2 of the Voting Rights Act, 3 J.L. Pol. 295, 299 (1986). One article argues that, all along, the reapportionment cases advanced "group" interests—the interests of the majority. Note, The Constitutional Imperative of Proportional Representation, 94 Yale L.J. 163, 175–79 (1986). On further aspects of treating the majority as a group interest, see Blacksher and Menefee, At-Large Elections and One Person, One Vote, in Minority Vote Dilution 203, 230 (C. Davidson ed. 1984).

33. Parker, Racial Gerrymandering and Legislative Apportionment, in Minority Vote Dilution 89–99 (C. Davidson ed. 1984). "Cracking" involves isolating and submerging minority voters in areas within white majority districts. "Stacking" and "packing" are methods of concentrating minority voting strength in a few districts and thus "wasting" minority votes.

34. Nondilutionary districting seeks to secure a group's potential electoral power; it cannot establish proportional representation for that group. The reason is that a group's potential power is less than proportional to its total statewide numbers, given some geographic dispersion of its voting strength. Because the American electoral system is one of geographically based single-member districts, the geographic contiguity of an electoral bloc is significant in determining its "proportional" political influence. I owe this clarification to correspondence with Bernard Grofman.

decidedly demographic emphasis in districting—an approach termed "affirmative action gerrymandering" by some critics.[35]

Epithets aside, it is difficult to determine the actual objective or expected result of the nondilution criterion. Most commentators see its objective as giving minority voters a fair chance to elect the representatives of their choice.[36] A fair chance, however, does not entail securing a fixed number of minority officeholders. The latter goal leans toward descriptive representation—in this context, that individuals can only be represented by members of their own racial group. Descriptive representation of this sort would lead to claims for proportionality that, in the American electoral system, might translate into safe, homogeneous districts nearly proportional to racial groups' statewide population.[37] Given the limited geographic contiguity among racial group populations,[38] proportional representation of racial group interests through demographic districting is an unrealistic objective.[39]

Another possible definition of nondilutionary districting is districting that compensates black or Hispanic voters as a *numerical* minority for their potentially diminished competitiveness in a majoritarian electoral system. Such compensation recognizes an aggregate voting

---

35. See, e.g., Wells, Affirmative Action Gerrymandering, 67 Natl. Civ. Rev. 10 (1978); Note, Group Representation and Race-Conscious Apportionment, 91 Harv. L. Rev. 1847 (1978).

36. See, e.g., Grofman, Criteria for Districting, 33 U.C.L.A. L. Rev. 77, 148 (1985).

37. This leaves aside the question of whether alternative electoral systems—single transferable vote, list PR, etc.—would better serve the goal of fair representation. No doubt proportionality would be better served by jettisoning the territorial conception of single-member districts with plurality winners, but such wholesale electoral reform was not an option open to the federal judiciary. On the possibilities for such systemic reform of the American electoral process, see Brams, Approval Voting, in Representation and Redistricting Issues 137 (B. Grofman, A. Lijphart, et al. eds. 1982); Engstrom and Taebel, Cumulative Voting as a Remedy for Minority Vote Dilution, 5 J. Pol. (1988); Grofman, Alternatives to Singlemember Plurality Districts, in Representation and Redistricting Issues 107 (B. Grofman, A. Lijphart, et al. eds. 1982); Still, Alternatives to Singlemember Districts, in Minority Vote Dilution 249 (C. Davidson ed. 1984).

38. Grofman and Handley, Why Are There So Few Black Congressmen from the South? (paper presented to the American Political Science Association, Chicago, Ill.) (Sept., 1987).

39. It would also be a dangerously divisive objective in racially plural society. It would arguably invite myriad claims from other potentially "districtable groups." See Cain, Perspectives on *Davis v. Bandemer,* in Toward Fair and Effective Representation: Political Gerrymandering and the Courts (B. Grofman ed. 1990). Cain argues that "it is virtually impossible to overestimate the number of groups who will become interested in districting and electoral arrangements if given the chance."

right, a political right exercised effectively only by individuals acting in concert.[40] In other words, to guarantee minority voters a fair chance to elect delegates of their choice, nondilutionary districting must prevent minority groups from being disadvantaged by a majoritarian selection process. "Being disadvantaged" means losing elections, the usual fate of minority interests in the process of majority rule. The nondilution criterion accepts the use of demographic districting to alter anticipated majoritarian outcomes; thus, it entails a theory of political competition—at least for racial minorities—whose goal is compensatory majoritarianism.

The second results-oriented districting criterion also has a decidedly group-compensating focus. It, too, represents an attempt to modify the operations of a majoritarian system of electoral competition. But instead of being a single guideline for reform, it proposes a series of recommendations seeking partisan fairness in districting. The objective of partisan fairness, however, is a matter of dispute, since reapportionment scholars are divided over the definition of stable partisan competition.[41] Some favor a bipartisan scheme of proportional safe seats for each major party, or a seats-votes ratio that is "symmetrical" to each party's statewide strength.[42] Others champion a districting scheme with the greatest number of unsafe, competitive seats, with each district seat highly responsive to swings in the popular vote.[43] Distinguishing each of these approaches to stable partisan competition from intentionally discriminatory partisan gerrymandering necessitates attention to incumbency protection, whereby a districting plan may not provide for differential treatment of the two parties' incumbents.[44]

---

40. Note, Primary Elections and the Collective Right to Freedom of Association, 94 Yale L.J. 117, 121 n.20 (1984). See also Note, Group Representation and Race-Conscious Apportionment, 91 Harv. L. Rev. 1847, 1852 (1978).

41. See Alfange, Gerrymandering and the Constitution, 1986 Sup. Ct. Rev. 175, 240.

42. Niemi, The Effects of Districting on Tradeoffs among Party Competition, Electoral Responsiveness and Seats-Votes Relationships, in Representation and Redistricting Issues 35 (B. Grofman, A. Lijphart, et al. eds. 1982). Some reapportionment scholars feel that a "base race" method of estimating seat share is preferable to a seats-votes ratio. See Backstrom and Robins, What's Next in Gerrymandering (paper presented to the American Political Science Association, Washington, D.C.) (Sept., 1988).

43. Lowenstein and Steinberg, Districting in the Public Interest, 33 U.C.L.A. L. Rev. 16, 37–43 (1985).

44. Owen and Grofman, Optimal Partisan Gerrymandering, 7 Pol. Geog. Q. 5 (1988).

Admittedly, the partisan fairness criterion for districting is somewhat confusing and not terribly precise, and thus is the source of a great deal of dissent among scholars. The very objective of partisan fairness in districting exacerbates the existing tension between pluralist and majoritarian conceptions of political competition. On the one hand, fairness presumably requires that parties win seats "roughly proportional to their share of the popular vote."[45] On the other hand, representation weighted toward the majority facilitates implementation of the majority's policies and enhances its accountability.[46] Clearly, the kinds of electoral outcomes one associates with competitive districts will influence one's criteria for fair partisan districting.

Despite scholarly disagreements over the objectives of partisan fairness in districting, consideration of partisan demographics in the districting process is significant in and of itself. It acknowledges that race is not the only group interest that can be diluted or disadvantaged by the electoral system. The burgeoning literature on compatible standards for racial and partisan districting[47] suggests that scholars view partisan fairness as a results-oriented districting criterion with a compensatory thrust similar to racial nondilution. In the context of districting for partisan fairness, compensatory majoritarianism repudiates "to the victor belong the spoils." At a minimum, the partisan fairness criterion would deprive the party victorious in the state house from implementing the sort of electoral competition it sees fit. Removing districting from the hands of incumbent legislators[48] or, at least, tying those legislative hands with fairness criteria,

---

45. This language is from Dixon, Fair Criteria and Procedures for Establishing Legislative Districts, in Representation and Redistricting Issues 9 (B. Grofman, A. Lijphart, et al. eds., 1982).

46. Lowenstein and Steinberg, Districting in the Public Interest, 33 U.C.L.A. L. Rev. 16, 52 (1985).

47. The volume of literature is immense. A selection of important articles would include: B. Cain, The Reapportionment Puzzle (1984); B. Grofman and A. Lijphart, eds., Electoral Laws and Their Political Consequences (1986); Alfange, Gerrymandering and the Constitution: Into the Thorns of the Political Thicket at Last, 1986 Sup. Ct. Rev. 175; Baker, Judicial Determination of Political Gerrymandering: A "Totality of Circumstances" Approach, 3 J.L. Pol. 1 (1986); B. Grofman, ed., Toward Fair and Effective Representation: Political Gerrymandering and the Courts (1990); Gerrymandering Symposium, 33 U.C.L.A. L. Rev. (1985).

48. There has been some discussion of transferring authority for redistricting decisions from elected legislators to nonpartisan or bipartisan electoral commissions. See, e.g., B. Cain, The Reapportionment Puzzle (1984).

would be a significant—and compensatory—modification of majority party hegemony over redistricting.

The criteria for districting accepted by modern reapportionment theory underlie the conceptual type of demographic representation. To a much greater degree than the previous conceptualization of group representation, the demographic conceptualization is the product of scholarly consideration of the political goals of the representation process. Of course, the impetus for considering the technicalities of districting came from the decisions of the Warren and Burger Courts.

We have already mentioned that one of the first objectives of the 1960s reapportionment decisions was to make a majoritarian electoral system truly majoritarian. But almost from the start of the reapportionment revolution, the Court was urged to make a majoritarian system more plural as well. One early Warren Court ruling should suffice to show that the tension between majoritarian and plural representation was present not only in the history and theory of reapportionment, but in the Supreme Court's own decisions as well. The nature of political competition resulting from a districting plan was central to the Warren Court's debate in *Wright v. Rockefeller,* in 1964.[49] Because of insufficient evidence of discriminatory gerrymandering, the Court upheld a New York congressional districting plan that "packed" black and Hispanic voters into a single electoral district.[50] Concentrating the ethnic voters did guarantee them the delegate of their choice, but at the price of "wasting" their electoral strength within that district. The dissenters, led by Justice Douglas, focused on the wisdom of "separate but better off" for racial minorities in districting.[51] Douglas argued that a race-based districting system "is a divisive force in a community, emphasizing differences between candidates and voters that are irrelevant in the constitutional sense."[52] As an alternative, he proposed coalition building within heterogeneous districts to facilitate pluralist representation. Douglas's dissent was arguably motivated by concern that homogeneous, safe

---

49. 376 U.S. 52 (1964).
50. The record did suggest that the reason for the "packing" was to create a safe, white district for the Republican party in Manhattan. See Parker, Gerrymandering and Reapportionment, in Minority Vote Dilution 85, 99 (C. Davidson ed. 1984).
51. 376 U.S. at 67.
52. 376 U.S. at 66.

districts (especially when excessively safe) diluted the value of individual participation by circumscribing electoral choice.[53]

Wright was one of the first cases to ask the Court to define interest group representation in republican government.[54] The case raised questions about how the demographics of districting were related to electoral competition and, indirectly, to legislative accountability. The case also showed that, particularly with respect to racial voting power, the Court would be urged to reform the electoral districting system to facilitate plural representation. As future decisions gradually expanded the Court's power to restructure state and local electoral systems, the interrelationship between district demographics and electoral competition became an increasingly critical issue for the Burger Court.

We shall use the conceptualization of demographic representation to test the sophistication of the Burger Court's view of this interrelationship. Accordingly, our focus will be the decisions' acceptance of two premises: (1) the idea that political competition depends on the demographics of districting, and (2) the conception of electoral competition as compensatory majoritarianism. The cases in this area consider both racial and partisan districting issues, and involve redistricting as well as the choice of electoral systems. I subdivide the cases into two categories for analysis. The first category of cases considers the effect of the electoral structure on racial political strength and involves the federal government's efforts to remedy racial dilution. These cases concern the Court's interpretation and application of a major antidiscrimination statute, the Voting Rights Act.

The second group of cases highlights the Burger Court's approach to group-biased gerrymandering as a violation of the equal protection clause. These decisions reveal that the Court embraced a theory of group representation that went beyond remedying past racial disenfranchisement. For both categories of cases, we will look to see if the decisions show (1) consistency, (2) confirmation, (3) irrelevance, or (4) contradiction with respect to the conceptual type of demographic representation. The concluding section of the chapter will discuss the implications of the assertion that recent districting decisions "view legislators not as representatives of individuals who happen to re-

---

53. Stephens, Provisions for Apportionment, 72 Natl. Civ. Rev. 174, 176 (1982).
54. Cf. Packer, Tracking the Court through a Political Thicket, 22 Urb. L. Ann. 227, 241, 257 (1982).

side ... in a single geographic area, ... but as represent[atives] of specific groups *as groups*."[55]

The Excluded Constituency: The Voting Rights Act and Racial Political Equality

No other problem in representation law validates the dictum "voting does not equal representation"[56] as authoritatively as does racial vote dilution. The history and early judicial interpretation of the Voting Rights Act show all too well that as minorities overcame barriers to casting ballots, "new barriers were being erected to ensure that while blacks might vote, they couldn't win."[57] The gap between voting and representation led the Burger Court to strike down electoral practices that deprived minorities of political influence. As will become clear, the Court's interpretation of the Act was generally consistent with the ideals of both demographic districting and compensatory majoritarianism.

Congress passed the Voting Rights Act in 1965, after nearly a century of failure to enforce the Fifteenth Amendment, a Reconstruction Era guarantee against race-based deprivations of the vote. The Voting Rights Act prohibited denial or abridgment of the right to vote on the basis of race and authorized federal remedies for such violations. For judicial scrutiny of state electoral practices, the two most important parts of the statute were sections 2 and 5. Section 2 broadly stated that "no voting qualification or prerequisite to voting, or standard, practice or procedure, shall be imposed or applied by any state or political subdivision to deny or abridge the right to vote of any citizen ... on account of race." Section 5 established a preclearance procedure for electoral changes made by "covered jurisdictions" with a history of low black voting registration or turnout. Electoral changes meriting special scrutiny included changes from ward to at-large district elections, and municipal annexations to existing electoral jurisdictions.[58] The act specifically authorized federal judicial

---

55. Wells, Affirmative Action Gerrymandering, 67 Natl. Civic Rev. 10, 14 (1978).

56. R. Dixon, Democratic Representation 267–70 (1968).

57. Derfner, The Voting Rights Act Amendments of 1982, in Minority Vote Dilution 145, 149–50 (C. Davidson ed. 1984).

58. Parker, Gerrymandering and Reapportionment, in Minority Vote Dilution 85, 102 (C. Davidson ed. 1984). The initial focus of the act was on black registration and

enforcement and articulated a clear role for courts in supervising electoral structures.

One question dominated the Court's debate over the construction of the Voting Rights Act: what constituted proof of abridgment of the right to vote on the basis of race? Was an electoral districting system to be judged on its procedural fairness or its substantive outcome? Initially, courts interpreted section 2 of the act to require proof of intentional discrimination—the so-called smoking-gun finding. In other words, without evidence that a districting plan had been adopted with the intent to abridge or dilute black votes, the electoral results of that plan were presumed to reflect fair majoritarian competition.

A brief synopsis of racial considerations in districting elucidates the origins of the intent requirement. As noted earlier, in its 1960 decision in *Gomillion v. Lightfoot,* the Warren Court invalidated the districting plan for the city of Tuskeegee, Alabama, which excluded almost all blacks from voting in municipal elections. As the plan employed the quintessentially noncompact district, the Warren Court inferred an intent to deny the right to vote on the basis of race. This racial intent standard,[59] which *Gomillion* implied from the Fifteenth Amendment, was the same standard applied by the Court under the equal protection clause of the Fourteenth Amendment. Thus, a constitutional challenge to a districting plan required proof that composition of the district was motivated by an intent to discriminate.[60]

The first cases interpreting the Voting Rights Act focused on the preliminary issue of the federal government's enforcement power under the act, particularly its preclearance authority under section 5.[61] Until federal authority to enforce the preclearance provision was established, the issue of what constituted proof of discriminatory electoral changes was not specifically addressed. The first case to consider the latter issue was *Allen v. State Board of Elections,* a Mississippi case decided by the Warren Court in 1969, which concerned the applica-

---

voting; scrutiny of the impact of certain electoral structures on the value of black votes followed. For a comprehensive treatment of the history and meaning of the Voting Rights Act, see A. Thernstrom, Whose Votes Count? (1987).

59. Gelfand, Voting Rights and the Democratic Process, 17 Urb. Law. 333, 338 (1985).

60. Wright v. Rockefeller, 376 U.S. 52, 56–58 (1964). See also Engstrom, Racial Vote Dilution, in The Voting Rights Act 16–17 (L. Foster ed. 1985).

61. See South Carolina v. Katzenbach, 383 U.S. 301 (1966).

tion of the intent requirement to section 5 electoral changes.[62] The outcome was a clear victory for judicial authority to restructure local representative systems. The Warren majority held that in the context of racial bloc voting, changes from wards to at-large districts might not affect the numerical equality of votes but did tend to compromise minority voting strength. Significantly, the case also suggested that litigants challenging at-large electoral systems might be exempt from the requirement to show intent.[63] The majority argued that the Voting Rights Act was "aimed at the subtle, as well as the obvious, state regulations which *have the effect* of abridging the right to vote on the basis of race."[64] Essentially, *Allen* broadly defined evidence of intentional discrimination.

Did Warren's statement in *Allen* mean that the at-large system per se abridged the right to vote through racial dilution? Not in a strictly procedural sense, according to Justice Harlan. In a partial dissent, Harlan objected to the majority's intimation that the act granted a right to proportional representation for minority groups. He drew a distinction between preventing individual blacks from voting freely, and limiting blacks' group voting power through an at-large electoral system—only the former was a violation of the law. Harlan's dissent is important because of his observation about the relative competitive environments provided by the at-large and the single-member district election. With respect to the political competitiveness of a minority group, Harlan commented that it was unclear whether *more* influence over the election of *fewer* representatives was inherently preferable to *some* influence over the election of *many* representatives.[65] The *Allen* majority obviously leaned toward the former view, which was an argument for designing electoral competition so that it ensured a certain degree of minority political influence.

By the end of its tenure, the Warren Court had established the basic legitimacy of section 5 preclearance—that is, of federal scrutiny of proposed state electoral changes.[66] Its precedents also clarified

---

62. 393 U.S. 544 (1969).
63. A. Thernstrom, Whose Votes Count? 22–23 (1987).
64. 393 U.S. at 565.
65. 393 U.S. at 586 (Harlan, J., dissenting) (emphasis added).
66. See, for example, the early Burger Court ruling in Perkins v. Matthews, 400 U.S. 379 (1971) (dilutionary impact of municipal annexations combined with instigation of at-large elections covered by section 5).

which sorts of electoral changes were suspect under the act. Nevertheless, the difficult issues of section 5—those inherited by the Warren Court's successor—frequently turned on circumstantial evidence that a suspect practice was intentionally discriminatory. Adverse effects on potential minority voting strength were often considered a strong indicator of a practice's probable discriminatory origins. Discriminatory intent was also inferred from adverse effects that were linked to the decision to construct multimember districts rather than single-member districts. A clear division developed among the Burger Court justices over the necessity of racially demographic districting to provide fair electoral competition for minority groups. Those justices who favored such districting as a remedy for decades of disenfranchisement were prepared to see its absence as evidence of impermissible racial vote dilution.

One of the last cases to test the actual scope of section 5 preclearance was also the first Burger Court case to explore the discriminatory intent necessary to invalidate an at-large electoral change. *Georgia v. United States,* in 1973, concerned the preclearance of the state house reapportionment plan and the implications of its consolidation of single-member districts into several multimember districts. Georgia's initial argument—that section 5 was inapplicable because it did not reach the issue of reapportionment—was quickly dismissed by the Stewart majority in light of the *Allen* ruling.[67] As to the dilutionary impact of the plan on minority voting power, Stewart held that section 5 shifted the burden of proof to the state making electoral changes, so that the state would have to demonstrate the absence of intentional discrimination.[68] Because section 5 cases involved conscious changes in electoral practices, any resulting minority vote dilution could be presumed intentionally discriminatory. Although *Georgia* did not suggest that dilutionary results alone constituted a general violation of the act, the decision's attention to the racial demographics of at-large districting is consistent with the conceptual type of demographic representation.

Georgia indicated, at minimum, that the Burger Court would not immediately retreat from its predecessor's concern for minority political access. Another electoral change covered by section 5, and rele-

---

67. 411 U.S. 526, 532 (1973).
68. 411 U.S. at 538.

vant in terms of political access and the intent requirement, was municipal annexation. Annexation of white residential areas—absent any corollary change in electoral practices—could profoundly dilute minority voting strength. Nevertheless, because annexation could be legitimately defended as a measure to expand a growing city's tax base and jurisdictional reach, a dilutionary annexation might survive section 5 preclearance. To address this problem of "peripheral" discriminatory effect, the Burger Court endorsed what came to be known as the "nonretrogression" standard.

The first example of this approach occurred in *City of Richmond v. United States,* in 1975. The majority, led by Justice White, precleared the city's annexations, which reduced the proportion of blacks from 52 percent to 42 percent of the population. However, the Court mandated the institution of wards in city council elections in order to "afford blacks representation reasonably equivalent to their political strength in the enlarged political community."[69] The *Richmond* opinion constituted the first expression of a nonretrogression standard for municipal annexations: boundary changes were permissible as long as the reduced minority component of a city's population was able to maximize its revised political strength.

Beginning with *Richmond,* the Court avoided complete condemnation of annexations that diluted a minority group's total voting strength. This approach, White observed, also avoided the Hobson's choice of forbidding annexations entirely versus permitting them at the price of permanently overrepresenting the minority community.[70] The *Richmond* majority seemed aware that its nonretrogression standard implied a compensatory obligation on the part of the annexing municipality; the nonretrogression directive itself necessitated wards demographically drawn to aid minority voting potential. The breadth of the *Richmond* ruling is evidence of its confirmation of the conceptual type of demographic representation.

But the nonretrogression standard could also impede the goal of compensatory majoritarianism. As long as local electoral changes did not reduce a minority's current political strength, there was no proof of impermissible racial dilution. Such was the Court's finding in *Beer v. United States,* in 1976. *Beer* concerned a redistricting plan for the New Orleans city council, which retained two at-large seats and white

---
69. 422 U.S. 358, 370 (1975).
70. 422 U.S. at 371.

majorities in four of the five wards. While the plan failed to reflect numerical black voting potential, it maintained the previous black control of one ward. The Stewart majority held that in the absence of evidence of discriminatory purpose, an electoral change that did not further reduce minority voting power was permissible under the Voting Rights Act.[71]

Some commentators have argued that the basis of *Beer*'s nonretrogression formula was judicial fear that section 5 might be interpreted to require racial quotas in electoral districting.[72] Indeed, two of the *Beer* dissenters found racial quotas permissible under section 5: Marshall and Brennan specifically argued that dilution of voting power referred to any resultant voting strength that was less than a group's *potential* power.[73] Under this view, remedying noncompetitive electoral structures would not be limited to invalidating only systems reducing existing—and possibly already inequitable—minority voting power.[74] The *Beer* dissent made clear that the decision retreated somewhat from the concept of compensatory majoritarianism. We must, therefore, view the *Beer* decision—though not the nonretrogression test itself—as contradictory of the conceptualization of demographic representation.

The nonretrogression standard presumed that no clear intent to discriminate was involved. Despite its conservative interpretation by the Court in *Beer*, nonretrogression could be a progressive standard as it accepted dilutionary results as evidence of a voting rights violation. Indeed, in 1980, in *City of Rome v. United States,* the Court denied preclearance to the city's annexations and districting changes because of their retrogressive effect.[75] Marshall's opinion for the Court had

---

71. 425 U.S. 130, 141 (1976).
72. Parker, Gerrymandering and Reapportionment, in Minority Vote Dilution 105 (C. Davidson ed. 1984).
73. 425 U.S. at 156 (Marshall, J., dissenting).
74. White made the same point in his separate dissent in *Beer,* 425 U.S. at 130.
75. 446 U.S. 156, 172, 184 (1980). In addition to the annexation of white suburbs, the city's plan included provisions for a majority rather than plurality vote in the selection of city commissioners, as well as reduction of the number of wards and their replacement with multimember districts with numbered posts and staggered terms of office for commission members.

Both the old and the new election system called for at-large elections, which, as a practical matter, meant that the city's black minority could not elect a black candidate under either system without substantial white support. Nevertheless, the black vote constituted an important swing vote and provided the margin of victory for winning

broad implications; in essence, *Rome* barred a city from adopting a majoritarian election procedure—the at-large district plus majority-winner requirements—under which black voters as a group would lose. Powell's dissent, objecting to the Court's attempt to define the political rights of groups in representative government,[76] highlights the degree to which the decision confirms the conceptual type of demographic representation.

At the same time that the Burger Court broadened the reach of section 5, it also sharpened the intent requirement of section 2 of the Voting Rights Act. *Mobile v. Bolden,* a section 2 case decided in the same term as *Rome,* concerned a charge against the city's existing at-large city council elections and their alleged dilutionary effect on the minority vote. In an abrupt turnaround from Marshall's reading of the Fifteenth Amendment in *Rome,* Stewart's plurality opinion held that only actions motivated by discriminatory intent violated the amendment, and thus the act.[77] The at-large system had been adopted by the city in 1911 pursuant to an Alabama statute; Mobile's at-large electoral system thus was not, Stewart reasoned, the result of a *current* intent to dilute black votes.[78] Nevertheless, the retention of the at-large system could have been construed as an affirmative decision to allow the same citywide (white) majority to control all of the council seats.[79]

The Stewart plurality also dismissed a Fourteenth Amendment challenge to the electoral system by unequivocally rejecting the notion that every political group has the right to elect candidates in propor-

---

candidates; black voters were arguably participating effectively. According to this interpretation of the facts of *Rome,* the decision meant that even a theoretical decrease in the minority group's ability to elect a candidate of its choice would be "retrogression." See Butler, Denial or Abridgement of the Right to Vote: What Does It Mean? in The Voting Rights Act 44, 50 (L. Foster ed. 1985).

76. See 446 U.S. at 195ff. The dissent was also bothered by the Court's encroachment on "local control of the means of self-government, one of the central values of our policy." See 446 U.S. at 201 (Powell, J., dissenting).

77. 446 U.S. 1, 62 (1980). Cf. Marshall's argument in *Rome* that the Fifteenth Amendment outlawed action with a discriminatory effect as well. 446 U.S. at 173.

78. 446 U.S. at 59–60.

79. See Blacksher and Menefee, At-Large Elections and One Person, One Vote, in Minority Vote Dilution 203, 230 (C. Davidson ed. 1984).

Following this line of argument, Brennan, White, and Marshall argued that intent should be inferred from impact, or from the "totality of circumstances." See 446 U.S. at 94 (White, J., dissenting); 446 U.S. at 103 (Marshall, J., dissenting); 446 U.S. at 94 (Brennan, J., dissenting).

tion to its members. "Whatever appeal this claim has as political theory," Stewart concluded in a stinging rebuke, "it is not the law."[80] Stevens, one of the two justices who concurred in the result, seemed uncomfortable with the plurality's stringent intent requirement. Stevens's fence-straddling position distinguished between state action that inhibited an individual's right to vote and state action that affected the political strength of various groups.[81] *Mobile* fell into the latter category and, thus, was permissible under current law. Although it carefully skirted the issue, the Court indirectly recognized the possibility of group-based electoral districting in *Mobile*. But because of what transpired in Congress immediately after the ruling, our final assessment of the decision must be that it was legally irrelevant to the conceptualization of demographic representation.

Mobile disturbed civil rights advocates because it seemed to require historical documentation of discriminatory intent to challenge electoral systems with long-standing dilutionary effect; as one commentator trenchantly observed, "smoking guns" are rare in the districting process.[82] In response, in 1981 Congress began formulating amendments to the Voting Rights Act that would avert the potential adverse impact of *Mobile*. The 1982 amendments to section 2 specifically eliminated the intent requirement for proving racial vote dilution,[83] thereby overruling *Mobile*'s statutory construction.

Passage of the 1982 amendments to the act, including the language of the "results test" in section 2, has been documented extensively elsewhere.[84] In essence, the new language specified that a state could

---

80. 446 U.S. at 75.

81. 446 U.S. at 83. But cf. Stevens's dissenting opinion in Cousins v. City of Chicago, 466 F.2d 830 (7th Cir. 1972), in which he read the Fourteenth Amendment as protecting all politically cohesive groups from electoral practices that diminished some voters' influence. 466 F.2d at 848–49.

82. Blacksher, Drawing Singlemember Districts, 17 Urb. Law. 347, 350 (1985).

83. The Act had been renewed in 1970 and extended in 1975 to cover, among other things, discrimination against language-minority voters. The Voting Rights Act became a powerful political symbol, for, as one commentator observed, "the issue of section 2 and the 'intent' test as opposed to an 'effects' test were central to the larger debate that occurred regarding the individual or the group as the atom of political existence." See Foster, Political Symbols and the Enactment of the 1982 Voting Rights Act, in The Voting Rights Act 85, 87–88 (L. Foster ed. 1985).

84. See Derfner, Voting Rights Act Amendments of 1982, in Minority Vote Dilution 145 (C. Davidson ed. 1984); Foster, Political Symbols and the Enactment of the 1982 Voting Rights Act, in the Voting Rights Act 85 (L. Foster ed. 1985); McDonald, The Quiet Revolution in Minority Voting Rights, 42 Vand. L. Rev. 1249 (1989).

not impose a qualification on voting "in a manner which results in a denial or abridgment" of the right to vote on the basis of race.[85] For our purposes, one aspect of passage in the House and Senate should be noted: the concern in some quarters that section 2 was too open-ended and might allow courts to find that a lack of proportional representation established a violation of the act. To avert this, the following disclaimer was added to the results test of section 2:

> The fact that members of a minority group have not been elected in numbers equal to the group's proportion of the total population shall not, in and of itself, constitute a violation of this section.[86]

The enactment of the results test coincided with the Burger Court's acceptance of a revised evidentiary standard for proving vote dilution. This approach, known as the "totality of circumstances" test, was a method of inferring intentional discrimination from circumstantial evidence[87] The Court's first post-*Mobile* ruling, *Rogers v. Lodge,* invalidated an at-large system based on evidence that would not have been dispositive in 1980.[88] Though the White majority reaffirmed the constitutionality of at-large systems, it was willing to infer discriminatory intent from the totality of facts.[89] On such findings, the Burger Court deferred to the district court, affirming the lower court's ordering of single-member districts. The "totality of circumstances" test thus affected the interpretation of unconstitutional vote dilution, as well as the construction of the amended section 2.

The "totality of circumstances" approach still lacked precise evaluative standards for vote dilution and necessitated rather fulsome gathering of data regarding minorities' diminished voting power. It also allowed critics of the results test to continue their denunciation of "proportional representation." Dissenters on the Court argued

---

85. 42 USC § 1973, section 2 (a).

86. Derfner, Voting Rights Act Amendments of 1982, in Minority Vote Dilution 153–55 (C. Davidson ed. 1984).

87. The "totality of circumstances" or "aggregate of factors" test for dilution came from the appellate decision of Zimmer v. McKeethen, 485 F.2d 1297 (5th Cir. 1973). See Butler, Denial or Abridgement of the Vote: What Does It Mean? in The Voting Rights Act 54 (L. Foster ed. 1985).

88. 102 S. Ct. 3272 (1982). See Davidson, Minority Vote Dilution, in Minority Vote Dilution 18–19 (C. Davidson ed. 1984).

89. 102 S. Ct. at 3276.

that scrutiny of an electoral system's *effects* on the political strength of various groups failed to suggest any enforceable judicial remedies—"or at least none short of a system of quotas or group representation."[90] The problem of standardless equitable discretion also dogged later section 5 rulings, as the 1983 case of *City of Port Arthur v. United States*[91] illustrates.

Port Arthur concerned the Texas city's proposed annexation and districting changes, which reduced the black population from 45 percent to about 41 percent but modified city council elections so as to virtually ensure black control of one-third of the council seats. Though the black proportion of the city's voting population was reduced, the changes themselves were seemingly progressive, as the pre-annexation council elections had been conducted at large, with ward residence and majority-winner requirements. Preclearance of the new electoral system was nonetheless denied, because the changes "insufficiently neutralized any adverse effect on black voter participation."[92] Arguably, this meant that the plan did not fully compensate blacks for decreased influence, even "by adjustments in the electoral system that virtually guarantee[d] ... greater representational opportunities for blacks."[93]

Port Arthur confirmed the conceptual type of demographic representation because of its apparent concern for a system of political competition most favorable to minority electoral success. The decision also intimated that the gap between remedies required by section 2 and section 5 was narrowing in favor of the general objective of single-member districts attentive to racial demography.[94] Neverthe-

---

90. Rogers v. Lodge, 102 S. Ct. at 3282 (Powell, J., dissenting).

91. 103 S. Ct. 530 (1983). The quoted phrase comes from the dissenting opinion of Justice Powell in Port Arthur 103 S. Ct. at 536.

92. 103 S. Ct. at 534.

93. Butler, Denial or Abridgement of the Right to Vote: What Does It Mean? in The Voting Rights Act 53 (L. Foster ed. 1985).

94. See Note, Getting Results under Section 5 of the Voting Rights Act, 94 Yale L.J. 139 (1984).

Another example of this was the so-called 65 percent rule in remedial districting plans. This guideline was used by reviewing courts to prevent legislators from diluting minority votes by creating "disguised majority-white districts." The 65 percent minority population was necessary to afford minority voters a reasonable opportunity to control electoral outcome, given lower minority voter registration rates, lower minority voter turnout, and a smaller proportion of voting-age persons in minority populations. The 65 percent rule has operated as a rule of thumb for both lower federal courts and the

less, the imprecision of vote dilution standards allowed the Burger Court a certain amount of wavering on the stringency of nonretrogression. In a case decided the same term as *Port Arthur,* the Powell majority precleared another Texas city's alterations to its at-large electoral system.[95] The sole objection in *City of Lockhart v. United States* came from Marshall, who continued to resist reducing section 5 to a mere perpetuation of the political status quo.[96] *Lockhart* seemed to preserve a difference between dilutionary results as a violation of section 2, and retrogressive results under section 5. Evidence of intentional discrimination was not required for either type of violation, yet different standards for dilution continued to apply under the Voting Rights Act.

The definitive test of the amended section 2 and, potentially, of the compatibility of the results test and nonretrogression requirement, came in the Burger Court's last term. *Thornburg v. Gingles,* in 1986, prompted a unanimous ruling invalidating a North Carolina districting plan that diluted black voting strength, although the justices split over the standards for determining racial vote dilution. Brennan's majority opinion offered a variation on the totality of circumstances analysis: in light of past racial discrimination and polarized voting, the plan impaired black voters' ability to elect their preferred candidate.[97] The *Thornburg* majority's test for vote dilution was the *systematic frustration* or *exclusion* of minority groups from electoral competition. A finding of such denial of competitive access would legitimate the remedy of compensatory majoritarianism through districting changes.

Brennan's opinion also addressed another issue of demographic districting—which sorts of groups could challenge dilutionary electoral conditions. For the *Thornburg* majority, districtable—and therefore dilutable—groups had to be of a requisite size and geographic compactness and had to exhibit political cohesiveness and distinctive

---

Department of Justice. See Parker, Gerrymandering and Reapportionment, in Minority Vote Dilution 108–11 (C. Davidson ed. 1984); Blacksher, Drawing Singlemember Districts, 17 Urb. Law. 357–58 (1985).

95. City of Lockhart v. U.S., 103 S. Ct. 998, 1004 (1983). The Court found "no retrogression in fact" as a result of the city's increase in the size of the council, introduction of staggered terms for councilmen, and use of a numbered post system for election of council members.

96. 103 S. Ct. at 1005, 1010.

97. 106 S. Ct. 2752, 2772–74 (1986).

minority interests.[98] Though Brennan stopped short of granting such plural groups a right to collective representation, such groups could not be deprived of equal access to the electoral process. Indeed, Brennan's discussion of the rights of "politically cohesive groups" transcended the category of racial minority rights.[99] As much of the language of Brennan's opinion suggested the notion of aggregate voting rights, the decision was seemingly consistent with, if not confirmatory of, the demographic conceptualization of representation.

The question still raised about *Thornburg* is whether the ruling effectively condoned proportional representation by guaranteeing safe seats for minorities as the remedy for vote dilution. Most commentators do not see proportional representation as the proper standard against which dilution should be measured.[100] Proportional representation has been part of the rhetoric of remedial districting because it was an easily grasped, if not consistently appealing, concept of fairness. But the Burger Court's treatment of racial vote dilution claims under the Voting Rights Act can be more accurately described as compensatory majoritarianism. Clearly, the nonretrogression standard did not attempt to displace majoritarian elections or mandate anything close to racial proportional representation through districting—assuming such an objective were feasible. Similarly, the Court's "totality of circumstances"/results test mandates group political access, not group proportional representation.

Generally, the Burger Court's Voting Rights Act decisions were consistent with the conceptual type of demographic representation. With the exception of major rulings such as *Beer* and *Mobile,* the decisions accepted the legitimacy of compensatory alterations of majoritarian electoral processes. The decisions involved statutory questions and predominantly concerned the at-large electoral system; except for the *Thornburg* opinion, there was little discussion of the theoretical relationship between demographic districting and political competition. Indeed, the decisions may not conform to a theoretical

---

98. 106 S. Ct. at 2767.
99. O'Connor's concurrence—joined by Burger, Rehnquist, and Powell—parted company with the ruling on this issue of remedial districting. She argued that the "ruling result[ed] in the creation of a right to a form of proportional representation in favor of all geographically and political cohesive minority groups." 106 S. Ct. at 2785.
100. See, e.g., Engstrom, Racial Vote Dilution, in The Voting Rights Act 36–37 (L. Foster ed. 1985).

concept of group representation at all, whether of proportionality or compensatory majoritarianism. Rather, one could interpret the rulings as merely a practical response to the need for specifically race-based remedies.[101]

We shall test this assertion using the cases in the next section, which appear to reveal more about a general group theory of representation because they are not confined to statutory directives on racial political equality. These cases address the familiar problem of vote dilution and again raise the problem of majoritarian-biased competition in the at-large electoral system. But they focus specifically on "aggregate-level" gerrymandering—the drawing of district lines to affect the political strength of an identifiable group. The possibility of gerrymandering in our electoral system complicates efforts to talk about political competition in simple terms; the next section examines whether the Burger Court evaded the difficult task of defining a "competitive" electoral structure, or offered guidelines corresponding to a demographic conceptualization of representation.

Groups and Gerrymandering: The Jurisprudential Journey of Justice White

The Burger Court's Voting Rights Act opinions indicate that some of the justices viewed at-large elections as inherently discriminatory to minority groups because the at-large system is insensitive to the demographics of electoral coalitions and constituencies. The unanswered question looming behind the vote dilution issues was whether it was the at-large system of electoral competition *per se* that violated the equal protection clause of the constitution. If the at-large system was unconstitutional only when used to dilute a minority's political influence, such a conclusion strongly implied that other techniques for dilution of any group's electoral strength were also unconstitutional. Such "other techniques," of course, included gerrymanders.

The familiar difficulty with constitutional challenges to dilutionary gerrymandering was marshaling the evidence necessary to prove intentional discrimination. Some of the earliest allegations of unconstitutional racial vote dilution relied on cases such as *Reynolds* for their rationale; in cases involving numerical malapportionment, intent did

---

101. A. Thernstrom, Whose Votes Count? *passim* (1987).

not have to be proved.[102] Of course, multimember districts were frequently components of efforts to gerrymander political competition that nevertheless preserved a certain populational equity among electoral districts. Nevertheless, discriminatory intent could often be presumed from the maintenance of a districting system with foreseeable dilutionary effects. In response to this situation, the Burger Court began to evaluate an individual's political rights by reference to the voting strength of the group in which the individual was placed within the electoral structure.[103]

This means of analyzing voting strength implied that group-oriented demographic districting could be used to balance political competition. Thus, our conceptualization of demographic representation preserves a distinction between Voting Rights Act and gerrymandering cases. Each emphasized a different part of the conceptual type: the statutory cases focused on the remedy of compensatory majoritarian competition, while the gerrymandering cases explored the interrelationship between political competition and the demographics of districting.

The constitutional question regarding gerrymanders was twofold: in the districting plan under consideration, was a numerically equal vote equally effective, and, if not, was that discrepancy intentional? The evaluation of a vote's effectiveness depended on many demographic variables; one of the first variables the Court considered was race. However, racial political identity, racial composition of districts, and racial bloc voting were not the only group factors that affected a vote's meaningfulness and, thus, the demographics of districting. Factors associated with partisan electoral competition were also critical to the fairness of a districting system.

One of the Burger Court's most significant contributions to representation law was its recognition of the justiciability of these factors in gerrymandering allegations. We will look first at the relationship between gerrymandering and racial demographic factors, and then address the emerging importance of partisan demographics in reapportionment litigation, considering whether the Court has made any

---

102. Some of the earliest of these were Fortsen v. Dorsey, 379 U.S. 433 (1965), and Burns v. Richardson, 384 U.S. 73 (1966). See Butler, Constitutional and Statutory Challenges to Electoral Structures, 42 La. L. Rev. 875, 876 (1982).

103. Blacksher and Menefee, At-Large Elections and One Person, One Vote, in Minority Vote Dilution 229 (C. Davidson ed. 1984).

effort to develop compatible standards for racial and partisan vote dilution—or whether such standards are even possible within our model of demographic representation.

First, let us look at the constitutional challenges to racial gerrymandering. A review of the three leading racial cases reveals two important points. First, the "totality of circumstances" method of inferring intentional vote dilution had been part of the Burger Court's doctrinal repertoire since 1973. This tends to diminish the "revolutionary" nature of statutory developments such as the results test, which, arguably, only returned the law to status quo prior to *Mobile.* Second, these gerrymandering decisions reveal that compensatory districting is confined to particular racial minorities. Thus, as implemented by the Burger Court, racially demographic districting should not be interpreted as a new construction of representational "fairness" for all ethnic groups.

To explore the development of the "totality of circumstances" test, two decisions are instructive. The first, *Whitcomb v. Chavis,* in 1971, is widely interpreted as either Burger Court backsliding from Warren Court progressiveness or, perhaps simultaneously, frightened judicial retreat to the "safety" of one person, one vote in the face of racially based gerrymandering.[104] The lower court in *Whitcomb,* relying on the equal protection clause, invalidated an Indiana districting plan because of the racially dilutionary impact of a multimember district for the city of Indianapolis. The White plurality overruled the lower court's per se invalidation of the multimember district, but rejected the specific plan's population variance as too large.[105]

White recognized that at-large elections tend to submerge racial minorities and overrepresent the winning party, and, further, that unconstitutional vote dilution might result even if no intentional discriminatory gerrymandering had occurred.[106] But White could not

---

104. Engstrom, Racial Vote Dilution: The Concept and the Court, in The Voting Rights Act 22–23 (L. Foster ed. 1985); Alfange, Gerrymandering and the Constitution, 1986 Sup. Ct. Rev. 175, 201.

105. Recall that White was the first justice to split off from the Warren majority that had endorsed one person, one vote. After his 1969 dissent in *Wells v. Rockefeller,* he continued to resist rigid population equality for electoral districts. His subsequent tolerance of group-based justifications for population variance seemed to be an outgrowth of this attitude. See, for example, his opinion for the Court in *Gaffney v. Cummings,* discussed *infra* at 412 U.S. 735 (1972).

106. 403 U.S. 124, 144, 149–55 (1971).

agree that the facts in *Whitcomb* pointed to actual dilution or undervaluing of the black vote.[107] As one commentator summarized the decision, "To be freed from an electoral arrangement that minimized the impact of their vote, [plaintiffs] would have to prove discrimination at other points within the electoral process."[108] The *Whitcomb* Court concluded that unless plaintiffs were required to prove an aggregate denial of access to the political system, the district court finding in the case would require legislative representation for any group with distinctive interests.[109] The *Whitcomb* opinion was so confusing that it is difficult to distill any inherent theoretical implications. But, when coupled with the constitutional dilution case that followed, *Whitcomb* and its "denial of access" test are consistent with the conceptual type of demographic representation.

Its consistency with the demographic conceptualization is more apparent when one notes that the *Whitcomb* evidentiary standard for unconstitutional vote dilution—identified by a different name—was easily satisfied in the 1973 case of *White v. Regester*. *White* was one of three districting cases, decided concurrently that term, that forced the Court to consider the relationship of both population and demographic factors to the equality of voting power.[110] The demographic factors in these 1973 cases were not limited to race, although racial vote dilution was the crux of *White*. On the basis of "invidious exclusion of racial group[s]," *White*'s majority opinion invalidated a Texas legislative apportionment plan that included the use of multimember districts in areas with large concentrations of blacks and Hispanics.[111]

In finding evidence of "denial of access," the Court sought to distinguish the *White* situation from the multimember district upheld in *Whitcomb*. The majority maintained that outlawing invidious vote dilution was "not the same as declaring that every racial or political

---

107. The record showed that blacks were regularly slated as candidates by the Democrats, and when the Democrats won the black candidates won. The election returns tended to exhibit bloc voting along party lines to a greater degree than racial lines. The district court focused on the fact that ghetto blacks did not have legislative seats in proportion to their population. 403 U.S. at 150–53.

108. Engstrom, Racial Vote Dilution, in The Voting Rights Act 23 (L. Foster ed. 1985).

109. 403 U.S. at 155–56.

110. The other two cases, *Gaffney v. Cummings* and *White v. Weiser*, will be discussed in conjunction with the decisions on partisan-based districting, *infra* at U.S. 127–134 and accompanying text.

111. 412 U.S. 760, 765–68 (1973).

group has a constitutional right to be represented in the legislature."[112] Both decisions scrupulously avoided any implication of proportionality by focusing on minority groups' political access—the extent to which groups were capable of competitive political action in the political process as a whole.[113] Both the result of *White* and its establishment of a "totality of circumstances" test[114] for minority vote dilution were consistent with the conceptual type of demographic representation.

Arguably, the *White* decision could be seen as confirming the demographic conceptualization. After all, the ruling did not focus on discriminatory motives, but rather on participational barriers and the representational results for minority groups. But despite its concern with minority competitive access, the decision failed to define the connection between demographic criteria of districting and competitive elections. Thus, the *Whitcomb-White* "denial of access" analysis was insufficient to confirm the presence of demographic representation. However, White's approach to inferring intentional vote dilution remains an early form of an electoral "results test."

The third racial gerrymandering decision was not concerned with the totality of circumstances evidential standard. *United Jewish Organization v. Carey,* in 1977,[115] addressed the complex relationship between remedial action under the Voting Rights Act and nondilution requirements under the Constitution, stating quite explicitly that demographic districting had a restricted application as a competitive remedy. *UJO* showed that compensatory districting practices did not extend to voter groups who were already presumed to be represented in the majority—even if those voters were effectively denied influence in elections within their district.

UJO was an unusual case in that it involved a dilution allegation from a safe-district white minority. Members of the Hasidic Jewish community of Brooklyn challenged a state redistricting plan that increased the percentage of nonwhite voters to 65 percent in various borough districts. The race-based districting was done in compliance

---

112. 412 U.S. at 769.
113. One commentator asserts that *Whitcomb-White* established a "participation test" for racial vote dilution. Engstrom, Racial Vote Dilution, in The Voting Rights Act 34 (L. Foster ed. 1985).
114. 412 U.S. at 769.
115. 430 U.S. 144 (1977).

with section 5 of the Voting Rights Act, ensuring that nonwhite voters would no longer be denied the opportunity to elect candidates of their choice. But the cost of this compliance was borne by the Hasidim: their community was fractured among several redrawn assembly and senate districts. They argued that the plan constituted "reverse gerrymandering": as there was no reason other than race for dividing their community, their votes had been diluted in violation of the Fourteenth and Fifteenth Amendments.

In a judgment notable for its divisiveness,[116] the White plurality rejected the Hasidim's claim. White first acknowledged that, while the presumption in race-conscious districting was prior discrimination, "the permissible use of racial criteria was not confined to eliminating the effects of past discriminatory districting."[117] White, although somewhat ambiguous on this point, seemed to suggest that racial demographic districting was not limited to situations correcting historical discrimination. What was unambiguous was his conclusion that the Hasidim had failed to demonstrate dilution of their voting strength. The telling point for White was that "*whites as a group* were provided with fair representation" under the plan.[118] However legitimate the political classification, in reasoning that white voters as a whole controlled more than their fair share of seats and so had no cause of action,[119] the *UJO* plurality seemed to suggest that electoral outcomes were the test of competitive fairness in a districting system.

UJO has been viewed as the beginning of group voting rights in representation law, because the majority opinion was less concerned with the viability of the Hasidim's participation than with the relative representation of white and black voters generally.[120] *UJO* permitted districting that capitalized on geographically contiguous minority populations to achieve proportional minority influence. Indeed, both

---

116. White's plurality opinion was joined in full only by Stevens. Brennan, Blackmun, and Rehnquist in part; Stewart and Powell concurred in the result only. Burger was the sole dissenter who would have vindicated the Hasidim's reverse discrimination claim. Marshall took no part in the case.

117. In other words, neither the Fourteenth nor the Fifteenth Amendment mandated a per se rule against using racial factors in districting. 430 U.S. 144, 161 (1977). White noted that the plan did no more than what was required by the nonretrogression principle. 430 U.S. at 161–62.

118. 430 U.S. at 163.

119. 430 U.S. at 165–66.

120. A. Thernstrom, Whose Votes Count? 185–86 (1987); Note, *UJO v. Carey* and the Need to Recognize Aggregate Voting Rights, 87 Yale L.J. 571, 584–85 (1978).

the concurring and dissenting opinions were critical of the plurality's misguided approval of "racial gerrymandering."[121] Brennan, in his concurrence, expressed concern that a goal of "proportional distribution of voting power" for racial minorities could be used as a "contrivance to segregate the group, thereby frustrating its potentially successful efforts at coalition-building across racial lines."[122]

Brennan's comments raised the issue of what sort of political competition racially demographic districting was intended to accomplish. The question remains whether safe-districting practices facilitate minority groups' political competitiveness in the long run. Some have argued that race-based districts actually perpetuate the geographic and social segregation of minorities because any dispersion on their part cuts into their group electoral power.[123] Others argue that "ghettoization" itself created the particularized racial group interests that merit competitive parity through the districting process.[124] According to this line of argument, when the segregative forces in society disappear, so will the need for the political compensation of race-based districting.[125] This assertion about the goal of racially demographic districting, explainable under our conceptual notion of compensatory majoritarianism, has some plausibility.

The plurality never articulated what the relationship between dis-

---

121. The quoted phrase comes from Burger's dissenting opinion. 430 U.S. at 186. He labeled the 65 percent rule an unconstitutional "strict quota approach" to political representation. 430 U.S. at 182.

122. 430 U.S. at 171–72 (Brennan, J., concurring).

123. Thernstrom, The Odd Evolution of the Voting Rights Act, 55 Pub. Interest 49, 65 (1979).

124. I owe the substance of this comment to correspondence with Chandler Davidson.

From this observation, one might expect that ghettoized subsets of a minority group conform to voting patterns different from integrated subsets. If so, an at-large electoral system that dilutes the vote of integrated blacks might be tolerable, because these individuals' interests are not particularized through ghettoization. However, one study found that within a relatively limited geographic area, "differences in electoral preferences between black voters in homogeneous black precincts and black voters in mixed precincts are, on average, likely to be minimal." See Grofman, Migalski, and Noviello, The Totality of Circumstances Test, 7 Law and Policy 199, 203 (1985).

One might conclude that the reality of ghettoization only adds to the significance of race as an interest-cleavage in American political society.

125. Some commentators express doctrinal unease about "a constitutional 'right' that disappears when people move from one neighborhood to another." See Note, Group Representation and Race-Conscious Apportionment, 91 Harv. L. Rev. 1847, 1857 n.52 (1978).

trict demographics and electoral competition was supposed to be. The result of the *UJO* decision was to consign the Hasidic voting component of Brooklyn's white population to a form of "virtual" representation. This was due in part to the Court's concurrence with the district court's finding that the Hasidim did not enjoy a constitutional right to "separate community recognition" in apportionment as Hasidic Jews.[126] Because the Hasidim were not viewed as a distinct, dilutable group, they were not entitled to compensated competition in a majoritarian electoral process. The *UJO* decision can be interpreted as consistent with the conceptualization of demographic representation, despite the Court's fairly unsophisticated view of which groups deserve separate community recognition. Later decisions—including statutory rulings such as *Thornburg*—would partially remedy this paucity of analysis on the group demographics of districting.

UJO used an interesting analogy to explain why the intradistrict, racial bloc voting that disadvantaged the Hasidim did not, in and of itself, violate constitutional rights. The position of safe-district minority candidates, White's opinion argued, resembled "that of the Democratic or Republican minority that is submerged year after year by the adherents to the majority party, who tend to vote a straight party line."[127] White, of course, meant that neither situation involved a justiciable rights violation, but merely the hard luck of losing elections. Ironically, the partisan nature of a districting plan was eventually recognized as constitutionally significant.

Although the Burger Court ultimately did no better than its commentators in defining partisan fairness, its decisions were receptive to the use of partisan demographic districting to structure a competitive electoral system. However, most of its partisan districting decisions involved rather limited rulings. Even its coup de grace in 1986 held only that partisan vote dilution claims were justiciable. The real significance of these districting decisions is their receptivity to extending compensatory majoritarianism to partisan electoral competition. Indeed, the treatment of Democratic or Republican voters as an "aggrieved class" for the purposes of voting rights/equal protection

---

126. See White's plurality opinion, 430 U.S. at 153.
127. 430 U.S. at 167.

claims may prove extremely important for the future of American politics.[128]

The two crucial preliminary decisions on partisan districting occurred in 1973. These decisions considered whether population variance in legislative districting plans could be justified by partisan demographic factors. In the first case, *Gaffney v. Cummings*, a population variance of 7.83 percent among Connecticut legislative districts resulted from an alleged bipartisan sweetheart deal to achieve "political fairness" between the two major political parties.[129] Acknowledging that the districting plan aimed at "rough proportional representation of the statewide strength of the two parties," White's majority opinion found the partisan composition of the districts legitimate under the Fourteenth Amendment.[130] However, the *Gaffney* majority was more concerned with curtailing the unbridled excesses of equipopulous districting than with demographic districting per se.[131] Broadly construed, the decision is consistent with the conceptualization of demographic representation because it permitted partisan demographic districting that structured party competition.

The second 1973 case, *White v. Weiser*, concerned a congressional reapportionment plan for the state of Texas. This case also focused on population variance among districts, but the variance was the result of the promotion of "constituency-representative relations." The plan protected the constituencies of incumbent Texas congressmen so as to preserve the seniority of members of the state's delegation in the House of Representatives.[132] Arguably, the power and seniority of a state's congressional delegation is not negligible in assessing the quality of state citizens' national representation.[133] In his opinion for the Court, White admitted that incumbency preservation could be a districting factor considered among others. But incumbency preser-

---

128. This development came in the case of *Davis v. Bandemer*, in 1986, discussed *infra* at 134ff. See Grofman, Toward a Coherent Theory of Gerrymandering, in Toward Fair and Effective Representation: Political Gerrymandering and the Courts (B. Grofman ed. 1990).

129. 412 U.S. 735, 736 (1973).

130. 412 U.S. at 738, 752.

131. Foe example, White's majority opinion rejected "rigid and unyielding adherence to a strict population equality standard." 412 U.S. at 751.

132. 412 U.S. 783, 791 (1973).

133. Neither is the preservation of the continuity of districts unimportant to the quality of representation at the state level. See B. Cain, The Reapportionment Puzzle 184–85 (1984).

vation alone, he concluded, did not justify higher population variance between congressional districts.[134]

As the *Weiser* plan was less concerned with balancing partisan demographics than with avoiding races between incumbent legislators, the decision itself could be viewed as essentially irrelevant to the issue of demographic districting in the electoral process. Yet the White majority reversed the district court's adoption of an alternate plan, with population variance improved at the cost of reduced conformity with the old district lines; the reversal was based on insufficient attention to the state's goals in the districting process.[135] If White was tolerant, at least in principle, of Texas's goal of specially districted electoral competition, the *Weiser* opinion was purposefully inconclusive on the legitimacy of incumbency-protection districting. Such districting has not been considered by the Supreme Court since *Weiser*, but will likely be taken up in the near future given that partisan fairness in the districting process is now justiciable. Because incumbency preservation, as well as differential treatment of parties' incumbents, are intimately related to political gerrymandering,[136] I hesitate to say that *Weiser* is irrelevant to either partisan demographic districting or a policy of compensatory majoritarianism in the electoral process. Because of *Weiser*'s yet undeveloped principle, a new category of evaluation is needed: the decision was *not* inconsistent with the conceptual type of demographic representation.

The *Gaffney* and *Weiser* decisions intimated that group-based districting was not limited to race but could include various political factors. This was recognized in Justice Stevens's concurring opinion in the 1983 reapportionment case of *Karcher v. Daggett*,[137] where the equipopulous standard was applied with a vengeance to invalidate a New Jersey congressional districting plan. Stevens, casting the vital fifth vote, agreed that the plan was not a good-faith districting effort, but solely because of evidence of political gerrymandering. Though *Karcher* itself is irrelevant to our conceptual type, Stevens's concur-

---

134. White accepted the legitimacy of the maintenance of constituency-representative relations, but did not see it as proof of a "good faith effort" to reduce population discrepancies between congressional districts. 412 U.S. at 790–91.
135. 412 U.S. at 797.
136. Owen and Grofman, Optimal Partisan Gerrymandering, Pol. Geog. Q. 5 (1988).
137. 462 U.S. 725 (1983).

rence does suggest how the Court would approach future cases involving partisan fairness in districting. Following his own comments in earlier opinions,[138] Stevens was adamant that vote dilution claims were not confined to racial groups.

> The [equal protection] clause does not make some groups of citizens more equal than others.... As long as the clause proscribes gerrymandering against [racial] groups, its proscription must provide comparable protection for other cognizable groups of voters as well.[139]

For Stevens, "cognizable groups" were those whose "common interest was strong enough to be manifested in political action," those who constituted a "politically salient class."[140] As party voters were obviously such a class, Stevens proposed a test for justiciable claims of partisan vote dilution: a case could be made if the group's "*proportional* voting influence was adversely affected ... as a result of inattention or disregard for *group geographic distribution.*"[141] Stevens's concurrence described the conceptualization of demographic representation and its application to partisan electoral competition, but a concurrence is not a controlling precedent. The key question the Burger Court had left unaddressed was whether an otherwise permissible equipopulous plan would be invalid under the equal protection clause if it failed to approximate parties' statewide strength.

This question was finally considered in the Burger Court's last term, in the 1986 case of *Davis v. Bandemer.*[142] The case concerned an equal protection challenge by Democratic voters to an Indiana districting plan. The plan maximized the Republican party's electoral advantage, producing a discrepancy in the ratio between votes cast for the parties and their number of seats in the legislature. The political stakes were high in *Bandemer:* California Republicans were

---

138. See Stevens's concurrence in *Karcher,* 462 U.S. at 744 (referring to his opinions on the justiciability of partisan gerrymandering in Cousins v. City of Chicago, 466 F.2d 830, 848–50 (1972) (dissenting from denial of cert.); Mobile v. Bolden, 446 U.S. 55, at 86–89 (1980) (Stevens, J., concurring); and Rogers v. Lodge, 458 U.S. 613, at 652 (1982) (Stevens, J., dissenting).
139. 462 U.S. at 749.
140. 462 U.S. at 754 n.12.
141. 462 U.S. at 754–55.
142. 106 S.Ct. 2797 (1986).

waiting in the wings to challenge a similar partisan imbalance that favored Democrats in that state's legislative districting.[143] *Bandemer* has been analogized to the Court's 1962 decision in *Baker v. Carr* because it held only that partisan gerrymandering of electoral districts was a justiciable claim under the equal protection clause. Like *Baker*, *Bandemer* has also taken on a life of its own in the commentary of reapportionment scholars. Because many fine analyses of the case have already been written,[144] my summary of the various opinions in the case will be brief, and I will focus instead on the decision's implications for the demographic conceptualization of representation.

The first point to note about the case was the vote breakdown on the various issues considered by the Court. The ruling for justiciability in *Bandemer* was 6 to 3, with the majority opinion written by Justice White. But the justices were further divided about the threshold of discriminatory effects required to render a districting plan unconstitutional. Seven justices were against a finding that unconstitutional vote dilution was present in the Indiana plan, and only a plurality finally endorsed White's set of "manageable standards" for partisan vote dilution. Concurring Justices Powell and Stevens offered their own set of dilution guidelines, which they felt had been violated by the Indiana districting plan.

What was the definitive outcome of all this judicial disagreement? One substantive result of *Bandemer* was the White opinion's recognition that party adherents are a "politically salient/cohesive class" for the purpose of group voting rights.[145] In other words, *Bandemer* moved toward "symmetric treatment of group equal protection claims" by racial and partisan groups.[146] Less specific attention was

---

143. See Minisymposium on *Badham v. Eu, Political Science* 536ff. (Summer 1985).

144. See Alfange, Gerrymandering and the Constitution, 1986 Sup. Ct. Rev. 175; B. Grofman, ed., Toward Fair and Effective Representation: Political Gerrymandering and the Courts (1990); Backstrom, Robins, and Eller, Partisan Gerrymandering in a Post-*Bandemer* Era, 4 Const. Commentary 310 (1987). No doubt multitudinous others will exist by the time you read this.

145. Many commentators argue that anti-gerrymandering claims must rely on group rights; they cannot simply be regarded as an extension of *Reynolds*. See Engstrom, Post-Census Representational Districting, 7 S.U.L. Rev. 173, 205 (1981). Thus, once partisan gerrymandering is accepted as justiciable, it follows that a partisan group right has been recognized.

146. Cain, Perspectives on *Davis v. Bandemer,* in Toward Fair and Effective Representation: Political Gerrymandering and the Courts (B. Grofman ed. 1990).

given to the problem of identifying the members of the politically salient class. Several commentators have observed that "party identification is an evanescent concept," since party membership is not only fluid but also exists on many levels: voting behavior, registration, and political interests.[147] For purposes of justiciability of the claim of partisan vote dilution, White was not bothered that the characteristics of the partisan group were vague and mutable.[148] Instead, he pressed the simplistic analogy between racial and partisan vote dilution, emphasizing that politically significant group interests could be identified by one set of standards.

In theory, *Bandemer*'s treatment of parties as potentially districtable interests—that is, the justiciability ruling alone—is consistent with the possibility of demographic districting for balanced partisan competition. The problem, of course, is that the definition of "balanced partisan competition" remains unclear. This makes judicial recognition and remedying of partisan gerrymanders rather difficult. One commentator was fairly sanguine about the clarity of the *Bandemer* standard of unconstitutional political gerrymandering; such gerrymandering, he observed, must be intentional, severe, and "predictably nontransient in its effects."[149] White's opinion is fairly straightforward in certain respects: intent could be inferred from an aggregate of factors, and the severity of a gerrymander depended on "consistent" degradation of "a group of voters' influence on the political process" or "continued frustration" of voters' access.[150] But as to the threshold for discriminatory effects, White argued that a mere lack of proportional results or a discrepancy in the votes-seats ratio in one election did not prove unconstitutional vote dilution. He specifically

---

147. Lowenstein and Steinberg, Districting in the Public Interest, 33 U.C.L.A. L. Rev. 16, 27 (1985); Grofman, Toward a Coherent Theory of Gerrymandering, in Toward Fair and Effective Representation: Political Gerrymandering and the Courts (B. Grofman ed. 1990).

148. 106 S. Ct. at 2806. One commentator has argued that *Bandemer* was not a voting rights case at all, but a civil rights case that focused on the problem of suspect classifications under the equal protection clause. Only to the degree that party voters have been stigmatized like racial minorities do they have a case under the equal protection clause. Lowenstein, *Bandemer*'s Gap: Gerrymandering and the Equal Protection of the Law 40–41 (paper presented to the American Political Science Association, Chicago, Ill.) (Sept. 1987).

149. Grofman, Toward a Coherent Theory of Gerrymandering, in Toward Fair and Effective Representation: Political Gerrymandering and the Courts (B. Grofman ed. 1990).

150. 106 S. Ct. at 2810–11.

rejected *Gaffney*'s bipartisan maximization of safe seats as the requirement for competitive fairness in districting.[151] But his opinion does not settle questions about how much evidence is sufficient to demonstrate discriminatory districting.

As indicated earlier, reapportionment scholars have offered various formulas for determining whether a districting plan's electoral results are or will be politically biased. The common principle for determining bias is to examine the degree to which a plan maximizes the wasted votes of the opposition party while minimizing the wasted votes of one's own party. Wasted votes—those with redundant or diluted electoral impact—are an attribute of safe-district minorities and districts with supermajorities. Various formulas—the seats-votes ratio, the baseline race indicia, the asymmetrical majoritarian criterion, and the incumbent-displacement analysis—then attempt to measure the percentage of wasted votes. Nevertheless, as one commentator has observed, "no adequate formula has yet been established for distinguishing between a vote that is wasted due to natural causes and one that is wasted because of the discriminatory effect of a partisan gerrymander."[152]

Powell's approach to proof of political gerrymandering in his *Bandemer* concurrence illustrates the force of this observation. Powell supplied a laundry list of fairness criteria that the Indiana plan had violated, but no real guideline to distinguish political gerrymanders from legitimate plans that inevitably "give the majority party an advantage at the polls."[153] Without a reliable way to classify wasted votes, partisan electoral competition is susceptible to "I know it when I see it" jurisprudence.[154] It also elicits hyperbolic responses, such as the accusation in O'Connor's *Bandemer* dissent that the Court was moving toward "some rough form of proportional representation for all political groups."[155]

---

151. 106 S. Ct. at 2809.
152. Alfange, Gerrymandering and the Constitution, 1986 Sup. Ct. Rev. 175, 221. By "a vote wasted due to natural causes," the author means a vote that has no electoral impact due to unstrategic voting behavior or the overwhelming force of a countervailing majority coalition.
153. 106 S. Ct. at 2827–31. See also Alfange, Gerrymandering and the Constitution, 1986 Sup. Ct. Rev. 175, 252–53.
154. Shapiro, Gerrymandering, Unfairness and the Supreme Court, 33 U.C.L.A. L. Rev. 227, 252 (1985).
155. 106 S. Ct. at 2817. O'Connor's dissent was joined by the chief justice and by Justice Rehnquist.

If the *Bandemer* opinion moved in any direction, it was toward a policy of compensatory majoritarian competition through electoral districting. Thus, a conservative evaluation is that the decision was consistent with the conceptual type of demographic representation. What the *Bandemer* decision did was give constitutional imprimatur to judicial, legislative, and social science questioning of votes that were allegedly "wasted by 'natural causes.'" *Bandemer* destroyed the fiction that parties' competitiveness in American politics was some sort of unproblematic given. Rather, *Bandemer* made clear that the demographics of districting could legitimately alter that competitive environment—although the specific objectives of such alteration were not clearly outlined.

Of course, the *Bandemer* decision had more than this symbolic value; it is obviously a significant precedent on the justiciability of partisan vote dilution. As such, it will have great import in future reapportionment litigation. I see it as parallel, not to *Baker,* but to the 1971 racial gerrymandering decision in *Whitcomb.* Both cases were at the cutting edge of vote dilution challenges and offered new evidentiary standards based on electoral results. Neither decision accepted the evidence in the case itself as dispositive, so both were dismissed as dead letters. But with the benefit of hindsight, *Whitcomb*'s "denial of access" approach to group political rights has proven very influential, and the larger importance of both *Whitcomb* and *Bandemer* does lie in their symbolic meaning. The decisions acknowledged not only that majority rule is difficult to operationalize, but also that competition within a majoritarian political system is a matter of consciously designed electoral forums rather than unplanned market forces. *Bandemer* itself represents a call for plural representation beyond race, as well as an inherent skepticism about political competition in the American electoral system. While it falls short of a cry for an anti-gerrymandering standard that "thwarts majority control,"[156] *Bandemer* may suggest the beginning of a more compensatory attitude than winner-take-all politics.

One final note about the racial and partisan gerrymandering decisions. This section is subtitled "the jurisprudential journey of Justice White," for reasons that should now be evident: White wrote the opinion for the Court in all the major gerrymandering cases dis-

---
156. See Alfange, Gerrymandering and the Constitution, 1986 Sup. Ct. Rev. 175, 240.

cussed. No doubt, internal Court dynamics explain why White was so often the instrument of consensus. White's opinions on districting issues have always been cautious exercises, as far back as his sundering of the Warren majority on one person, one vote in 1969. White's "jurisprudential journey" was to move the Burger Court closer to the view of representation rights articulated by Stewart in his 1964 dissent in *Lucas v. Colorado General Assembly*. Stewart, one of the Warren Court justices least receptive to the one person, one vote doctrine, had proposed instead that districting plans should not "systematically frustrate the will of a majority."[157] Ironically, adoption of Stewart's approach in 1964 would have brought the Court to its *Bandemer* position much sooner—scrutinizing *group* power alignments within states to assess voters' relative political influence.[158]

The Demographics of Competition

To summarize, the case data described by the conceptual type of demographic representation concerned two kinds of districting policies—race-based and partisan-based districting. In analyzing the political and constitutional legitimacy of each, the chapter classified the cases according to whether they presented statutory or constitutional legal issues, to avoid conflating these distinct categories of voting rights. Race-based districting was both a statutory and constitutional issue, and partisan-based districting raised only constitutional questions; whether this jurisdictional difference was relevant to demographic districting policies is a point we can now consider.

Clearly, constitutional voting rights policies are more permanent, so it is especially important to understand how the Court derives and/or interprets them. Moreover, in segregating the statutory from the constitutional cases, we are able to highlight the interaction between the judicial and legislative branches over policies for racial political equality. I particularly wanted to avoid interpreting judicial decisions on a statute's construction as confirming the conceptualization of demographic representation, when those decisions were possibly more dependent on statutory directives than judicial initiative. Additionally, all the constitutional gerrymandering cases were ana-

---

157. 377 U.S. 713, 753–54 (1964).
158. This interpretation of Stewart's opinion is taken from J. Ely, Democracy and Distrust 123–24 (1980).

lyzed together to focus on the issue of compatible standards for racial and partisan vote dilution. This facilitates evaluation of what compatible standards do or do not imply about a districting policy of compensatory majoritarian competition.

To review the findings with respect to the case data, the statutory cases involving the Voting Rights Act are best summarized as "pre–results test" versus "post–results test" rulings. The results test of section 2, part of the 1982 amendments to the act, changed the tenor of that statute; arguably, the results test subtly affected judicial construction of the standards of preclearance under section 5 of the act. The Burger Court decided five "pre–results test" decisions: *Georgia, Richmond, Beer, Rome,* and *Mobile.* All but the last case dealt with section 5 preclearance and with the nonretrogression standard for local electoral changes; *Mobile* was the ruling that did much to precipitate the 1982 amendments to section 2. In the aggregate, the "pre–results test" rulings were consistent with the conceptual type of demographic representation, though their endorsement of compensatory majoritarian competition was somewhat tentative. Of the three "post–results test" rulings—*Port Arthur, Lockhart,* and *Thornburg*—only the latter actually interpreted the meaning of the new section 2. *Port Arthur* and *Thornburg* confirm the conceptual type of demographic representation because of their enthusiasm for demographic districting as political compensation for less competitive racial groups.[159] Generally, the statutory vote dilution decisions fall within the explanatory power of this conceptualization.

The second set of cases, those raising constitutional challenges to gerrymandered districts, should be subdivided by gerrymandered group rather than case chronology. The particular problem of the racial gerrymandering decisions was that district-based elections, which are supposed to partially accommodate plural interests, distorted the racial demographics of the electorate and biased the competitive environment. This bias was sometimes combined with the

---

159. *Thornburg,* of course, limits the compensatory remedy to "districtable" interests; noncompact minority populations would thus be unsuccessful in securing a remedy for aggregate level vote dilution. However, this is not to say that restructuring of the competitive environment depends exclusively on districting; one commentator argues that the remedial goal of *Thornburg* would permit alternative voting arrangements that would benefit "nondistrictable" groups. See Engstrom and Taebel, Cumulative Voting as a Remedy for Minority Vote Dilution: The case of Alamagordo, New Mexico, 5 J.L. Pol. 469 (1989).

competitive advantage that at-large electoral systems give to an electoral majority. The Burger Court decided three racial gerrymandering decisions—*Whitcomb, White v. Regester,* and *UJO*—the first two of which concerned the problem of the at-large competitive environment. Another interesting development of the first two cases was the emergence of a results test for racial vote dilution that predated the 1982 legislative amendments to the Voting Rights Act. Despite this, we interpreted all three decisions as merely consistent with the conceptual type of demographic representation, since none of them were specific as to the competitive goal of racially demographic districts. *UJO* clarified only one point: compensatory competition was available only to racial groups who were not deemed part of a majority coalition. Though the Court purported not to consider legislative responsiveness or accountability as factors relevant to vote dilution,[160] in *UJO* the majority seemed to presume that the white litigants had no case because there were white legislators responsive to their interests—albeit not from the litigants' own districts.

The other category of constitutional challenges, the partisan gerrymandering decisions, are also only consistent with the demographic conceptualization of representation. The three partisan decisions, *Gaffney, White v. Weiser,* and *Bandemer,* occasioned very limited holdings. Like their racial counterparts, the partisan districting decisions were long-winded on the warning signs of partisan gerrymandering, but inadequate when it came to defining fair partisan competition in district elections.[161] It has been alleged that the critical test both of manageable standards for detecting dilution and of the Court's commitment to partisan fairness in districting concern the use of at-large districts as part of a partisan gerrymander.[162] As the postcensus redistricting battles continue unabated, we should remember one point about the Burger Court's gerrymandering decisions: in general, they suggest that the Burger Court had waded into a demographic quag-

---

160. See Grofman, Toward a Coherent Theory of Gerrymandering, in Toward Fair and Effective Representation: Political Gerrymandering and the Courts (B. Grofman ed. 1990).
161. Not all commentators would agree with this assessment, particularly as it applies to *Bandemer*. See Engstrom and McDonald, Detecting Gerrymanders, in Toward Fair and Effective Representation: Political Gerrymandering and the Courts (B. Grofman ed. 1990).
162. I owe the substance of this comment to conversations with Bernard Grofman.

mire where "there are as many versions of a fair result as there are quantitative political scientists."[163]

The least one can say is that the Burger Court's trepidation in the gerrymandering area acknowledges the complexities of the redistricting process in the age of computer demographics. All districting is gerrymandering in the sense that spatially organized elections necessarily distort the proportional political influence of some interest groups within the electorate. The Burger Court did hold that for two groups—ghettoized racial minorities and members of major political parties—a districting plan may not undervalue their relative collective political influence. This naturally raises the question of whether undervalued political influence means the same thing and is susceptible to the same remedy in both situations. While the threshold level of discriminatory effects is not identical for racial and partisan vote dilution,[164] most commentators seem to desire compatible standards for fair districting practices. Little time has been spent, however, in addressing the preliminary question of why compatible standards are necessary or desirable to achieve "fair and effective representation." The topic of aggregate voting rights has been broached in some discussions of the Court's districting decisions, but, so far, group rights per se have not adequately justified the use of compensatory political procedures for racial or partisan groups.

The conceptualization of demographic representation can provide such a justification and, therefore, an explanation for the utility of compatible standards for group fairness in districting. The conceptual type does this by addressing the following dilemma: why are equipopulous and reasonably compact districting plans "competitive" electoral forums for most groups within the electorate, yet subject to additional demographic requirements when certain racial or partisan interests are at stake? The resolution to this districting dilemma lies in ameliorating the tension between majoritarian and plural representation, the theme that frames this chapter. Balancing majoritarian versus plural representation necessitates identifying which interest

---

163. Cain, Simple vs. Complex Criteria, 33 U.C.L.A. L. Rev. 213, 216 (1985).

164. Some differences are that partisan dilution must be more severe in its effects, because of the mutability of partisan affiliation and the subsequent predictability of partisan voting patterns. In addition, partisan vote dilution must imply undervaluing of a party's statewide strength, at least in challenges to state legislative redistricting. See Grofman, Toward a Coherent Theory of Gerrymandering, in Toward Fair and Effective Representation: Political Gerrymandering and the Courts (B. Grofman ed. 1990).

cleavages most "pluralize" a society. Because of historical and social forces, race is a critical, if not the critical, interest cleavage in American political society. Less obvious, certainly, is why partisanship is an equally important interest cleavage, especially since American political parties seem rather amorphous ideological entities and since party-label voting is allegedly on the decline. Nevertheless, partisanship pluralizes American society because it is essential to maintaining the political existence of the "official opposition" in deliberative politics. The political party is also significant as the mechanism by which other plural interests—economic, ethnic, religious, and occupational—are politically mobilized.

Thus, undervaluing the political influence of these two group interests directly undermines the balance between majoritarian and plural representation. Compensatory majoritarian competition—the remedy toward which demographic districting aims—theoretically restores that balance, Clearly, compatible standards of racial and partisan vote dilution are important to the viability of the demographic conceptualization of representation, and to an effective definition of compensatory majoritarianism. Regrettably, compatible standards— at least, both empirically workable and agreed-upon standards—await articulation in both the judicial discourse and scholarly literature on districting. The key stumbling block has been how to define proportional results, and then how seriously to consider the lack thereof as determinative evidence of vote dilution.[165]

Did the Burger Court, then, lay the groundwork for proportional representation in the United States? It has been suggested that if American politics does move toward proportional representation, it will not be the result of some conscious judicial stance, but of a legislative desire to avoid continual reapportionment litigation brought on by imprecise evidentiary standards.[166] There is already some evidence for this claim. Recently, several out-of-court settlements of dilution allegations in local elections have instituted semi-propor-

---

165. This very question is currently bedeviling litigation to remedy alleged racial vote dilution in state judicial elections. See Golden and Hayler, The Politics of Judicial Elections: Minority Representation and the Voting Rights Act Challenge in Chicago, Illinois (paper presented to the Law and Society Association, Berkeley, Ca.) (May 31– June 3, 1990); Lovrich and Sheldon, The Racial Factor in Nonpartisan Judicial Elections, W. Pol. Q. 807 (1988).

166. This point was raised in debate at the Roundtable on Gerrymandering, American Political Science Association, Washington, D.C. (Sept. 1–4, 1988).

tional voting methods such as cumulative and limited voting;[167] arguably, the Supreme Court's compensatory focus in decisions such as *Thornburg* provided the impetus for these kinds of settlements. In any case, true proportional representation is impossible within a district system of elections given the geographic dispersion of racial and partisan voting blocs. Political geography is also sufficiently complex to ensure conflicts between race-based and partisan-based districting; some commentators argue that districting to improve the competitive fairness of the black vote necessarily helps Republicans in surrounding districts.[168] In short, even demographic districting is a long way from proportional representation, as single-member district elections with plurality winners are inherently biased to overrepresent "the great middle." By retaining the archaic notion of territorially based constituencies, the United States has chosen to perpetuate the majoritarian bias at the expense of greater plural representation.[169] And because this bias is impossible to rectify without altering the entire electoral system, the best approximation of plural representation is to compensate selected disadvantaged groups within the structure of the existing district system.

The fact that solutions to the compatible-standards problem have not been forthcoming suggests that the conceptualization of demographic representation entails a fairly complex account of electoral competition. The reapportionment literature—the main source of the conceptual type—describes a theory of fair representation much more sophisticated than one person, one vote. Unfortunately, this sophistication threatens to remove districting from political to technocratic deliberation, and to render the issue of competitive fairness

---

167. Engstrom and Taebel, Cumulative Voting as a Remedy for Minority Vote Dilution, 5 J.L. Pol. 469 (1989).

168. A. Thernstrom, Whose Votes Count? 206 (1987).

169. G. Gudgin and P. J. Taylor, Seats, Votes and the Spatial Organization of Elections 203 (1979). One possible method to balance territorially based electoral districting with demographically proportional representation is the "additional member vote system." According to this system, additional legislators are selected by a previously agreed-upon formula in order to achieve a particular votes-seats ratio, while the physical connection between district members and their constituents is retained. Id. at 188–99. Though adaptation of this method to the American system of political representation might not facilitate partisan and racial pluralism, it has been recognized as attractive by some reapportionment scholars. See McDonald and Engstrom, Detecting Gerrymandering, in Toward Fair and Effective Representation: Political Gerrymandering and the Courts (B. Grofman, ed. 1990).

unintelligible to even the educated citizen. One of the virtues of the one person, one vote standard was its normative clarity. I have tried to argue that the normative objective of compensatory majoritarian competition helps to explain what the Court and its commentators have been attempting to achieve through demographic districting. Compensatory majoritarianism lacks the normative clarity of one person, one vote but, hopefully, articulates why compatible standards for racial and partisan districting are conceptually necessary. The demographic conceptualization illustrates the fine line between electoral pluralism and proportional representation, while recognizing that "the majority" is a "group" interest that must too be represented.

CHAPTER 6

The Dualistic Conception of Partisan Representation

In the previous chapter, I presented a conceptualization of group representation that focused on competitive fairness in the district system of elections. The chapter concluded on the somewhat melancholy note that workable standards for defining "fair" results in district elections were as yet unavailable. The demographic conceptualization was somewhat more successful in explaining why certain groups in a districting system merited attention *as groups*. The conceptual type justified group voting rights for racial minorities and party members as furthering the goal of compensatory majoritarian competition. With respect to groups of party voters, protection against dilution of electoral strength meant that a districting plan must preserve the viability of the "official" partisan opposition within a state.

The partisan districting cases considered the standards of fair two-party competition as well as the electoral contexts that preserved the effectiveness of partisan voting. Yet effective partisan representation involves more than just fair districting; it also concerns the political structure and operations of the party itself. Therefore, the question of individuals' political influence includes consideration of the extra-constitutional institution of the political party.

Our fourth conceptualization of group representation, that of partisan representation, concerns what definition of "responsible party government"[1] is mandated (or permitted) by the Constitution. The

---

1. This term has both a broad and a specific meaning in political science literature. Broadly, it simply refers to the idea of representation through parties, to the usefulness of parties as intermediary institutions. The term is used with this connotation by V. O. Key and Austin Ranney. "Responsible party government," in its narrower sense, refers to the school of thought that would model the American party system after the more

answer to this is complex, as the American concept of party responsibility—or partisan representation—is inherently dualistic. In order to explain the conceptual type of partisan representation, I will first articulate the functional attributes of party "responsibility." Then, I will explore the dualistic heritage of the political party in American politics, and examine how this historical tradition was partially responsible for the dualistic legal tradition of the party. Finally, the conceptualization of partisan representation will be used to explicate the Burger Court's decisions on party operations.

Broadly defined, the theory of responsible party government asserts that there are certain functions that parties perform in a system of representative government. This functional model of political parties has a pro-party bias, in that it presumes parties are necessary institutions for the aggregation of mass electorate preferences; even among political scientists who acknowledge the decline of party-label voting, electoral competition between party candidates is viewed as essential to converting diffuse popular opinion into specific electoral and policy choices.[2] Political scientists who study parties usually speak of three functions that political parties perform in the political system.[3] First, parties perform an *organizational function,* which provides effective accountability between the party's voters and their elected officials. Parties as organizations aggregate and accommodate the various policy preferences of their members or supporters through

---

centralized British parliamentary party system. E. E. Schattschneider, James MacGregor Burns, and Charles Hardin typify this perspective. See L. Epstein, Political Parties in the American Mold 29–37 (1986); A. Ranney, Curing the Mischief of Factions 42–48 (1975).

I will be using the term "responsible party government" in the more general sense, to connote the widespread feeling among party scholars that the indigenous American political party should be defended as an essential component of democratic politics. On the pro-party bias of political scientists, see S. Eldersveld, Political Parties 20–21 (1964); L. Epstein, Political Parties in the American Mold 16–18 (1986).

2. L. Epstein, Political Parties in the American Mold 22 (1986); E. Ladd and C. Hadley, Transformation of the American Party System 374 (1978). How strongly party labels influence voter choice is a matter of dispute among scholars of American electoral behavior. The recent emphasis of election studies is that issue voting is prominent, leading to ticket splitting and weakened party loyalty among voters. See N. Nie, S. Verba, and J. Petrocik, The Changing American Voter (1979); W. Crotty and G. Jacobson, American Parties in Decline (1980).

3. The functional approach to the political party, as well as that approach's generally positive assessment of American parties, has infiltrated most textbooks on American politics. I take this as a sign of the approach's acceptance by a majority within the political science discipline.

the process of internal party governance. Second, parties perform an *electoral function,* presenting the electorate with a choice between viable policy alternatives. Parties structure the vote in a democracy by sponsoring candidates who articulate party platforms, policy programs, and abstract ideological positions. Third, parties serve a *governmental function,* which includes structuring the government around party lines and party goals. The party-in-government articulates policies and provides services that rally legislative coalitions behind certain programs.[4]

"Responsible" partisan representation can be defined as the performance of these three functions. However, political parties perform these functions differently, depending on whether they are centralized or decentralized organizations and on whether they operate within a highly competitive partisan environment. Generally, the quality of a party's performance of the three representative functions depends on the degree of both intraparty and interparty democracy.[5] Intraparty democracy concerns the openness of decision-making processes within the party organization; it refers to the power of party elites relative to party regulars, as well as to how broadly party "membership" is defined. Interparty democracy concerns the kind of partisan competition that exists at the various levels of the electoral system; it focuses on whether electoral choice is confined to one or two partisan alternatives, or whether third-party and independent challengers are relatively competitive.

Both intraparty and interparty democracy are significant for political and legal evaluations of party operations. Yet neither political nor legal evaluations of the political party have uniformly favored greater party democracy. In fact, the American conception of partisan representation is rooted in a dualistic historical tradition in American politics, a dualism between a hierarchical party tradition and a populist party tradition. The former describes a bureaucratically centralized party organization, and the latter an antihierarchical and progres-

---

4. For discussion of party functions, see A. Ranney, The Doctrine of Responsible Party Government 11ff. (1962); Ladd, Party Reform since 1968, in The American Constitutional System under Strong and Weak Parties 90ff. (P. Bonomi ed. 1981); R. Clabby, The Supreme Court and State Regulation of Political Parties 9 (unpublished M.A. Thesis, Johns Hopkins University, 1976).

5. R. Clabby, The Supreme Court and State Regulation of Political Parties 5 (unpublished M.A. Thesis, Johns Hopkins University, 1976).

sively democratic party entity.[6] The key difference between the two party traditions turns on how the party organization reconciles representation of the organization's collective interests with individual members' and mass voters' participation.

Historically, the heyday of the hierarchical tradition was the age of machine politics in the late nineteenth century, though elements of this tradition were still present in the highly disciplined partisan politics of the post–World War II era. The hierarchical party tradition was one of bureaucratically centralized party institutions, which monitored partisan loyalty and directed the membership. Accordingly, control of the party is highly structured, with leadership in the party based on political apprenticeship and proven loyalty to the evolving policy positions of the party. Direct participation and influence by mass membership is limited to balloting for candidates, enhancing the power of party insiders.

The prototype for the hierarchical tradition was, of course, the party boss system. Machine politics provided for upward mobility of the rank-and-file membership through apprenticeship, and for indirect representation of membership interests through the coalition-building and patronage system that bossism required.[7] But even as an example of the hierarchical tradition, the party machine was never a nationally centralized political organization, such as European parliamentary parties are.[8] The chief attributes of the hierarchical party

---

6. Thelan, Two Traditions of Progressive Reform, in The American Constitutional System under Strong and Weak Parties 37ff. (P. Bonomi ed. 1981). Cf. Sundquist, Strengthening the National Parties, in Elections American Style 197ff. (A. Reichley ed. 1987).

Another commentator has offered a different typology of party models, identifying four prevailing definitions of the party in American politics. His typology takes into account the history of two-party cleavages, as well as the change in functions performed by the parties over time. Nevertheless, his four models—the factional party, the machine-based party, the mass solidarity party, and the policy-making party—can be collapsed into a dualistic typology as well. See Brisbin, Federal Courts and the Changing Role of Political Parties, 5 N.U. Ill. L. Rev. 31, 40–41 (1984).

A more recent articulation of the dualistic tradition of parties labels the two traditions of party organization the "party-as-political-machine" and the "party-as-peripheral-organization." See P. Herrnson, Party Campaigning in the 1980's, at 8–29 (1988).

7. R. Merton, Social Structure 73–82 (1964).

8. Indeed, it was during the period of the hierarchical party tradition that Schattschneider criticized the American political party organization because it was built around state and local politicians. To Schattschneider, a proponent of "responsible party government" in the strict sense, a party that was "a loose confederation of state

were its synthesis of conflicting group interests and its function as an instrument of local political consensus in the democratic system.[9]

The populist tradition offers a competing view of the political party in American politics and the role of group interests within and peripheral to the party organization. Rather than focusing on the synthesis of group interest within a bureaucratically centralized structure, the goal of the populist party tradition was broader participation for plural group interests. This tradition originated in the late nineteenth- and early twentieth-century reforms of the Populist and Progressive Eras. The Populist movement initiated democratically based third parties and broadened the notion of interparty competition.[10] The Progressive movement sought to minimize the role of intermediaries within the party organization in favor of more direct popular sovereignty. The Progressives conceived of an antihierarchical party organization, in which the power of party regulars and bosses would be curbed, and the corruption of legislative politics by partisan patronage would be eliminated.[11]

The Progressives also advocated control of nominations for party candidates by direct popular primaries rather than by party organizations. Their reforms restricted party regulars' domination of internal operations, fostering greater intraparty democracy.[12] The trends in party reform initiated by the Progressives were later taken up by the reform commissions of the Democratic party in the 1960s and 1970s. These commissions advocated greater popular representation in the party to make the organization stronger, more competitive, and more responsive.[13] An example was the National Democratic Party's popu-

---

and local bosses" would necessarily lack policy coherence. See E. E. Schattschneider, The Struggle for Party Government (1948); L. Epstein, Political Parties in the American Mold 33 (1986).

9. P. Herrnson, Party Campaigning in the 1980's 9–18 (1988); Auerbach, Commentary, in Reapportionment in the 70's, at 78 (N. Polsby ed. 1971).

10. Thelan, Two Traditions of Progressive Reform, in The American Constitutional System under Strong and Weak Parties 48 (P. Bonomi ed. 1981).

11. Ranney, Comment, in The American Constitutional System under Strong and Weak Parties 68 (P. Bonomi ed. 1981).

12. Ladd, Party Reform since 1968, in The American Constitutional System under Strong and Weak Parties 85 (P. Bonomi ed. 1981).

13. Ladd, Party Reform since 1968, in The American Constitutional System under Strong and Weak Parties 86–87 (P. Bonomi ed. 1981). See E. Ladd and C. Hadley, Transformation of the American Party System, 344–45 (1978), on the specific Democratic party reforms of 1968 and 1972. The Republican party also sought to streamline

lar reform of the delegate-slating process in 1968 and 1972. The new nominating processes in the Democratic party were intended to increase direct responsiveness of delegates to rank-and-file wishes; among the reforms was the use of affirmative-action guidelines to increase the representation of women and minorities in the party convention.[14]

The Democratic reforms did not escape censure—testimony, perhaps, to the fact that the populist party tradition has not been the dominant conception in American politics. The reforms were criticized for changing the integrative, collectivizing role of the so-called umbrella party within the American political system; some commentators argued that greater democratization within the party organization weakened the party's ability to integrate competing interests within its electoral platforms and governing coalitions.[15] Thus, the Democratic party's internal reforms, combined with the growing weakness of local parties in candidate recruitment activities, seemed to contribute to the party organization's disunity and disorganization.[16] Class-sensitive party scholars commented that the destruction of bossism, patronage, and party leadership through party apprenticeship were goals of a new professional elite, who sought influence in their party's operations comparable to their influence in society through the communications media.[17]

A variant of the dualistic tradition of political parties has emerged in contemporary electoral politics. Historically, responsibility for aggregation of interests and communication with the electorate rested

---

the national convention and enhance communication between delegates and constituents, but it has not challenged states' requirements regarding delegate selection. Republican reform has not been as participation-oriented as that of the Democratic party, but has instead emphasized the coordinating function of the national committee. However, rule 38 of the 1968 charter recommended more broad-based participation in party affairs at the state level. See A. Gitelson, American Political Parties: Stability and Change 93 (1984).

14. A Ranney, Curing the Mischief of Faction 149ff. (1975).

15. See generally, W. Elliot, The Rise of Guardian Democracy (1974); P. Herrnson, Party Campaigning in the 1980's, at 18–19 (1988); L. Maisel, Parties and Elections in America (1987); K. Polakoff, Political Parties in American History (1981); Schlesinger, The Crisis of the American Party System, in Political Parties and the Modern State 71 (R. McCormick ed. 1984).

16. See E. Ladd and C. Hadley, Transformation of the American Party System 344–45 (1978); N. Polsby, The Consequences of Party Reform 140ff. (1983).

17. E. Ladd and C. Hadley, Transformation of the American Party System 184, 367 (1978).

with political parties. Arguably, these functions are now performed by the electronic media.[18] Some political scientists argue that the "populism" of media-centered politics has dispensed with the need for party organizations to serve as aggregative intermediaries of the party organizations.[19] The role of the media, and of money, in party campaign operations facilitates an electoral version of the dualistic party tradition—with the dualism now between the party and the political action committee.

Political action committees, political fund-raising and issue-oriented pressure groups, theoretically allow candidates greater independence from their party base and from accommodationist politics. PACs are defended as populist institutions that allow for more balanced accommodation and more direct representation of citizens' plural interests than party bureaucracies can provide. But PACs have also been criticized for encouraging corruption in the electoral process and vitiating existing party institutions.[20] Parties remain a convenient means for organizing Congress and structuring electoral choice, as well as a useful theoretical label, but the presence of PACs arguably erodes party political functions and relegates the party to a mere administrative role in the nominating process.[21] Undoubtedly, the nature of the party's electoral function has been most affected by competition with PACs. Ironically, the legal legitimacy of the PAC

---

18. See N. Polsby, The Consequences of Party Reform 141 (1983).

19. For a discussion of the rise of "personalistic politics," see Orren, The Changing Styles of American Party Politics, in The Future of American Political Parties 4–41 (J. Fleishman ed. 1982).

20. See generally H. Alexander and B. Haggerty, PACs and Parties: Relationships and Interrelationships (1984); A. Etzioni, Capital Corruption (1984). But cf. A Matasar, Corporate PACs and Federal Campaign Financing Laws (1986); Adamany, Political Parties in the 1980's, in Money and Politics in the United States 38, 70 (M. Malbin ed. 1984); Jacobson, Money in the 1980's, in Money and Politics in the United States 38, 70 (M. Malbin ed. 1984).

21. See E. Ladd and C. Hadley, Transformation of the American Party System 337 (1978); Ladd, Party Reform since 1968, in The American Constitutional System under Strong and Weak Parties 87 (P. Bonomi ed. 1981).

While he does not explicitly defend PACs, Sorauf is one commentator who is relatively sanguine about the possibility of "politics without parties." See F. Sorauf, Party Politics in America (1984). For a positive assessment of the national parties' adaptation to a post-PAC electoral environment, see P. Herrnson, Party Campaigning in the 1980's (1988).

organization had its roots in doctrines the Supreme Court developed to protect party autonomy.[22]

Attention to the political and legal status of PACs leads naturally to the question of the party's dualistic legal tradition. The party's legal dualism does not exactly parallel its historical dualism, but ambiguity over the party's public, open character versus its private, exclusive character is common to both traditions.[23] Further, the party's dualistic heritage makes the notion of a dualistic legal identity conceptually more familiar.

Development of a coherent doctrine of the party's constitutional status was hampered by its legal identity as both an agent of the state and a private association.[24] Examination of an early Supreme Court ruling reveals that the ambiguity of the party's legal identity produced a tension between the organization's associational freedom and an individual's right to vote. In the well-known "white primary case" of *Smith v. Allwright*,[25] in 1944, the Texas Democratic party operated a whites-only primary election that was tantamount to determining the winner of the general election. The Court held that, as an entity cloaked in state authority, the Texas party organization could not

---

22. See the discussion of the collective freedom of association and the case of Buckley v. Valeo, 424 U.S. 1 (1976), *infra* at 173ff.

23. Some commentators explain the jurisprudential difficulties with the political party as the product of several competing—and, at times, irreconcilable—visions of politics. For example, Moeller identifies three theories of politics that run through the Supreme Court's party decisions. He argues convincingly that the party cases can be seen as part of a systemic debate between the theories of "fair politics," First Amendment primacy, and "Madisonian politics." Moeller, The Federal Courts Involvement in the Reform of Political Parties, 1987 W. Pol. Q. 717, 718–21. For a similar thesis but a different typology, see McClesky, Parties at the Bar, 46 J. Pol. 346, 367 (1984).

Other commentators argue that the constitutional treatment of parties—particularly, the Court's accommodation of minor parties into the existing two-party structure—has had more to do with temporal and political dimensions of particular judicial eras. See Epstein and Hadley, On the Treatment of Political Parties in the U.S. Supreme Court: 1900–1986, 52 J. Pol. 413, 427–29 (1990).

24. See Brisbin, Federal Courts and the Changing Role of Political Parties, 5 N.U. Ill. L. Rev. 31, 67–69 (1984). Some commentators go further in criticizing the public/private entity dispute, seeing it as a doctrinal obfuscation of the real issues in the party cases. Lowenstein, Constitutional Rights of Major Political Parties: A Skeptical Inquiry (paper presented to the American Political Science Association, Washington, D.C.) (Sept., 1988).

25. 321 U.S. 649 (1944). See also Terry v. Adams, 345 U.S. 461 (1953). On the doctrinal tension of these white primary cases, see Note, *Cousins* and *LaFollette:* An Anomaly Created by a Choice between Freedom of Association and the Right to Vote, 80 N.W.U.L. Rev. 666, 679ff. (1985).

conduct a racially exclusive primary election that abridged individual voting rights.[26] Because the party primary was "an integral part of the election process," the party had to be treated as a state agency, obligated to respect antidiscrimination guarantees.[27] In other words, in *Allwright* the legal identity of the party was as a publicly regulated and public-character organization.

A dualistic legal conception of the party developed when decisions subsequent to the white primary cases characterized the party as a rights-bearing "voluntary association of individuals" protected from state interference.[28] This development had its origin in the Warren Court's recognition, in *NAACP v. Alabama,* that the First Amendment protected freedom of association and, indeed, *collective* freedom of association.[29] The Warren Court's party decisions suggested that the collective advocacy rationale articulated in the *NAACP* ruling might extend to parties' electoral activities.[30] The rights of party members as a group were asserted in *Williams v. Rhodes,* in 1968, which held that the equal protection clause was violated by certain ballot access restrictions on minor parties.[31] One year later, in *Hadnott v. Amos,* the Warren Court specifically stated that the freedom of association applied to party organizations.[32] In *Hadnott,* the Warren Court invalidated an Alabama ballot access provision used to discriminate against black political organizations. The majority noted that the regulation restricted the ability of the black members of the National Democratic Party of Alabama to "band together for the advancement of political beliefs."[33] The series of party cases from 1944–69 show that the

---

26. *Smith v. Allwright* involved the application of the state-action doctrine. See Chemerinsky, Rethinking State Action, 80 N.W.U.L. Rev. 503 (1985).

27. See L. Epstein, Political Parties in the American Mold 176–78 (1986); McClesky, Parties at the Bar: Equal Protection, Freedom of Association and the Rights of Political Organizations, 46 J. Pol. 346, 355 (1984).

28. The quoted phrase comes from the per curiam opinion in O'Brien v. Brown, 409 U.S. 1, 4 (1972).

29. NAACP v. Alabama, 357 U.S. 449 (1958).

30. See McClesky, Parties at the Bar, 46 J. Pol. 346, 356 (1984).

31. 393 U.S. 23 (1968). The Court's chief concern in *Williams* was equal access of major and minor parties to the ballot; it did not address the First Amendment association rights of party members directly.

32. 394 U.S. 358 (1969). The discussion of the freedom of association occurred only in dicta; technically, the ruling relied on the antidiscrimination provisions of the Fourteenth and Fifteenth Amendments.

33. 394 U.S. at 364.

party's dualistic legal tradition involved a conflict between the private associational party and the publicly controlled electoral party.[34]

The Warren Court's legacy of judicial supervision of parties was limited to issues of interparty competition and to indirect references to parties' collective freedom of association.[35] The Burger Court, however, systematically applied the First Amendment freedom of association to protect the rights of party members as a group. Recognition of party members' collective rights prompted fresh judicial appraisal of the freedom of association as an important political right. One could also argue that it paved the way for later judicial conceptions of partisan electoral politics as a group activity.[36] Most important, unlike the Warren Court, the Burger Court faced legal questions about the party on all three functional levels. Therefore, its decisions raised the more general issue of responsible party government.

Did the Burger Court's decisions define or attempt to define responsible party government? The Burger Court did consider issues relevant to parties' organizational, electoral, and governmental functions. I therefore use the functional conception of responsible party government to organize the discussion and evaluation of the Court's party decisions. Each of the cases will be grouped according to its functional subject matter.

The organizational function cases raise questions about candidate selection and nomination procedures. The primary issue in these cases is the extent to which the party bureaucracy should have autonomous control over primary election results and delegate selection processes. The governmental function cases focus on the issue of party patronage. Certain members of the Court questioned the validity of party patronage employment, as well as the legitimacy of

---

34. L. Epstein, Political Parties in the American Mold 155ff. (1986). Epstein argues that it is useful to analogize parties' semi-public/semi-private legal status to that of public utilities.

35. The Warren Court's party rulings could be summarized as embodying the view that "all political [expression] cannot be channeled into the programs of our two major parties." This statement comes from Sweezy v. New Hampshire, 354 U.S. 234, 250–51 (1957). The decision invalidated on due process grounds state investigation into the activities of the Progressive party; Warren's plurality opinion discussed party freedom of association in dicta.

36. See Maveety, The Burger Court and Group Access to the Political Process (paper presented to the American Political Science Association, Chicago, Ill.) (Sept., 1987).

partisan participation by civil servants. Thus, the patronage cases explore what the party-in-government may do with its popular mandate. In both the organizational and the governmental function cases, the Court had to evaluate conditions of intraparty democracy.

The electoral function cases concern both getting on the ballot and financing a candidacy. With respect to issues of political mobilization by "subversives" and third parties, the Court considered what constitutes equal access to the ballot and viable electoral competition by minor political parties. The electoral cases also involve judicial scrutiny of financial competition among parties and their candidates. In a series of campaign-financing decisions, the Court policed the integrity of the electoral process and examined the extent to which unequal fiscal resources of political groups undermine partisan electoral competition.[37] The electoral function cases forced the Court to evaluate—if not broadly conceive—interparty democracy.

The Burger Court's point of departure in its party decisions was generally the associational rights of party members as a group.[38] In adjudicating questions about different party functions, the Court increasingly acknowledged that the distinct rights of party organizations and party members must be balanced. Balancing the associational claims of the party "establishment" with those of the "partisan fringe"—third parties, independents, PACs, intraparty factions, and so on—was difficult because numerous political groups claimed to represent "partisan freedom of association."[39] This difficulty was

37. The Court construed monetary contributions for political purposes as political speech protected by the First Amendment. See Buckley v. Valeo, 424 U.S. 1 (1976); First National Bank of Boston v. Bellotti, 435 U.S. 765 (1978); Federal Election Commission v. National Conservative Political Action Committee, 105 S. Ct. 1479 (1985). The implications of this trend in group representation—and the Court's concomitant reading of freedom of association—will be further assessed in the concluding chapter.

38. Recall that in the partisan districting decisions discussed in the previous chapter, the focus was on party members' aggregate right to nondiluted votes. See Davis v. Bandemer, 106 S. Ct. 2797 (1986). A difficulty common to both districting and party operations controversies is determining whether party "members" speak for the collective right of the party. This issue is formally one of plaintiff representativity.

39. Brisbin alludes to a version of this problem, namely, who represents the interests of partisan representation *generis:* the major party organizations or independent/unaligned party members? He argues that the Court vacillated between a conception of the party as a private association unregulatable by the state, and a conception of the party as a public organ of the state. This vacillation is especially apparent if the results of ballot access cases such as *Williams* are compared with the rulings in the white primary cases. See Brisbin, Federal Courts and the Changing Role of Political Parties, 5 N.U. Ill. L. Rev. 31 (1984).

compounded by what one commentator calls "careless reification of the concept 'party.'"[40] In both political science literature and legal discussions, the term "party" has many disparate referents. This terminological ambiguity is troublesome, but does not present an absolute barrier to evaluating the Court's approach to issues of partisan representation.

While it would be imprecise to characterize all the party cases as essentially intraparty disputes, one cannot overemphasize the jurisprudential importance of rivalries between different groups of party members. The party cases ensnared the Court in the tension between the hierarchical and populist traditions of the party. Therefore, before we can determine whether the Burger Court arrived at a coherent definition of responsible party government, we must examine how its decisions reconciled the dualistic historical tradition of the party.

We shall evaluate the party case data using the dualistic conceptualization of partisan representation to answer three questions. First, is a particular party decision best described as a confirmation or contradiction of one historical tradition, or is the decision merely consistent with a party tradition? Second, does the distribution of decisions within each functional category suggest the endorsement of one particular party tradition? In other words, do the electoral function decisions—for example—generally and overwhelmingly support the populist and not the hierarchical party tradition? Third, do the answers to the previous questions demonstrate judicial cognizance of the necessary interrelationship of the organizational, governmental, and electoral functions of the party? The answers to these questions will assist in evaluating whether the Burger Court developed a coherent doctrine of the constitutional status of the political party.

When examining a decision's correspondence with the hierarchical or populist party tradition, we will use the following guidelines. The hierarchical tradition emphasizes collective representation of interests and organizational responsibility. The populist tradition emphasizes direct popular participation within, and competition between, political parties. In other words, for a case to be consistent with a party tradition, it must do more than address a certain set of ques-

---

40. Lowenstein, Constitutional Rights of Major Political Parties: A Skeptical Inquiry (paper presented to the American Political Science Association, Washington, D.C.) (Sept., 1988).

tions or issues; the decision must reach a result or espouse a policy view corresponding to one of these traditions. If a decision's result is irrelevant to the assumptions of either party tradition, or explicitly contradictory of a particular tradition, this will undermine the explanatory value of the dualistic conceptualization of partisan representation. Hopefully, however, the dualistic conceptual type of partisan representation will elucidate that, like so many of the Burger Court's representation decisions, the party decisions fundamentally concerned the problem of political competition.

The Organizational Function of Parties

E. E. Schattschneider once commented that centralization of national political parties and destruction of local party machines would vitalize local self-government.[41] While this seems an unlikely hidden agenda for the Burger Court's "states' rights" scrutiny of the party nomination process, one could argue that the Burger Court's decisions on primary procedures and delegate selection support national party organs at the expense of state authority.[42] The Court's tendency to support party freedom of association at the expense of state regulation of elections was at odds with the earlier trend in the white primary cases. Rather than viewing the party's actions as those of an agent of the government—if not *the* government—the organizational function cases reveal a strong tendency to separate the entity of "the party" from "the state."

Because of the continued vitality of the hierarchical party tradition, party nomination operations retains a "regulars only" character. Even when primary elections became more prevalent as candidate selection procedures, and despite the white primary rulings, primaries were not conceived of as entirely public operations. There is an instrumental reason for this view of primaries. As a political organization, the political party must fulfill both expressive and competitive goals. Its method of internal governance and delegate selection must

---

41. E. E. Schattschneider, Party Government 182–83 (1977).

42. See Note, Cousins and LaFollette, 80 N.W.U.L. Rev. 666, 692 (1985); Lawson, How State Laws Undermine Parties, in Elections American Style 247ff. (A Reichley ed. 1987). But cf. Lowenstein, Constitutional Rights of Major American Parties (paper presented to the American Political Science Association, Washington, D.C.) (Sept., 1988). Lowenstein argues that the cases I label as organizational function controversies are not simply conflicts between the state and the party.

allow for the expression of party members' political characteristics and preferences. At the same time, its internal processes must not detract from "combat effectiveness," from the mobilization of a party's resources toward winning elections.[43] Nevertheless, the correct balance between expression and competition is something over which different groups of party members or adherents may disagree, and this disagreement becomes legally as well as politically troublesome when each group claims protection under the theory of partisan associational freedom.

Two trends in the organizational function cases lend credence to an initial claim that the decisions endorsed the hierarchical tradition. First, the Court supported party autonomy over state regulation in delegate selection/candidate nomination procedures. Second, the Court supported the authority of the national party committee over state party committees—what might be called support for party centralization American style.[44] In reviewing the organizational case data, it is evident that at a rhetorical level, at least, the hierarchical tradition was an important influence.

In one way or another, the organizational function cases all revolved around the problem of choosing delegates to party conventions; therefore, the cases all presented the question of which party "member" votes count the most. Often, the division between groups of party members was federalist. The first decision to address such an issue, *O'Brien v. Brown*,[45] in 1972, upheld the validity of national party rules over state regulation. The petitioners in *O'Brien* challenged the recommendations of the Credentials Committee of the 1972 Democratic National Convention regarding the seating of certain delegates at the party convention. The committee had recommended the unseating of some delegates from Illinois and California for violations of the Democratic National Party's slate-making guide-

---

43. See A. Ranney, Curing the Mischief of Factions 134–35 (1975).

44. Party "centralization" in the United States would always be tempered by our system of divided government, or separation of powers. Truly centralized responsible party government presupposes single-party control of the executive and legislative branches, as is the case in a parliamentary system. See Sundquist, Strengthening the National Parties, in Elections American Style 207 (A. Reichley ed. 1987). One party scholar argues that strengthening and institutionalization of the national party organizations has occurred since the late 1970s. See P. Herrnson, Party Campaigning in the 1980's, at 128 (1988).

45. 409 U.S. 1 (1972).

lines. *O'Brien* does not provide particularly solid evidence of the hierarchical tradition because the Court summarily upheld the committee's application of party rules. The per curiam majority viewed a lower court's reversal of the committee action as judicial interference into what was possibly a political question. Parties came into being as "voluntary associations of individuals," the Court argued, so the party's convention was the only proper forum for determining intraparty disputes.[46]

O'Brien was a prelude to subsequent organizational function rulings, in that the Court deferred to the decision of the central party organization on delegate selection rules. The *O'Brien* decision was consistent with the hierarchical party tradition, though it supported a central party organization that had reformed and broadened intraparty democracy.

Probably the most fundamental question of the organizational function cases was whether national party guidelines for primary suffrage and delegate selection should take precedence over the state's electoral code. Central to this question was the issue of "closed" primaries—primary elections open only to registered party voters. Many states, through different regulatory devices, provided for such closed primaries, and justified them as protecting the integrity of the major parties' internal decisions. Two rulings in 1973 on state-mandated closed primaries demonstrated mixed support for the hierarchical party tradition. *Rosario v. Rockefeller*[47] upheld a New York law requiring voters to declare their party affiliation thirty days before the general election in order to vote in the next primary. The law permitted voters to participate in a different primary each year, as long as they planned ahead. *Kusper v. Pontikes*[48] concerned a challenge by a voter to Illinois' primary participation restriction. The state's twenty-three-month qualification period barred an individual who voted in a Republican party primary for municipal offices from voting in a Democratic party primary for state elections. This regulation

---

46. 409 U.S. at 4–5. This statement was significant since some lower courts were beginning to apply "one Democrat, one vote"—a judicially enforced conception of "fair politics"—to every step of the party nomination process. Bode v. National Democratic Party, 452 F.2d 1302 (1971). See Moeller, Federal Courts Involvement in the Reform of Political Parties, 1987 W. Pol. Q. 717, 723.
47. 410 U.S. 752 (1973).
48. 414 U.S. 51 (1973).

was rejected by a majority of seven justices, while the New York law in *Rosario* was upheld only by a majority of five.[49]

The Stewart majority in *Kusper* identified the problem with state-mandated closed primaries: their interference with "the right to associate with the political party of one's choice, ... an integral part of freedom of association."[50] Both *Rosario* and *Kusper* demonstrated the conflict between state concerns for party solidarity and voters' claims for freer, broader intraparty participation. It should be noted that these cases concerned private, individual associational rights, not associational claims of the party as a group;[51] this seemed to make a jurisprudential difference, for *Rosario* was only weakly consistent with the hierarchical party tradition, and *Kusper* was only weakly contradictory of it. Neither objected to the state goal of protecting party integrity; the decisions simply focused on the state's choice of the "least drastic means" to achieve that goal.

Partisan freedom of association received stronger validation when asserted by the party organization, as it was in *Cousins v. Wigoda*,[52] in 1975. *Cousins* concerned the Democratic party reforms of 1972 and the resulting dispute over the seating of certain Illinois delegates at the Democratic National Convention. The Court held, as it had in *O'Brien*, that national party rules for delegate selection took precedence over the state election code. But unlike *O'Brien*, *Cousins* specifically relied on the party's claim that it was protecting its members' freedom of association.[53] Brennan's majority opinion argued that the national party's guidelines furthered uniform party policy and strengthened the party's performance of its electoral function. Collective associational integrity required that the party's interest in national representation take precedence over any state interest.[54] *Cousins* is strongly affirmative of one side of the party's conceptual

---

49. Stewart's majority opinion rejected the state's justification of preventing "raiding" of the primary by the opposition party. 414 U.S. at 61. Justices Blackmun and Rehnquist dissented, finding that the provision was carefully drawn to tie disqualification to the vote in another party's last primary. 414 U.S. at 64, 68.

50. 414 U.S. at 57.

51. For further discussion of this point, see L. Epstein, Political Parties in the American Mold 185ff. (1986).

52. 419 U.S. 477 (1975).

53. 419 U.S. at 488.

54. 419 U.S. at 490.

dualism: through its ruling for the national party over state controls[55] and its application of freedom of association to the party collective, the decision confirms the hierarchical party tradition.

In spite of the decisive *Cousins* ruling, the Burger Court's conception of partisan freedom of association remained ambiguous. This ambiguity clouded its interpretation of the party organizational function; decisions permitting the centralization of internal party governance were still not reconciled with the qualified support for open primaries in *Kusper*.[56] This latent tension within the organizational function decisions surfaced in the 1979 ruling of *Marchioro v. Chaney*.[57] This case concerned a Washington state statute requiring each major political party to have a state committee consisting of two representatives from each county, in order to facilitate regional representation within each political party. The state law conflicted with a 1976 amendment adopted during the Democratic National Convention requiring one representative from each state electoral district on all state party committees. As a result of reapportionment rulings, county and electoral district boundaries were not coterminous; thus, the national party's "one Democrat, one vote" formula resulted in a less geographic-based distribution for state party committees.

Marchioro was made even more problematic by the Washington state committee's refusal to comply with the national party amendment. The case was thus a combination of intraparty conflict and state versus party conflict. The Court unanimously ruled that because the state committee legitimately ran internal party affairs when the national convention was not in session, its decision to follow the state law must be upheld.[58] The Court reasoned that the statute could not be construed as burdensome to the party's associational rights because

---

55. The justices who had resisted the one person, one vote doctrine in the reapportionment cases expressed concern over the majority's support for national party rules regarding collective representation. Rehnquist, Burger, and Stewart concurred, but emphasized the continuing need for attention to state participation in the delegate selection process. 419 U.S. at 491, 496. Powell, in a partial dissent, was the strongest advocate for the state mandate over uniform party rules. He argued that the party committee could not force on the people of Illinois delegates to represent them that were contrary to their elective choice. 419 U.S. at 497. The separate opinions in *Cousins* suggested that federalism tensions would reappear in the Burger Court's discussions of states' regulations on parties.
56. See McClesky, Parties at the Bar, 46 J. Pol. 346, 361 (1984).
57. 442 U.S. 191 (1979).
58. 442 U.S. at 193.

the source of the problem was the national party's own decision to delegate authority to the state committee.[59] Oddly enough, the Court's deference to the national convention's delegation of intraparty governance resulted in a restriction of the central party's power to set its own guidelines for state party committees. While an interesting problem of delegation, the *Marchioro* ruling was essentially irrelevant to either tradition of the party.

This disposition of *Marchioro* only highlighted the unresolved conflict between two notions of partisan freedom of association. One notion stressed the right of the organization "regulars" to collective autonomy, which included the right to exclude. The other notion addressed the right of peripheral members, who were nevertheless party voters, to greater inclusion in internal party decision making. When the central party organization itself objected to open primaries as part of the nomination process, the two notions of partisan association rights directly conflicted. *Democratic Party v. LaFollette*,[60] in 1981, concerned just such a conflict between national party rules for delegate selection and Wisconsin's system of open primaries for party candidates. The state's election code provided for primaries open to non–party members and separate, closed elections for convention delegates. However, the Wisconsin delegates were instructed to vote at the convention in accordance with the open primary results. The statute contravened the party rules that only those who publicly affiliate themselves with the party may influence the selection of national convention delegates; as a result, the convention commission refused to seat the Wisconsin delegates on the grounds that the state's election system underrepresented party regulars.

The conflict in *LaFollette* was between the state's interest in furthering popular participation and the national party's definition of its group associational rights. The Stewart majority endorsed the party's choice of procedures for self-governance, relying on the *Cousins* rul-

---

59. 442 U.S. at 199. Epstein offers a different interpretation of *Marchiano*, emphasizing that the state wished to regulate the party committee because it performed specific electoral, quasi-public functions. Strictly in this context, the Court allowed the state regulation to stand. See L. Epstein, Political Parties in the American Mold 191–92 (1986); McClesky, Parties at the Bar, 46 J. Pol. 346, 360 (1984). Cf. Moeller, The Federal Courts Involvement in the Reform of Political Parties, 1987 W. Pol. Q. 717, 722–23.

60. 450 U.S. 107 (1981).

ing.⁶¹ Stewart's opinion was unambiguous in its application of freedom of association to the party organization as a group. He accepted the party's view that the Wisconsin system underrepresented rank-and-file Democrats in the party's own governing body,⁶² reasoning that "freedom of association would prove an empty guarantee if associations could not limit control over their decisions to those who share the interests and persuasions that underlie the association's being."⁶³ The Stewart majority in *LaFollette* reiterated the centralized notion of party authority and the protection of collective autonomy articulated in *Cousins*. Thus, *LaFollette* was also a confirmation of the hierarchical party tradition, as it solidified the Court's support for the national party organization.

The dissenters' position in *LaFollette* is worth mentioning because of its partial endorsement of the populist party tradition. Powell's dissenting opinion praised the broad-based partisan representation of the Wisconsin system: its virtue was that it allowed independent voters who leaned toward the policy position of a particular party to influence that party's strength and ideological identity.⁶⁴ The dissent's populist position in *LaFollette* was thus more consistent with the anti–closed primary ruling in *Kusper*.

The split among the justices in *LaFollette* seemed motivated by the conflict between the rights of the party establishment and party adherents.⁶⁵ In its last organizational function decision, the Burger

---

61. 450 U.S. at 120.
62. 450 U.S. at 116.
63. 450 U.S. at 122 n.2. Stewart was careful to add that the party rules did not forbid Wisconsin from holding an open primary; they only provided that the state could not require its party delegates to vote in accordance with the primary result. 450 U.S. at 126.
64. 450 U.S. at 132.
65. In a case dealing with electoral procedures in Puerto Rico, party self-government was again upheld over broad-based individual participation. The 1982 decision of Rodriguez v. Popular Democratic Party, 102 S. Ct. 2194 (1982), concerned the procedure for filling a midterm vacancy of a legislative seat held by a member of the Popular Democratic Party. The governor of Puerto Rico had called a by-election open to all qualified electors of the seat's district. The appellee party challenged the governor's action as a violation of a Puerto Rico statute limiting participation to electors affiliated with the party.

A unanimous Court upheld Puerto Rico's party appointment statute as the fairest way to ensure the stability and continuity of the partisan balance in the legislature and to protect the electoral mandate of the previous election. 102 S. Ct. at 2197. The Court analogized the interim appointment procedure to a primary election, over which the states have authority. Though *Rodriguez* supported collective partisan representation,

Court reiterated its support for party centralization and control over intraparty participation. In *Bellotti v. Connolly*, in 1983, the Court sustained a Massachusetts Democratic party requirement that state primary candidates demonstrate a threshold of support at the state party nominating convention.[66] This time, a dissenting faction of the Court questioned whether the party rule improperly elevated the associational rights of party regulars (convention delegates) over those of other party members.[67] The dissenters felt that the issue of competing First Amendment rights of two groups of party members deserved fuller consideration; *Bellotti* thus represented a missed opportunity for the Burger Court to clarify its position on partisan freedom of association.[68] As such, the decision is irrelevant to either party tradition.

Despite its shortcomings, *Bellotti* fits in with the Burger Court's pattern of support for autonomous party control over state regulation of intraparty governance, the pattern evident in *O'Brien, Kusper, Cousins,* and *LaFollette*. Only in *Marchioro* did the Court permit antihierarchical party organization. Yet even *Marchioro* could be construed as contributing to party centralization, as the legitimacy of the state party committee's decision in the case depended on a delegation of authority from the national convention. The organizational function decisions linked the centralization and autonomy of parties to a collective right of freedom of association, yet, paradoxically, the Court's support for party centralization may contribute to disorganization within the Democratic party because of the antihierarchical nature of the party reforms in delegate selection.

Partisan implications aside, the organizational function decisions generally endorsed the hierarchical tradition of the American political party. The direction of these decisions is further clarified if we consider the Rehnquist Court's first rulings on party organization.

---

the Court managed to justify its theoretical position in terms of individual rights of participation. The party appointment process was here the best reflection of voter will. 102 S. Ct. at 2201.

66. 103 S. Ct. 1510 (1983) (cert. denied).

67. 103 S. Ct. at 1512. Stevens's dissent was joined by Rehnquist and O'Connor.

68. However, in its last term, in *Tashjian v. Republican Party of Connecticut*, the Burger Court let stand an appeals court ruling preventing the state from forcing the party to run a closed primary. 106 S. Ct. 1257 (1986) (aff'd on appeal). The case was later decided on the merits in the first term of the Rehnquist Court. As in *LaFollette*, authority to choose the members of the association was lodged with the party organization. 107 S. Ct. 544 (1987).

In *Tashjian v. Republican Party of Connecticut,* in 1986, and *Eu v. San Francisco County Democratic Central Committee,* in 1989, the Court overturned state restrictions on internal policy governance of political parties. *Tashjian* is particularly illustrative of the hierarchical tradition, as the five-judge majority endorsed the state party's choice to run closed primary elections at the expense of registered independent voters.[69] *Eu,* in invalidating California's regulation of the endorsement and internal governance activities of state party committees, relied heavily on *Tashjian,* as well as *LaFollette* and *Kusper*.[70] Clearly, the Burger Court principle of party organizational autonomy has been embraced and extended in the Rehnquist Court's party decisions. Provisionally, this demonstrates the impact and importance of one category of Burger Court representation decisions.

The Electoral Function of Parties

In addition to a certain degree of organizational centralization and autonomy, an attribute of the hierarchical party tradition is two-party electoral competition. American parties have often been described as constituent rather than governing parties, more concerned with structuring political competition and recruiting electoral coalitions than with dictating legislative policy.[71] If this thesis is valid, then the parties' performance of the electoral function will be the most critical to their continued viability as American political institutions.

The Burger Court's electoral function decisions supported, though not uniformly, two-party political competition. The Court did allow the relaxation of ballot access restrictions on minor parties as a means of furthering broader electoral choice for voters. However, its sensitivity to third parties' rights was tempered by concern that the relaxed ballot structure might fragment majority will. Thus, the Burger Court broadened interparty democracy only with a qualified "yes."

As interparty competition also depends on candidates' relative parity in campaign financing, the electoral function cases included con-

---

69. 107 S. Ct. 544, 548–49 (1986). The Marshall majority primarily relied on the partisan freedom of association precedent of *Anderson v. Celebrezze;* this case, which concerned the associational rights of independent candidates and their supporters, will be discussed in the next section.

70. 109 S. Ct. 1013, 1020–21 (1989).

71. E. Ladd and C. Hadley, Transformation of the American Party System 337 (1978).

troversies over campaign financing as well as issues of formal ballot access. Arguably, the former has a great deal more to do with the competitive parity of parties in the electoral system. The campaign finance decisions are hard to classify in terms of the dualistic tradition of the party, since they did not involve conflicts between the rights of groups of party members. Rather, the decisions extended freedom of association protection to the campaign activities of political action committees.

A possible interpretation of the campaign finance decisions is that they interjected populism into an electoral structure characterized by major-party dominance. But one could also interpret the campaign finance rulings as broadening group political access at the expense of direct partisan appeals to the electorate,[72] as the PAC decisions contested the idea that electoral mobilization was the exclusive domain of political parties. Such a view goes beyond even the populist tradition; it would seem to be antiparty. The ambiguity of the electoral function decisions with respect to interparty competition lends credence to the claim that the decisions did not contribute to a coherent theory of partisan representation.

Let us test this assertion by first reviewing the electoral function decisions dealing with ballot access. Brief mention should be made of an earlier ruling by the Warren Court, *Williams v. Rhodes,* in 1968. In this case, the Court invalidated an Ohio ballot access restriction on third-party presidential candidates. The Black majority found that the requirement's differential treatment of major and minor parties violated the equal protection clause. Black's view seemed to be that the legal right to participate was only meaningful if participation is readily possible and not subject to obstacles.[73]

Williams intimates that, like so many of the party cases, the ballot access cases concerned the clash between the rights of dissenting major-party members. However, the Burger Court did not follow *William's* adjudication of this clash in its first ballot access decisions. In

---

72. For an example of this view of the effects of PACs, see W. Crotty, American Political Parties in Decline 133–43 (1984).

73. Moeller, Federal Courts' Involvement in the Reform of Political Parties, 1987 W. Pol. Q. 717, 728–29. Curiously, Chief Justice Warren dissented in *Williams,* supporting the state's interest in fashioning its own electoral laws by regulating party activities. 393 U.S. at 63, 66. Since partisan freedom of association was not an issue in *Williams,* it is possible that Warren's opinion was motivated by a conception of the party as an agent of the state, as in the white primary cases.

Jenness v. Fortson, in 1971, the Court sustained Georgia's nominating petition requirements for minor-party candidates,[74] endorsing the state interest in providing stable party competition. Similarly, in *Storer v. Brown,*[75] in 1974, the Court upheld California's petition requirements and related restrictions for independent candidates. For the White majority in *Storer,* the statute legitimately curtailed independent candidacies motivated by short-term political goals. White's concern in *Storer* was with the integrity of the general election as "reserved for major struggles . . . , not [as] a forum for continuing intraparty feuds."[76] In other words, a state might legitimately restrict independent candidacies because many are motivated by major party "renegades." As both *Jenness* and *Storer* protected major-party solidarity and two-party dominated competition, both decisions were consistent with the hierarchical tradition and contradictory of the populist tradition of parties.

The early ballot access decisions speak to both party traditions because they were an effort to accommodate the accepted tradition of two-party competition with the emerging rights of minor parties. However, equal protection, not First Amendment association, was the predominant legal question in *Williams, Jenness,* and *Storer.* The trend toward viewing ballot access restrictions as partisan freedom of association issues began in a contemporaneous series of filing-fee cases. In unanimous opinions in 1972 and 1974, the Court held that a candidate's prospective popular support bore no relation to his or her financial ability to get on the ballot; a filing fee, absent alternative measures, was unrelated to determining a candidate's seriousness of

---

74. 403 U.S. 431 (1971). Georgia's balloting provision distinguished the political access of "political parties" and "political bodies." Under the statute, political parties were political organizations whose candidates had polled at least 20 percent of the vote in the most recent gubernatorial or presidential election; any other organization was a political body. Only political parties could conduct primary elections and automatically list their winning candidate on the state ballot; political body nominees gained ballot positions by submitting a nominating petition and fee.

75. 415 U.S. 724 (1974).

76. 415 U.S. at 735. See also American Party of Texas v. White, 415 U.S. 767 (1974); Mandel v. Bradley, 432 U.S. 173 (1977). In both cases the Court ruled against the associational rights of independent candidates and their supporters, deferring to state interests in regulating interparty competition.

The dissenters in *Storer*—Brennan, Douglas, and Marshall—argued that California's requirement froze the political status quo and removed the opportunity for progressive candidates to react to partisan nominees or issues. 415 U.S. at 758. The dissenters espoused the participationist line in *Williams* and in the one person, one vote decisions.

intentions.[77] The impermissibility of filing fees was based on the burden they imposed on the associational freedom of potential supporters of minor party candidates.[78]

Despite their broad reading of associational freedom, the filing-fee cases suggest a reason for the less than enthusiastic endorsement of populist interparty competition in the ballot access decisions: candidacy was not a fundamental right. This view of candidacy predominated in the ballot qualification case of *Clements v. Fashing*, in 1982. The plurality opinion, authored by Rehnquist, sustained a Texas officeholder eligibility regulation imposing a "resign to run" requirement. Rehnquist argued that because candidacy is not a constitutional right, the regulation did not burden freedom of association.[79] Oddly, but understandably, both factions of the Court in *Clements* claimed commitment to party competition and accountability. The Rehnquist plurality opinion—joined by Burger, Powell, and O'Connor—emphasized a party representative's current governmental responsibility. The dissenters—Brennan, Marshall, Blackmun, and White—emphasized a party representative's access to the electorate, as well as his or her *private* First Amendment rights.[80]

While the result of *Clements* was essentially irrelevant to either party tradition, it did reveal the contradictory objectives of partisan representation in American politics. In the ballot access cases generally, the Burger Court's main concern was a candidate's effective representation of majority will. As a result, its decisions tended not to favor the populist party tradition and its broad conception of electoral competition. But neither did the Court uniformly defer to state structuring of the ballot: the justices unanimously invalidated an Indiana loyalty oath for certain minor parties in *Communist Party v. Whitcomb*, in 1974.[81] The controlling factor was the burden on freedom of association of the minor party's supporters.

Additionally, in its last ballot access ruling, the Burger Court soft-

---

77. Bullock v. Carter, 405 U.S. 134, 143–44 (1972). *Bullock* invalidated the Texas filing fee under equal protection requirements only. In Lubin v. Panish, 415 U.S. 707 (1974), a similar California filing fee was struck down under equal protection and freedom of association guarantees. 415 U.S. at 716–18.
78. Lubin v. Panish, 415 U.S. at 712, 716.
79. 102 S. Ct. at 2843–44.
80. 102 S. Ct. at 2850.
81. 414 U.S. 441 (1974). *Whitcomb* is a fairly minor case; still, its result could be interpreted as consistent with the populist party tradition.

ened its bias toward two-party electoral competition; a five-judge majority in *Anderson v. Celebrezze,* a 1983 case, invalidated Ohio's early filing deadline for independent candidates. According to Stevens's majority opinion, the restriction placed an unconstitutional burden on the electoral and "associational choices" of voters.[82] The majority argued that an independent candidate's potential supporters possessed the freedom "to associate in the electoral arena to enhance their political effectiveness as a group."[83] *Anderson* was significant in that the Court expressly defined electoral participation as a group activity. Arguably, the Burger Court viewed collective association as instrumental to some, as yet inchoate, conception of group representation rights.[84]

Anderson has been described as an antiparty ruling, rather than as a broadening of interparty competition.[85] While *Anderson* did treat independents with special deference, it retained a fairly conservative, case-by-case analysis of ballot access restrictions—the same approach found in *Storer. Anderson* is probably best described as irrelevant to either party tradition, in that it is consistent with both. Interestingly, the Rehnquist Court cited *Anderson* in support of partisan freedom of association in its rulings in *Tashjian* and *Eu.* Although these cases dealt with party organizational functions, their protection of party autonomy could be viewed as confirmation of the hierarchical party tradition.[86] Marshall, who wrote both opinions, had joined the majority in *Anderson;* clearly, he is qualified to evaluate that precedent's meaning and to determine that it is not "antiparty." Though the Burger Court's ballot access rulings, taken as a whole, can hardly be construed as defining a theory of party government, they do acknowledge the importance of group association for effective political action.

The group association principle proved an even more dramatic aspect of the second category of electoral function cases, those dealing with campaign finance. In an age of expensive, mass-media cam-

---

82. 460 U.S. 780, 793 (1983). The four *Anderson* dissenters—Rehnquist, White, Powell, and O'Connor—stressed the state interest in preserving the integrity of republican government and preventing intraparty factionalism.

83. 460 U.S. at 794.

84. See Maveety, The Burger Court and Group Access to the Political Process, (paper presented at the American Political Science Association, Chicago, Ill.) (Sept., 1987).

85. McClesky, Parties at the Bar, 46 J. Pol. 346, 353 (1984).

86. See *supra* notes 68–69 and accompanying text.

paigning, the distribution of political capital has the greatest potential impact on interparty electoral competition. Oddly enough, the federal campaign regulations were contemporaneous with national party organizational reforms of the 1970s; both movements reflected a national policy aimed at preserving the popular character of the electoral process. The Burger Court supported both areas of reform, but the reforms had different implications for the performance of party functions. The Court regarded freedom of association as applicable in both areas, even though associational rights protected party centralization in one instance and partisan decentralization in the other. In essence, collective association freedom ensured that parties and PACs would be competitors for individuals' political and associational loyalties.

The most obvious result of the campaign finance rulings was the application of association rights to political entities other than parties; the decisions treated party organizations no differently from PACs or individual contributors for the purpose of campaign-financing regulations.[87] Some commentators summarize the campaign finance rulings as contrasting sharply with the Court's tendency in other cases to free parties from legislative regulation.[88] While this generalization may be valid, it does not capture what was so important about the campaign finance decisions. In fact, the Court's tendency to free PACs from legislative restrictions most affected the partisan electoral function. Thus, the campaign finance rulings facilitated other political organizations' performing what is usually thought of as the party's function of mobilizing electoral coalitions behind certain candidates. Yet, arguably, the proliferation of interest groups and the extension of their sway only reinforces the need for partisan electoral responsibility,[89] and may have also facilitated a new, influential role for parties as intermediaries or "brokers" in electoral politics.[90]

Potential impact aside, the campaign finance decisions demonstrated imperfect awareness of the political tension between parties and PACs. Even when decisions discussed the matter, it was as a

---

87. See generally Sabato, Real and Imagined Corruption in Campaign Financing, in Elections American Style 155 (A. Reichley ed. 1987).
88. David Adamany, Political Parties in the 1980's, in Money and Politics in the United States 74 (M. Malbin ed. 1984).
89. Ladd, Party Reform and the Public Interest, in Elections American Style 227 (A. Reichley ed. 1987).
90. P. Herrnson, Party Campaigning in the 1980's, at 47, 123 (1988).

decidedly secondary issue. This can be seen in the first case to address the constitutionality of campaign finance regulation, *Buckley v. Valeo*, in 1976.[91] The case concerned a First Amendment challenge to the 1974 amendments to the Federal Election Campaign Act (FECA). The act established contribution and expenditure limitations for individual candidates, parties, and political action committees; public disclosure requirements for federal campaigns; and public financing provisions for presidential campaigns. The per curiam opinion upheld all FECA provisions except those limiting personal and independent campaign expenditures, justifying the invalidation of expenditure ceilings by distinguishing contributions and expenditures in terms of the First Amendment. The distinction hinged on the possibility of corruption of candidates; independent expenditures, by definition, were not coordinated with the campaign's activities. The Court viewed such expenditures, expressing advocacy of candidates, as no less protected by the First Amendment than discussion of public policy generally,[92] and saw no critical difference between advocacy by individuals and advocacy by political action committees.

By allowing unlimited expenditures by PACs, yet applying contribution limitations to parties, *Buckley* diminished the parties' role as sponsors of candidates. PAC spending thus competes with the electoral function of parties, as PAC funding increases candidates' reliance on and obligation to PACs rather than their party. This development has been of some benefit to challengers of incumbent legislators.[93] *Buckley* theoretically broadened electoral competition by supporting interest group associations, if not third-party competitors. The Court's reasoning, in the spirit of *NAACP v. Alabama*, seems to have been that PAC association was protected because it enhanced effective political advocacy. PACs were simply a new form of collective advocacy; their expenditures were protected by the First Amendment to prevent dilution of "the right to join together for the advancement of beliefs and ideas."[94] As in the ballot access rulings,

---

91. 424 U.S. 1 (1976).
92. 424 U.S. at 48.
93. F. Sorauf, Money in American Elections 161ff. (1988); Sabato, Real and Imagined Corruption in Campaign Financing, in Elections American Style 164–65 (A. Reichley ed. 1987). A countervailing point is that PACs disproportionately support incumbents, solely because they *are* incumbents.
94. 424 U.S. at 65–66.

individual associational choices merited protection and could not be constitutionally limited to formal (major-party) organizations.

The Court's acceptance of the public financing provisions in *Buckley* also affected interparty competition more directly. The public financing provisions established three categories of public funding, based on a party's percentage of popular support in the last presidential election. Major parties received full funding; minor parties received a lesser percentage; and independents and new parties received, at best, post-election funds. Justice Rehnquist was the sole critic of the provisions' "invidious discrimination" against minor parties, independents, and new parties; he argued that the categories of the act "financially enshrined the two major parties in a permanent position of dominance."[95]

Taken together, judicial support for PAC political activity and for the public financing provisions render *Buckley* enigmatic with respect to party traditions. The former aspect of *Buckley* is weakly consistent with the populist tradition, while the latter is weakly consistent with the hierarchical tradition. The clearest result of the decision was that the associational rights of party and PAC adherents were constitutionally equivalent.

The combination of upholding contribution limitations on parties and extending associational rights to PAC organizations implied a presumption that parties were no more important to electoral repre-

---

95. Both phrases come from Rehnquist's partial dissent. 424 U.S. at 293. Regulation of minor-party electoral financing raised the interparty democracy issue of the ballot access cases, although no members of the *Anderson* majority were sympathetic to it. Rehnquist himself dissented from the *Anderson* Court's relaxation of ballot access for independent candidates. Arguably, he felt that financial disincentives on third-party presidential candidacies would have more impact on interparty competition than formal ballot access restrictions.

Irrespective of the *Buckley* ruling on public funding, minor parties are unlikely to win elections. The Burger Court seemed to view minor parties not so much as vehicles for electoral competition, but as organizations for free association and political debate. Cf. Epstein and Hadley, On the Treatment of Political Parties in the U.S. Supreme Court: 1990–1986, 52 J. Pol. 413, 427 (1990). This interpretation of minor parties was clear in Brown v. Socialist Workers '74 Campaign Committee, 103 S. Ct. 416, 1983. The Court invalidated the application of Ohio's campaign disclosure law to the Socialist Workers party. Marshall's opinion for the Court observed that since minor parties are unlikely to win elections, the state interest in preventing vote buying is hardly substantial. *Brown* was little more than a symbolic victory for interparty democracy, for it confirmed the Court's implicit assessment of electoral competition as essentially a two-party battle. In the last analysis, the decision is irrelevant to either tradition of political parties.

sentation than other political groups. The Court did permit state party committees to channel funds for campaigns of federal party candidates through a central, coordinating party-campaign organization.[96] It also remained sensitive to the corruption possible from PAC campaign war chests and continued to uphold limitations on contribution solicitation by corporations.[97] Yet *Buckley*'s view of the importance of financial parity between the major parties in presidential elections did not arrest the Court's broad reading of PAC freedom of association. In 1985, in *Federal Election Commission v. National Conservative Political Action Committee,* the Burger Court struck down the PAC expenditure ceiling in the Presidential Election Campaign Fund Act. Broadening opportunities for public political discourse was the Rehnquist majority's stated purpose. Allowing presentation of political views while limiting speech-related expenditures, Rehnquist argued, was like allowing a speaker in a public hall to express his views while denying him the use of an amplifying system.[98] Still, the *NCPAC* decision, in essence, permitted the party with the strongest financial network to dominate media campaigning. The long-term significance of the decision, nevertheless, was its reaffirmation that the old-style coalition building in which the two major parties traditionally engaged is also the prerogative of PACs.

In the campaign-financing decisions, the Court equated the electoral function of PACs with that of political parties, analogizing the collective associational rights of the PAC with those of the party. In *NCPAC,* for example, the Court argued that PACs were "mechanisms by which large numbers of individuals of modest means can join together in organizations which serve to amplify the voice of their

---

96. Federal Election Commission v. Democratic Senatorial Campaign Committee, 454 U.S. 27 (1981).

97. California Medical Association v. Federal Election Commission, 453 U.S. 182 (1981); Federal Election Commission v. National Right to Work Committee, 459 U.S. 550 (1982).

98. 105 S. Ct. 1459, 1467 (1985). White, Brennan, Marshall, and Stevens dissented from the Court's seeming endorsement of a "money talks" attitude toward political competition. See also *Buckley,* 424 U.S. at 265–66 (White, J., concurring). While they objected that protecting spending as opposed to speech destroyed both the appearance and the reality of equal access to the political arena, neither White's nor Marshall's dissent addressed the impact of unlimited PAC expenditures on the role of parties themselves. 105 S. Ct. at 1474–76 (White, J., dissenting); 105 S. Ct. at 1480–81 (Marshall, J., dissenting).

adherents."[99] Taken alone, this statement suggests that the decision could be viewed as consistent with the populist party tradition of broadened electoral competition. However, as is now probably evident, PACs do not fit comfortably within either the hierarchical or populist traditions of political parties. PACs are a symptom of parties in transition, not a cause. More than anything else, the electorate's tendency to respond to issues and personalities, rather than party labels, accounts for the prominence of PACs.

In sum, the electoral function decisions draw from both party traditions without endorsing either; indeed, they are as dualistic as the historical tradition of the party itself. Unlike the organizational function decisions, the spirit of the electoral function decisions was to make major-party organizations more accessible to ancillary adherents. The electoral function decisions upheld the major parties' dominance in the electoral process, yet recognized new political intermediaries for mobilizing individual interests. These new political intermediaries were generally independent candidacies or PACs, not third-party competitors. Like the organizational function cases, the electoral function decisions demonstrated insensitivity to the doctrinal ambiguity of "partisan freedom of association." Did that freedom imply that intraparty factions should be permitted to organize through PACs, or did it mean that parties should enjoy preferential or exclusive status with respect to financing candidates? Arguably, the campaign finance rulings—especially *Buckley*—attempted to harmonize conflicting associational rights by allowing financial and expressive avenues that broaden political debate.

The harmony between the associational rights of different groups of party members proved tenuous in both the ballot access and the campaign finance decisions. However, such harmony was absent entirely from the decisions addressing the governmental function of parties. In these cases, the Burger Court's concern for freedom of association and for balanced interparty competition led to a repudiation of an important element of responsible party governance.

The Governmental Function of Parties

The freedom of association of like-minded individuals seemed to animate the Court's decisions in *Democratic Party v. LaFollette, Anderson*

---

99. 105 S. Ct. at 1467.

v. Celebrezze, and *FEC v. NCPAC*. The organizational and electoral function cases concerned the rights of the members of political associations, whether they were parties or other types of groups. In terms of our dualistic conceptualization of partisan representation, the result of these rulings was an endorsement of a weak hierarchical tradition. "Weak" implies a hierarchically organized two-party system that, nevertheless, incorporates elements of issue-oriented politics. This uneasy blend was a prominent feature of decisions concerning PAC activity and the rights of independent voters. Still, the decisions presumed that political parties were the essential link between elected officials and the electorate.

In contrast, the third category of party cases, the governmental function decisions, directly challenged certain assumptions of the hierarchical party tradition. More clearly than the other party decisions, the governmental function rulings supported elements of the populist party tradition by striking at the heart of partisan political control: the patronage, or "spoils," system. Disciplining public officials and directing their actions is the key element of the party's governmental function. Historically, the major parties used patronage employment to distribute government jobs as rewards for political "good behavior" and support. This patronage system was an important element of the hierarchical party tradition, as it maintained party solidarity and provided party members with representation in the policy-making process. Our examination of the Burger Court's governmental function decisions will focus on the degree to which their result repudiated this aspect of the hierarchical party tradition.

Despite defenses of the "latent functions of the machine,"[100] patronage has had its share of critics. The original critics were of course the Progressives, who led the battle in the early twentieth century to rid city politics of corruption, graft, and inefficiency. As a recent study indicates, the Progressive reformers' motives were not altogether pristine, for "eliminating fraud meant eliminating clientelist parties riddled with corruption and associated with rowdy immigrants, and efficiency was understood as government run on business principles in business' interests."[101] To the Progressives, invalidating patronage practices would weaken the partisan nature of governmental structure.

---

100. R. Merton, Social Structure (1964).
101. F. Piven and R. Cloward, Why Americans Don't Vote 71 (1988).

Part of the goal of the Progressive movement, as of the populist party tradition, was a nonpartisan civil service. Initially, this objective entailed the elimination of partisan favoritism in governmental administration. Beginning about 1904, Progressive-oriented party organizations gained control of many state legislatures, adopting statutes that restricted partisan political activity by civil service employees.[102] The first example of the Burger Court's supervision of the party governmental function involved consideration of such a state restriction on bureaucratic partisanship.

In *Broadrick v. Oklahoma*,[103] in 1973, the Court upheld a state statute prohibiting certain partisan political conduct by classified civil servants. The majority's explanation for the ruling centered on the application of the First Amendment's overbreadth doctrine. In terms of a theory of partisan representation, the most striking feature of *Broadrick* was the strong dissent it elicited.

Both the major and minor dissents were ostensibly concerned with the First Amendment rights specific to public employees. They differed, however, on the reasons for such concern. Justice Brennan, joined by Stewart and Marshall, objected to the statute's failure to distinguish between private and public partisan conduct on the part of state civil servants.[104] Justice Douglas's separate dissent went beyond questions of First Amendment doctrine; he challenged the very notion of a nonpartisan civil service. Douglas's condemnation of the regulation stemmed from more theoretical arguments about democratic government; fairly explicitly, Douglas rejected assumptions of the populist party tradition, arguing that "a bureaucracy that is alert, vigilant and alive is more efficient than one that is quiet and submissive."[105] On the basis of the dissenters' statements, *Broadrick* could be interpreted as both contradicting the hierarchical tradition and confirming the populist tradition. A more conservative evaluation, based on the less hyperbolic majority opinion, is to view *Broadrick* as consistent with the populist tradition.

The justices who objected to the result in *Broadrick* were generally

---

102. F. Mosher, Democracy and the Public Service 67, 71 (1968); Thelan, Two Traditions of Progressive Reform, in The American Constitutional System under Strong and Weak Parties 41 (P. Bonomi ed. 1981).
103. 413 U.S. 601 (1973).
104. 413 U.S. at 624 (Brennan, J., dissenting).
105. 413 U.S. at 621.

the same justices who favored broad interparty competition through relaxed ballot access, as well as greater party autonomy in internal organization. Clearly, their reading of associational liberties across different party contexts did not produce a uniform endorsement of either the hierarchical or populist party tradition. Arguably, the inconsistent views of *Broadrick*'s dissenting contingent were a manifestation of a more general attribute of the party rulings—the rulings often seemed more attentive to the associational claim of a particular litigant than to the party tradition that the litigant seemed to represent. The governmental function decisions are thus noteworthy for building an edifice of doctrine somewhat removed from the reality of partisan politics.[106] In other words, the Court seemed preoccupied with the connection between certain party functions and associational rights, while deemphasizing the necessary *interdependence* of party functions.

Lack of attention to the interrelatedness of party functions similarly marked the rulings on patronage practices. Whether or not this was a factor, in *Elrod v. Burns*,[107] in 1976, the opinion of the Court was supported by only four votes, plus two concurrences. Brennan's judgment for the Court overturned the discharge of a non–civil service employee because he was not a member of the incoming administration's political party. Patronage dismissals not only restrained freedom of association, Brennan argued, but were "at war with deeper traditions of democracy embodied in the First Amendment."[108] His conclusion that patronage was not essential to a meaningful system of democratic government[109] was an extraordinary break with the traditional conception of partisan-organized government.

---

106. Lowenstein makes this claim about another subset of party rulings, those dealing with organizational disputes. While I disagree with his assessment of those decisions, his general observation about the "preoccupation with the manipulation of abstract categories" has merit with respect to other party decisions. See Lowenstein, The Constitutional Rights of Major Political Parties: A Skeptical Inquiry (paper presented to the American Political Science Association, Washington, D.C.) (Sept., 1988).
107. 427 U.S. 347 (1976).
108. 427 U.S. at 357. This language came from an earlier circuit court opinion written by then Judge Stevens. Illinois State Employees Union v. Lewis, 474 F.2d 561, 576 (1972). See Moeller, The Federal Courts' Involvement in the Reform of Political Parties, 1987 W. Pol. Q. 717, 729.
109. 427 U.S. at 370. Brennan found no relationship between the employee's duties and demonstrable political loyalty to the incoming party. Burns was a ministerial, nonconfidential government employee with limited policy-making authority.

Stewart and Blackmun's concurrence, stopping short of a complete subversion of patronage, emphasized that the *Elrod* rule should be limited to partisan dismissal of ministerial government employees.[110] Though they accepted Brennan's application of freedom of association in the case, they were more sensitive to the party-in-government's own associational freedom. Stewart and Blackmun represented a more moderate position than Brennan, since they were unconvinced that a party could not exact some price for performing its function of organizing the government. Because of the faceted nature of the *Elrod* ruling, it is difficult to evaluate in terms of our conceptual type. While the rhetoric of Brennan suggests repudiation or contradiction of the hierarchical party tradition, the decision itself is best characterized as confirming the presence of the populist tradition.

The argument of the dissent supports this reading of the decision. Powell's dissenting opinion clung both to the value of patronage for party accountability and solidarity and, by implication, to the hierarchical party tradition. Powell's dissent spoke directly to the interrelated functions of political parties. Patronage employment, he argued, had played a significant role in democratizing American politics; by broadening popular participation in government, patronage strengthened the parties' electoral function as political intermediaries.[111] Powell's argument suggested that while the case was a conflict between *two* claims for partisan associational freedom, the claim of the party-in-government had the stronger functional component. He made this point rather bluntly: hope of reward, not "good government," was the mainstay of local party activity.[112]

Elrod's tentative confirmation of the populist tradition was tested in 1980, in *Branti v. Finkel*.[113] *Branti* extended the ban on patronage dismissals from ministerial employees to state public defenders. The Stevens majority read the *Elrod* ruling broadly, arguing that patronage practices were invalid when party affiliation was irrelevant to the

---

110. 427 U.S. at 374.

111. 427 U.S. at 379. Powell's dissent was joined by Rehnquist; Burger wrote a separate dissenting opinion. He insisted that out of judicial respect for matters of political administration, state government appointments deserved the same deference as those of the federal executive branch or Congress. 427 U.S. at 376.

112. See McCleskey, Parties at the Bar: Equal Protection, Freedom of Association and the Rights of Political Organizations, 46 J. Pol. 346, 363 (1984).

113. 445 U.S. 507 (1980).

state employee's performance of his or her public duties.[114] Stevens felt that the patronage dismissal in *Branti* contravened the freedom of association indirectly, by distorting the results of the electoral process. The distortion arose from the power to "starve" the opposition out of public policy-making by commanding partisan support from governmental employees.[115] The *Branti* majority came close to recommending bipartisan governmental administration, elevating what are arguably short-term interests of opposition party officers over the associational rights necessary to a party's governmental function. *Branti* was not a complete and explicit condemnation of the hierarchical party tradition, but the language of the opinion was more hostile to the party-in-government's collective interests than was the language in *Elrod*. Unlike *Elrod*, *Branti*'s effect was more negative than positive; rather than confirming the presence of the populist tradition, *Branti* contradicted the hierarchical tradition.

This assessment of *Branti*, while largely inferential, is confirmed by the language of the dissent. Again, Powell authored a dissenting opinion notable for its defense of patronage practices and of the overall partisan role in government.[116] As in *Elrod*, Powell reiterated the important political interests served by patronage employment—the building of stable political parties and party organizations.[117] Without patronage as a tool, Powell argued, party solidarity and discipline would break down and decrease the party's ability to mobilize electoral and legislative coalitions. For Powell, effective popular representation required partisan patronage; he saw the *Branti* ruling as having an antidemocratic effect on the representation of local voters' wishes.[118]

Powell's explicit recognition of the interdependence of the party's political functions underscores the neglect of the subject in the majority opinion. Decisions such as *Elrod* and *Branti* reduced the party's governmental function to a legal status secondary to the other party functions. Thus, the party-in-government's function of structuring

---

114. 445 U.S. at 517.
115. 445 U.S. at 514 n.8.
116. Moeller calls Powell's opinion a "Madisonian defense of political parties" because of its view of patronage as part of a complex political balance that developed over time. Moeller, The Federal Courts' Involvement in the Reform of Political Parties, 1987 W. Pol. Q. 717, 720.
117. 445 U.S. at 527–28.
118. 445 U.S. at 532–33.

governmental administration—and the associational rights that function implies—yielded to competing associational claims made by other groups of party members. One commentator summed up the impact of the patronage decisions quite astutely: "More than any other political party reform issue—only the political gerrymander might rival it—patronage cases engender controversy and call forth strong theoretical discussion about the role of political parties in the American democracy."[119]

Though the governmental function decisions uniformly applied associational freedom to support the populist party tradition, doctrinal consistency was bought at a high price. The price was a disregard for the reality of partisan competition: a weaker governmental function does not further interparty democracy but rather intraparty disorganization. Traditionally, partisan political competition has not included bipartisan governmental administration. Yet in settling conflicting claims of partisan associational freedom by restricting patronage, the governmental function decisions have a potentially broad effect on parties' competitive activities. Arguably, the decisions offer a new vision of partisan electoral competition between more diffuse party organizations.

This vision seems to have captured the imagination of the Rehnquist Court. In a 1990 decision that was the coup de grace to *Branti*, a five-judge majority invalidated patronage hirings and promotions as violating pubic employees' First Amendment rights. In the words of Justice Brennan's majority opinion, "To the victor belong only those spoils that may be constitutionally obtained."[120] The Rehnquist Court ruling essentially eliminates patronage practices that do not serve "vital governmental interests." The dissent's assessment of the decision was even more dramatic, alleging that the majority

---

119. Moeller, The Federal Courts' Involvement in the Reform of Political Parties, 1987 W. Pol. Q. 717, 730.
120. Rutan v. Republican Party of Illinois, 58 U.S.L.W. 4872 (June 19, 1990). Four justices—all of them Reagan appointees—dissented from the ruling. The most interesting opinion for the partisan conceptualization of group representation was the separate concurrence of Justice Stevens. Citing a "critical distinction between partisan interest and the public interest," Stevens rejected the dissent's assertion that party patronage was part of the democratic tradition. "The tradition that is relevant in this case," Stevens concluded, "is the American commitment to examine and reexamine past and present practices against the basic principles embodied in the Constitution." 58 U.S.L.W. at 4879–80.

had constitutionally established an antipartisan "merit civil service" at war with the American tradition of "party discipline."[121] What is important for our purposes is that the current Court took this step by following the populist reasoning of the Burger Court patronage precedents.

Whether to welcome this development depends a great deal on one's theoretical and practical perspective on political parties. This chapter has argued that legal reform of party operations is likely to be misguided if it disregards the parties' dualistic heritage. But another issue arises specifically from decisions such as *Elrod* and *Branti*. The governmental function cases raise major problems of democratic governance because, like the partisan gerrymandering cases, they pose the fundamental question of what constitutes competitive fairness for parties. Unfortunately, the patronage and gerrymandering cases were also similar in their outcomes: the Court ultimately did not arrive at a standard of fair partisan competition, either for governmental administration or districting.

In general, the party decisions discussed in this chapter reflect an ad hoc balancing of various party functions and assertions of partisan freedom of association. The results perpetuated the dualistic tradition of political parties; this was not unexpected, given that the party's quasi-public–quasi-private legal status is rooted in this historical dualism. However, the Burger Court's party decisions also tended to evaluate assertions of partisan associational freedom without attending to the relationship between the doctrine and the actual performance of party functions. The doctrine of partisan freedom of association thus threatened to take precedence over the entity the doctrine was supposed to protect. The result was an almost studied ignorance of the interdependence of the organizational, electoral, and governmental functions, whatever the theory of partisan representation. The implications of this result for a coherent constitutional theory of responsible party government are addressed in the concluding section.

The "Baneful Effects of the Spirit of Party"

Before evaluating the party decisions in terms of the dualistic conceptualization of partisan representation, let us review the case data.

---

121. 58 U.S.L.W. at 4880 (Scalia, J., dissenting).

Following the accepted format of "responsible party government," we classified the cases into three categories, corresponding to the party's three political functions. The organizational function decisions concerned the autonomy of the central party organization on matters of delegate selection and candidate nomination. Collectively, these decisions were consistent with the hierarchical party tradition. The electoral function decisions, which included issues of ballot access and campaign finance, irregularly endorsed strong two-party electoral competition. The ballot access rulings equivocated on this point; the campaign finance decisions gave preference to major parties for public funding, but also protected the political activities of new electoral intermediaries, PACs. We concluded that, in general, the electoral function decisions were consistent with a "weak" hierarchical tradition—a two-party electoral structure that extended electoral access to independent candidates and organizations. Finally, the governmental function decisions restricted patronage practices and partisan activities by civil servants, objectives both strongly associated with the populist party tradition.

Clearly, no one tradition of political parties predominated in the Burger Court's party decisions. Indeed, the justices could be accused of giving primacy to their individual views of what constitutes freedom of association in party operations. Conjecture about judicial behavior and motivations aside, my purpose is to present a more systematic account of the rulings than the rulings themselves provide. Initially, I argued that American parties could be characterized by their dualistic heritage, identified as the hierarchical versus the populist tradition. As noted, this historical dualism was partly responsible for the party's dualistic legal heritage as both a private and a public entity. The party's legal dualism occasionally made partisan freedom of association difficult to define, particularly in cases in which the associational rights of two groups of party adherents conflicted—as in the primary election cases. The party decisions' employment of the freedom of association to protect *collective* political action is a corollary of the study's general thesis that the Burger Court embraced a group-based approach to representation questions. However, for the freedom of association to be a doctrinal tool that furthers responsible party government, it must be applied with a goal in mind. With the political culture itself of two minds about the purpose of parties in democratic government, it is hardly surprising that the Supreme

Court's decisions were also caught in this historical dualism. Therefore, while the party's legal dualism complicates a coherent constitutional theory of party government, it is less central than historical dualism to the Court's difficulties with party reform.

Table 1 provides a systematic description of the party case data in terms of the dualism between the hierarchical and populist party traditions. The table indicates that the Burger Court's party decisions were not chaotic, but evenly balanced between the two party traditions.

Although we faulted the Court for neglecting the interdependence of the organizational, electoral, and governmental functions for effective party government, on closer examination what seemed like neglect may have been an effort at compromise. According to the taxonomy in table 1, the Court's decisions slightly favored the hierarchical tradition. However, two significant developments—those in the

TABLE 1. The Dualistic Conceptual Type and the Party Case Data: a Taxonomy According to the Party Function Categories

	Hierarchical Tradition	Populist Tradition
Confirmation	Organizational function (2 decisions)	Governmental function (1 decision)
Consistency	Organizational function (2 decisions)	Electoral function (2 decisions)
	Electoral function (3 decisions)	Governmental function (1 decision)
Irrelevance	Organizational function (2 decisions)	Electoral function (1 decision)
Contradiction	Organizational function (1 decision)	Electoral function (2 decisions)
	Electoral function (1 decision)	
	Governmental function (1 decision)	

PAC and patronage rulings—repudiated important elements of that tradition. In spite of this, the party decisions only intermittently supported the populist tradition. The overall pattern of the decisions thus suggests the endorsement of a participatory variation of the hierarchical party tradition.

This variation of the hierarchical tradition was implicitly endorsed in many of the delegate selection and ballot access decisions. Moreover, it provides an account of partisan representation that justifies the populist aspects of rulings such as *Elrod*. Support for the populist party tradition in the patronage rulings (and, to a lesser degree, in the PAC rulings) was not evidence of disregard for interrelated party functions, but, rather, evidence of extension of the participatory variation of the hierarchical tradition. In other words, the results of *Buckley, NCPAC, Elrod,* and *Branti* were integral to a consistent theory of responsible party government, because the opposite outcomes would have been inconsistent with a "weak" hierarchical tradition.

Thus, the dualistic conceptualization of partisan representation aids in construction of an alternative explanation for cases otherwise construed as "inattentive to the interdependence of party functions." In terms of our dualistic conceptual type, that apparent inattention comes to resemble overt balancing of two disparate conceptions of the political party. Without attributing either tendency to conscious judicial motivation, I offer an explanation of the party case data that also provides a coherent theory of partisan representation. The coherence of any such theory is constrained by the party's historical dualism; yet, since the influence of history is difficult to repudiate, I am suggesting that a constitutional theory of responsible party government must develop within the confines of party tradition.

The party's development and performance of certain political functions has—until recently—had little to do with constitutional law. To be precise, avoiding the baneful influence of party was the original "party tradition" in America. Madison's *Federalist X* reflected a widespread and rather negative conception of parties as "factions," yet the Constitution itself is not hostile but silent on the question of parties.[122] As a result, the American tradition of party government flourished

---

122. Some of the Madisonian hostility to parties lingers in our political culture; arguably, it is a hostility vented on a recent political invention, the PAC. PACs are often viewed as destructive to party government in the same way that parties were once thought to be destructive to democratic government.

outside of the constitutional framework. What, then, are we to make of the party's long aconstitutional heritage? Perhaps, simply that the party institution is unlikely to conform very neatly to lawyerly doctrinal categories. Thus, much of the constitutional debate over the party has not been directly related to a coherent theory of partisan representation. The Burger Court's contribution to the case law on parties—the impact of its precedents—lies in its decisions' attempt to reconnect questions of party rights to the process of representation.

Despite some doctrinal confusion over associational freedom, the Burger Court's party decisions did employ the theory to further group representation and group political action. As the Warren Court first noted in the 1958 decision of *NAACP v. Alabama,* individuals are too weak, as individuals, to make democratic machinery work. Individuals must therefore combine to act as groups, and parties have been the traditional groups for collective political action. Parties antedate *Reynolds v. Sims,* but the Burger Court's application of "fair and effective representation" guidelines to the electoral forum has modified the concept of partisan competition. The Burger Court's party decisions showed that representational reforms and party functions must be viewed as interdependent if a coherent constitutional theory of partisan representation is to be developed.

CHAPTER 7

Administrative and Litigational Representation

Thus far, we have presented four conceptual types of representation that focus on political forums in which group political action is primarily electoral. We have used these conceptualizations to illustrate that while the Burger Court embraced a group-based approach to representation problems, its decisions did not reflect a monolithic view of group rights of representation. Indeed, a fifth category of decisions involved political representation without concerning voting rights or the electoral process at all. These were decisions about the popular accountability of the administrative branch of government. Popular access to agency proceedings is not usually thought of as part of our representative government, but if the recent proliferation of administrative law studies by political scientists is any indication,[1] the conflict between administrative policy-making and democratic politics is of great moment.

Renewed interest in integrating the administrative branch into the constitutional system unites much of this political science commentary. Historically, the principle means of such integration has been judicial scrutiny of administrative agency decisions. The federal court's involvement in the administrative process was precipitated by a series of congressional statutes requiring agencies to conform to certain procedures. These procedural requirements constitute a body of statutory and case law that regulates the regulators. At first glance, the technocratic complexity of administrative procedure would seem to have little to do with issues of representation. Yet if we keep in mind that one goal of administrative law has been controlling bureau-

---

1. G. Bryner, Bureaucratic Discretion (1987); L. Carter, Administrative Law and Politics (1983); P. Cooper, Public Law and Public Administration (1988); J. Rohr, To Run a Constitution (1986); D. Yates, Bureaucratic Democracy (1982).

cratic discretion, then judicial review of agency action becomes a form of political "representation" in the administrative process. The courts represent a political check on the agencies through the actions of the litigants who appear before them. Thus, citizen access to judicial supervision of the administrative branch is a modern manifestation of a representation right.

This conception of administrative accountability accentuates the role of the judiciary in facilitating popular representation. Judicial supervision of the political process is important to other conceptualizations of representation; for example, the reapportionment revolution concerned a judicially fashioned right to an equally weighted vote. Popular representation in the administrative branch also assumes an active judicial involvement in defending rights of political access. But unique to the judicial scrutiny of administrative accountability is litigation itself being a form of popular representation.[2] Since litigation is central to administrative accountability, we define "administrative representation" as plaintiff access to the federal courts in order to challenge agency rule-making.

The general description of the conceptual type of administrative representation is citizen or group use of litigation to facilitate participation in the administrative process. This conceptual type seeks to reconcile administrative policy-making with the goal of pluralist representation. However, before measuring the Burger Court's decisions against this conceptualization, we must more precisely pinpoint the case data relevant to administrative representation. Recently, an expert on administrative law commented that the first step in "pluralizing" agency decision making was the expansion of *standing,* the legal right to bring a complaint before a court.[3] Arguably, the doctrine of standing directly and immediately relates to furthering administrative accountability, because it is itself a representative concept. Standing concerns whether a litigant has sufficient personal interest in judicial relief, or can appropriately represent a group of interested

---

2. The notion that litigation is a form of access to the political process is common to studies of interest group lobbying of the judicial branch. See K. O'Connor, Women's Organizations Use of the Courts (1980); T. O'Neill, *Bakke* and the Politics of Equality (1985); Krislov, The Amicus Curiae Brief: From Friendship to Advocacy, 71 Yale L.J. 694 (1963); O'Connor and Epstein, The Rise of Conservative Interest Group Litigation, 45 J. Pol. 479 (1983); Vose, Litigation as a Form of Pressure Group Activity, 319 Annals 20 (1958).

3. M. Shapiro, Who Guards the Guardians? 45 (1988).

parties seeking legal redress.[4] Since standing to sue is an essential prerequisite of "litigational representation," we will confine our survey of Burger Court administrative law decisions to those involving the standing of citizens and groups to challenge agencies in court.

An enduring problem with any conception of administrative accountability is that since the birth of the administrative branch in 1887,[5] it has coexisted rather uneasily with the constitutional branches. Because the first independent agencies were framed as "above politics,"[6] the terms of their relationship to democratic government were unclear. Thus, one cannot really evaluate the status of modern administrative law—or the significance of a conceptualization of administrative representation—without attending to the "illegitimate birth" of the administrative state. Accordingly, the first section of this chapter sketches the development of the administrative law state, and the accommodation of the administrative process to democratic politics. Before we can assess the Burger Court's contributions to administrative accountability and litigational representation, we must show the connection between our conceptual type and the history of the tension between administration and politics in American government.

The Administrative "Bill of Rights"

Although the first independent federal agency was created in 1887, administrative accountability did not become a major political issue until the expansion of the federal bureaucracy during the New Deal. Woodrow Wilson and other early proponents of administrative government christened it an "apolitical science" because of the administrative agency's technocratic approach to serving the public interest.[7] From its inception, the administrative branch was conceived of as antithetical to the political process; as a result, its conformity with the constitutional doctrine of separation of powers was a point of contro-

---

4. Hart and Wechsler, Federal Courts 156 (2d ed. 1973).

5. This date is used because it marks the creation of the first independent federal agency, the Interstate Commerce Commission. J. Rohr, To Run a Constitution 90 (1986). It is also the date of the publication of Woodrow Wilson's influential essay "The Study of Administration."

6. Breger, Thoughts on Accountability and the Administrative Process, 39 Admin. L. Rev. 399, 400 (1987).

7. J. Rohr, To Run a Constitution 65–69 (1986).

versy. By the 1930s, the "apolitical" administrative branch was being challenged from two viewpoints. One view, represented by the organized bar and conservative critics of the New Deal, urged that agencies behave procedurally more like courts. The other view, that of certain New Dealers themselves, was that independent commissions should be susceptible to greater presidential control and political accountability.[8] These two views were incorporated in the Administrative Procedures Act of 1946, the first major regulatory statute for administrative agencies.

The Administrative Procedures Act of 1946 (APA) attempted to codify and regularize existing agency practices and to provide uniform standards for judicial review of the procedural fairness of agency decision making. The APA is akin to a bill of rights for the administrative state.[9] While basically a reflection of the way agencies already behaved, it did set new general standards for hearing practices and for more judicialized adjudication procedures within agencies.[10] The APA also included a sketchy provision for agency rule-making procedures; the objective was to provide for public comment on, and thus popular input into, agency decision-making procedures.[11] The APA specified that agency rules were subject to judicial review to provide a judicial check on possible arbitrary actions or abuses of rule-making discretion.[12] Section 702 of the APA attempted to codify nonstatutory rules about standing, to afford access to court to a "person suffering legal wrong or adversely affected or aggrieved by agency action within the meaning of a relevant statute." Federal courts did not read section 702 as a static codification, and modified standing doctrines in accordance with contemporary policy needs.[13]

In the 1950s and 1960s, issues of administrative procedure took a backseat to more critical and immediate political problems. But Congress did commission several studies during this period to explore the

---

8. Breger, Thoughts on Accountability and the Administrative Process, 39 Admin. L. Rev. 399, 403 (1987).

9. J. Rohr, To Run a Constitution 157 (1986).

10. M. Shapiro, Who Guards the Guardians? 39–40 (1988).

11. M. Shapiro, Who Guards the Guardians? 43–44 (1988). The provision is for what is known as "notice and comment" rule-making. See 5 U.S.C. §553(b)–(c).

12. P. Cooper, Public Law and Public Administration 115 (1988).

13. S. Breyer and R. Stewart, Administrative Procedure and Regulatory Policy 922 (1979).

status of popular access to administrative proceedings,[14] and partially in response to some of these findings on agency operations, federal programs of the late 1960s began to mandate more procedural protections for citizens' rights in the agencies' implementation of policy. Although many of these programs endorsed the broad objective of administrative accountability, the precise scope of that objective was often left to judicial construction.

For example, beginning with the social service programs of the Johnson administration, the federal government encouraged "maximum feasible participation" in the administration of certain federal grants. Several federal programs, including Housing and Urban Development's "Model Cities" program, required community participation, either in the form of citizen boards with legal authority over program decisions or citizen advisory committees.[15] The federal courts soon were involved in an endless round of litigation over the specific meaning of this "maximum feasible participation" requirement. The Supreme Court averted the conflict by denying certiorari in *Rizzo v. North City Area-Wide Council*,[16] a case dealing with citizen participation in the implementation of the Model Cities program.[17] The objective of widespread citizen participation in the administration of federal programs failed to come to fruition, partly because judicial intervention was ineffective in securing this kind of administrative accountability. Technological expertise tended to reinforce the dominance of program boards by administrative elites within the program's policy area.[18]

Statutory mandates for direct citizen participation in the administration of federal grants eventually gave rise to agency enabling statutes providing broader public access to rule-making proceedings. The "pluralization" of the federal administrative process meant encouraging participation by interested parties other than those under agency regulation. Such pluralization included statutory provisions granting "private rights of action" and compensation for litigation

---

14. P. Cooper, Public Law and Public Administration 86–89 (1988).

15. This requirement is found at 42 U.S.C. §3303(a)–(c) of the Demonstration Cities and Metropolitan Development Act. See M. and R. Kweit, Implementing Citizen Participation in a Bureaucratic Society 5–6, 106 (1981).

16. 406 U.S. 963 (1972).

17. See D. Horowitz, The Courts and Social Policy 68ff. (1977).

18. Advisory Commission on Intergovernmental Relations, Citizen Participation in the American Federal System 123, 131 (1979).

costs of public interest intervenors.[19] Various regulatory statutes enacted in the 1970s included broad standing provisions and citizen suit clauses expanding the class of persons who could enforce administrative regulations.[20] Agency statutes also awarded attorney and expert witness fees to public interest litigators; a plaintiff serving as a "private attorney general" could potentially recover costs if Congress had specifically provided for fee shifting in the relevant statute.[21] The thrust of the standing and compensation provisions during this period was to facilitate citizen representation in agency proceedings through litigation, and to supply an indirect popular check on administrative discretion.

In addition to statutory standing provisions and fee awards, the class-action suit—a claim by a litigating party that represents the unified interest of an injured group—also became an important representative tool in public interest litigation. The availability of the class action since the mid-1960s was enhanced by judicial decisions naming groups as rights bearers; the Warren Court decision of *NAACP v. Button,* in 1963, identified the lawsuit as a vehicle for vindicating social and political rights.[22] The class-action suit became an important legal device in mass tort, reapportionment, and civil rights litigation,[23] and the prevalence of such actions clearly indicated judicial receptivity to interest group representation through litigation.

---

19. M. Shapiro, Who Guards the Guardians? 116–17 (1988). "Private rights of action" extend to procedures for bypassing recalcitrant or lethargic agencies. For a comprehensive survey of such actions, see Brisbin, The Politics of Private Rights of Action (paper presented to the Southern Political Science Association, Atlanta, Georgia) (Nov. 3–5, 1988).

20. For example, the Federal Communications Commission specifies which parties are entitled to seek judicial review of licensing actions. See S. Breyer and R. Stewart, Administrative Law and Regulatory Policy 922 (1979). See also Clean Air Act of 1963, Amendments of 1970, 42 U.S.C. §7604(a); Occupational Safety and Health Act of 1970, 29 U.S.C. §660(a) (1982); and Consumer Product Safety Act of 1972, 15 U.S.C. §2060 (1982).

21. Note, Federal Agency Assistance to Impecunious Intervenors, 88 Harv. L. Rev. 1815, 1825 (1975); Alyeska Pipeline Service Co. v. Wilderness Society, 421 U.S. 240 (1975).

22. 371 U.S. 415, 429–30 (1963); Chayes, Public Law Litigation and the Burger Court, 96 Harv. L. Rev. 4, 27 (1982).

23. Congress sanctioned the class action as an important representative tool. For example, Title VII of the Civil Rights Act of 1964 made the victim of discrimination "the chosen instrument of Congress to vindicate a policy Congress considered of the highest priority." On studies of litigation as a political pressure tactic, see L. Epstein, Conservatives in Court 5–15 (1985); C. Vose, Caucasians Only (1959).

The early 1970s proved a significant period for administrative law reform. Standing to seek judicial review of agency actions was broadened, as was the right to participate in formal agency proceedings. Legal scholars were divided over which form of access accommodated the need for "public action" in administrative government, but there was consensus on the "interest representation" approach to administrative law.[24] The notion of "regulating the regulators" directly resulted from the predominance of pluralist political theory, which held that good public policy implied open competition among group interests. Not surprisingly, administrative law, following a pluralistic conception of politics, emphasized access to the rule-making process.[25] During this period, the gulf between politics and administration narrowed; the reforms increased administrative accountability to the public interest and thus the political legitimacy of the rule-making process.[26]

The federal courts, particularly the D.C. Circuit Court of Appeals, were actively involved in developing the interest-representation model of administrative law. A ground-breaking decision was *United Church of Christ v. Federal Communications Commission,* a D.C. Circuit case decided in 1966. Writing for a majority of the court, Judge Burger held that the FCC could not foreclose participation by members of the listening public in agency proceedings concerning the renewal of broadcast licenses.[27] The court expanded the standing of parties challenging the agency's decisions; further, in a reconsideration of the merits of the license denial, it held that the FCC was responsible for the legal fees of such public interest intervenors.[28] The result of *Church of Christ* encouraged further public interest litigation.

In addition to broadening statutory standing provisions, the interest-representation model of administrative law fostered "public ac-

---

24. See S. Breyer and R. Stewart, Administrative Law and Regulatory Policy 1013–14, 1024 (1979); R. Stewart, The Reformation of American Administrative Law, 88 Harv. L. Rev. 1669 (1975).

25. M. Shapiro, Who Guards the Guardians? 4–5, 110 (1988).

26. This was done, in the words of one scholar critical of the reforms, by introducing appeals procedures and dispute processes of "debilitating complexity." Harrington, Regulatory Reform: Creating Gaps and Making Markets, 10 Law and Poly. 293, 298 (1988).

27. 359 F.2d 994 (D.C. Cir. 1966).

28. 465 F.2d 519, 527–28 (D.C. Cir. 1972). See Note, Federal Agency Assistance to Impecunious Intervenors, 88 Harv. L. Rev. 1815, 1823 (1975).

tions,"[29] suits initiated by citizen and taxpayer plaintiffs in which the class of injured persons is the public at large, and the injury alleged is shared and abstract. Standing guidelines for public actions are usually not statutory, but derived from the "adverseness" requirement of Article III of the Constitution. Constitutional standing requires that a plaintiff prove injury-in-fact, governmental causation of the injury, and the suitability of a judicial remedy.[30] In addition to the formal Article III criteria, the Supreme Court added additional prudential requirements for constitutional standing. One prudential restriction of long duration concerned citizen and taxpayer plaintiffs' assertions of "undifferentiated injury" or generalized interest in constitutional governance.[31] Such public actions were usually denied standing, on the assumption that the political process best addressed generalized complaints about the operations of the federal government.[32]

In 1968 the Warren Court reassessed the prudential limits on standing in public actions and reconsidered the accountability function of taxpayer suits. In the case of *Flast v. Cohen,* the Court held that a taxpayer plaintiff had standing to challenge a federal expenditure on the grounds that it violated the establishment clause of the First Amendment.[33] *Flast* has been interpreted as consistent with the pluralization or interest-representation model of administrative law, and its liberalization of access to the federal courts affected judicial construction of statutory standing provisions.[34]

---

29. See, e.g., L. Jaffee, Judicial Control of Administrative Action 524–26 (1965).

30. Connelly, Congressional Authority to Expand the Class of Persons with Standing to Seek Judicial Review of Agency Rulemaking, 39 Admin. L. Rev. 139, 141–42 (1987).

31. P. Cooper, Public Law and Public Administration 192–93 (1988).

32. See Frothingham v. Mellon, 262 U.S. 447 (1923). See also S. Breyer and R. Stewart, Administrative Law and Regulatory Policy 922–23 (1979).

33. 392 U.S. 83 (1968). *Flast* articulated what was called the "nexus requirement," which plaintiffs in public actions had to satisfy to merit standing to sue. The plaintiff had to demonstrate a relationship between his status as a taxpayer and the challenged expenditure, as well as the fact that the challenged enactment exceeded a specific constitutional prohibition. See G. Gunther, ed., Constitutional Law 1545ff. (11th ed. 1985).

34. It is important to recognize the limits of *Flast,* particularly with respect to administrative accountability. The Warren Court was clearly more receptive to public actions than its predecessors. Nevertheless, the *Flast* majority was unequivocal that taxpayer status would "not be sufficient to allege an incidental expenditure of tax funds in the administration of an essentially regulatory statute." 392 U.S. at 102. See B. Schwartz, Administrative Law 460 (1976).

Judicial sponsorship of the interest-representation model of administrative law also occurred in other areas of administrative procedure. For example, courts began to require that agencies keep "rule-making records" of public comments and agency responses made during rule-making hearings. In reviewing agency actions, courts employed the "hard look" doctrine, scrutinizing these written records and requiring that agencies reach their final rule through consideration of the facts in the record.[35] Both judicial reformers and scholars of this period held that good rule-making procedures should accurately sum group preferences, thereby producing tenable substantive rules.[36] Clearly, administrative law during the 1970s assumed that the bureaucracy need not be elected to fulfill a representative function.[37]

This belief in the political responsiveness of public administration began to break down as reformers were confronted with the realities of public intervention in the administrative process. Commentators on group litigation began to be less confident about the possibility of pluralism within administrative government. Attention turned to special interest lobbies, whose narrow interest base made them "nonmediating groups"—forces likely to attempt to co-opt or constrain administrative agencies.[38] The consensus of this post-pluralist commentary was to reject the assumption that competing interests would be equally represented, or that a rough balance among interest groups would exist in agency proceedings.[39] Given the possibility of agencies'

---

35. M. Shapiro, Who Guards the Guardians? 48–49 (1988); Breger, Thoughts on Accountability and the Administrative Process, 39 Admin. L. Rev. 399, 406 (1987). See also C. Sunstein, Deregulation and the Hard Look Doctrine, 1983 Sup. Ct. Rev. 177.

36. This goal is even more clearly illustrated by a recent reform known as "negotiated rule-making." Negotiated rule-making requires that administrative disputes be settled through arbitration proceedings between an agency and relevant interest groups. It has been used by OSHA in rule-making to settle what are recognized as interest rather than rights disputes. See Perritt, Negotiated Rule Making before Federal Agencies, 74 Geo. L.J. 1625, 1630 (1986); Perritt, A Broad View of Dispute Resolution, 29 Vill. L. Rev. 1221, 1221–29 (1984); Susskind and McMahon, The Theory and Practice of Negotiated Rulemaking, 3 Yale J. on Reg. 133 (1985); Administrative Conference of the U.S., Recommendation 82-4 (1982), codified at 1 C.F.R. §305 (1986). For a critical discussion of regulatory negotiation, see C. Harrington, Regulatory Reform: Creating Gaps and Making Markets, 10 Law and Poly. 293 (1988).

37. J. Rohr, To Run a Constitution 100 (1986).

38. A. Etzioni, Capital Corruption 202–8 (1984).

39. D. Yates, Bureaucratic Democracy 117 (1982); Stewart, The Discontents of Legalism: Interest Group Relations in Administrative Regulation, 1985 Wis. L. Rev. 655.

"capture" by special or regulated interests, and the belief that bargaining among competing groups could not be relied on to produce rules serving the public interest, courts took a different approach to administrative accountability. By the late 1970s, courts were demanding that rule-making be synoptic—that agencies demonstrate that they had made the substantively best policy.[40] Administrative law during the 1980s required once again a technocratic rationality from agencies.

Oddly enough, the post-pluralist critique of "politics as usual" for administrative government was somewhat nostalgic—recalling the nineteenth-century conception of the administrative process as insulated from group forces in politics.[41] The revival of the "apolitical science" concept included the abandonment of the pluralist enterprise of administrative representation. As a contemporary scholar of administrative procedure has argued, "Attempts to constitutionalize participation in the formation of governmental administrative policy ... to capture it somehow as a determinate constitutional right that goes beyond participation in electoral politics ... are unlikely to yield satisfaction."[42]

Such comments would seem to deflate the whole enterprise of articulating a conceptualization of administrative representation. Yet the present cynicism about administrative accountability does not vitiate the importance of access to courts as a vital link between politics and administration. Neither does a determined nostalgia for apolitical administrative government eradicate the need for accountability. Our review of the history of the administrative branch inspires an obvious question: did the decisions of the Burger Court resist or conform to the trends of the 1970s and 1980s in administrative law? More specifically, were the decisions of the Burger Court responsive to the post-pluralistic revisions of administrative procedure? To address the relationship between the work of the Burger Court and the changing conceptions of administrative accountability, this chapter

---

40. M. Shapiro, Who Guards the Guardians? 52–54, 126 (1988).

41. Breger, Thoughts on Accountability and the Administrative Process, 39 Admin. L. Rev. 399, 415 (1987).

42. J. Mashaw, Due Process in the Administrative State 260 (1985). Mashaw's fear in constitutionalizing participation in administrative processes is the judicial creation of "dysfunctional" innovations. Id. at 261. Even the language this commentator uses to criticize an interest-representation model of administrative law is technocratic, in keeping with the contemporary mentality about the administrative branch.

focuses on one procedural device—litigant standing to challenge agency actions. We will examine the Court's interpretation of standing provisions in agency enabling statutes, as well as its view of public actions brought under Article III guidelines.

The conceptualization of administrative representation will be employed to examine whether the Court's decisions on statutory and constitutional standing reflect a unified vision of the representative function of court access. As the conceptual type posits only that plaintiff access is the precondition of litigational representation in the administrative process, a very restrictive view of access might indicate judicial rejection of the notion of administrative representation. However, we must also be ready to see renewed judicial concern for plaintiffs' "representativity" as a refinement of representation through litigation.[43]

Following the methodology of previous chapters, we will classify each decision to ascertain whether it is consistent with, confirms, or contradicts the conceptualization. However, in order to accurately assess the significance of the decisions for the model of administrative representation, these categories must be defined more precisely. A decision will confirm the conceptual type if it broadly endorses pluralization of the administrative process through relaxed access to the courts. A decision will be consistent with the conceptual type if plaintiff standing is qualified—for example, if the plaintiff's representativity is emphasized—but not abrogated. Finally, a decision will contradict the conceptual type if it constitutes a clear repudiation of the representative utility of access to court.[44] This more rigorous system of classification avoids erroneously interpreting differences between the Warren and Burger Courts as absolute rejection of the conceptualization of administrative representation.

We will first examine the Burger Court's decisions on the parameters of statutory grants of standing to challenge agency actions. Statutory standing, sometimes referred to as a grant of a "private right of action," involves greater judicial deference to congressional judg-

---

43. "Representativity" is a legal term, denoting whether a plaintiff in a class-action suit has the ability to "fairly and adequately protect the interests of the class." See Sosna v. Iowa, 419 U.S. 393 (1975); Fed. R. Civ. P. 23(a). On class actions and representativity generally, see P. Low and J. Jeffries, Civil Rights Actions 659–64 (1988).

44. For purposes of classification in this chapter, the "irrelevant" category will not be employed.

ment. However, within the limits of statutory construction, the Burger Court left its mark on administrative accountability. Since statutory standing intertwines with other developments in administrative procedure, I will also note the interaction between the Court's decisions on access and its decisions on the rule-making procedures governing agency deliberations.

A subsequent section discusses the Burger Court's decisions on public actions—the use of litigation to represent generalized public grievances against the government or its agents. This section focuses in particular on whether the Court's determinations about constitutional standing under Article III contributed to a unified vision of litigational and, ultimately, administrative representation.

Representation through Litigation I: Statutory Standing

As noted in the previous discussion of the historical developments in administrative law, the early 1970s was a period of great reform of agency procedures. The Burger Court began its scrutiny of the administrative process during the pluralization of access to administrative proceedings, and on the heels of *Flast*'s liberalization of public actions. The relaxation of standing requirements for plaintiffs challenging agency rule-making was a large part of broader access. Not surprisingly, the first Burger Court decisions on issues of statutory standing were consistent with the changing attitude of the federal government toward administrative accountability.

A good example of this heightened accountability is *Association of Data Processing Service Organizations v. Camp*,[45] decided in 1970. The case concerned a competitor's suit against banks offering data processing services. Under the Bank Service Corporation Act of 1962, "no bank service corporation may engage in any activity other than performance of bank services for banks."[46] The standing question in *Camp* was whether the complainant data processing service organization fell within the class of "persons" protected or regulated by the act. The plaintiff's standing in *Camp* turned on the meaning of the APA's grant of a right of action to a person "aggrieved by agency action within the meaning of a relevant statute."[47]

---
45. 397 U.S. 150 (1970).
46. 12 U.S.C. §1864.
47. 5 U.S.C. §702.

Writing for the Court, Justice Douglas held that the economic harm that the data processing service organization stood to suffer plainly constituted injury-in-fact under Article III. As to whether the organization's legal rights were protected by the act, Douglas argued that the organization was "arguably within the *zone of interests* to be protected or regulated by the statute."[48] Thus, no explicit statutory provision in the Bank Service Act was necessary to confer standing. The result of *Camp* and its companion case, *Barlow v. Collins*,[49] broadened the availability of judicial review for groups affected by agency action. The zone-of-interests test was clearly a pluralist approach to the administrative process; both the result and the reasoning of *Camp* are confirmation of the conceptual type of administrative representation.

The Court's tightening of the formal rule-making procedures that agencies employed under the APA roughly coincided with *Camp*'s relaxation of standing barriers. *Camp*'s extension of the availability of judicial review presupposed that agency rule-making generated a comprehensive written record, as such a record would be necessary for courts to determine whether agencies had exercised their discretion reasonably.[50] The 1971 decision of *Citizens to Preserve Overton Park v. Volpe*[51] complemented *Camp*'s position on standing; rule-making reforms became part of the interest-representation model of administrative law.

In *Overton Park*, the Court held that the rule-making guidelines of the APA required that, before courts could rule on an agency's action, they had to review the record of notice and comment proceedings. This record was to be a transcript of proceedings, supplemented by the agency's explanation of the grounds for its decision. *Overton Park* was an activist step toward pluralization of administrative procedure for a simple reason: the APA did not specify that such a supplementary record of explanation was necessary in agencies' informal adjudication.[52] *Overton Park* acknowledged that the notice and comment

---

48. 397 U.S. at 156.
49. 397 U.S. 159 (1970) (standing of tenant farmers to challenge regulations under the Food and Agriculture Act upheld).
50. Stewart, Vermont Yankee and the Evolution of Administrative Procedure, 91 Harv. L. Rev. 1804, 1815 (1978).
51. 401 U.S. 402 (1971).
52. The APA does not require an evidentiary record of either notice and comment rule-making or informal adjudication of agencies. See 5 U.S.C. §556(e); 5 U.S.C. §553 (1976).

proceedings required by the APA did not always provide an adequate record for judicial review; to overcome this, the decision mandated "hybrid" rule-making procedures that would produce a documentary record for administrative and court review.[53]

Despite *Overton Park*'s confirmation of the pluralization of the administrative process espoused in *Camp,* the Burger Court did not demonstrate unwavering support for representation through litigation; subsequent standing decisions abandoned *Camp*'s broad zone-of-interests analysis.[54] In a series of statutory standing decisions in the early 1970s, the Court sharpened the requirement of litigants' injury-in-fact, while narrowing the standing provisions of the APA. This development is illustrated by *Sierra Club v. Morton,*[55] in 1972, which concerned a public interest organization seeking an injunction against the U.S. Forest Service to prevent development of national parkland. Representatives of the Sierra Club argued they had standing to sue based on section 702 of the APA;[56] however, they did not assert a specific injury on the part of individual members. Instead, the Sierra Club sued as a membership corporation with "a special interest in the conservation of national parkland," arguing that development would adversely affect the natural scenery of the park and impair its enjoyment by future generations. *Sierra Club* almost qualifies as a "public action" of generalized grievance, except that the plaintiffs were premising their standing claim on an act of Congress.

Stewart's opinion for the Court avoided the zone-of-interests test by holding that the plaintiffs had not satisfied the injury-in-fact requirement of Article III. Therefore, the organization's standing to sue was denied. Stewart argued that a "special interest" in the subject of conservation did not entitle the Sierra Club to access to the courts—absent personal injury to a club member.[57] Stewart stressed that organizational litigants must show that they represent individual members' interests. Because of this emphasis, and particularly in light

---

53. Harrington, Regulatory Reform: Creating Gaps and Making Markets, 10 Law and Poly. 293, 297–98 (1988); Stewart, Vermont Yankee and the Evolution of Administrative Procedure, 91 Harv. L. Rev. 1804, 1813–14 (1978).

54. Mashaw, Rights in the Federal Administrative State, 92 Yale L.J. 1129, 1141 (1983).

55. 405 U.S. 727 (1972).

56. See discussions supra at n.13.

57. 405 U.S. at 735.

of the Sierra Club's success in an amended suit,[58] it is reasonable to view the decision as consistent with the conceptual type of administrative representation.

In *Sierra Club,* and in several standing decisions that followed it, the Burger Court emphasized the plaintiffs' representativity. The Court focused on whether the interests of the aggrieved class were adequately represented by the party claiming standing.[59] In a 1972 civil rights action, *Trafficante v. Metropolitan Life Insurance Co.,*[60] the Burger Court recognized the standing of white plaintiffs to bring an action under the fair-housing provision of the Civil Rights Act of 1968. Although the complaint was directed against a landlord who discriminated against nonwhite apartment-seekers, the *Trafficante* plaintiffs asserted an injury indirectly resulting from this landlord's discriminatory behavior: whites' stigmatization for living and conducting business in a "white ghetto." Because these white plaintiffs' personal injury was representative of a class of interests, the Court granted standing. In terms of our conceptual type, *Trafficante* was a recognition of Congress's power "to create new interests, the invasion of which will confer standing."[61] Therefore, the decision is best viewed as confirming a pluralistic conceptualization of the administrative process.

The issue of plaintiff representativity of an injured class also figured prominently in the 1973 decision of *United States v. SCRAP.*[62] In *SCRAP,* the Court granted standing to representatives of a conservationist group seeking an environmental impact statement on actions by the Interstate Commerce Commission. The members of SCRAP asserted "economic, recreational, and aesthetic harm" resulting from the impact of increased rail freight charges on the recycling industry. Like the *Sierra Club* litigants, they based their standing claim on section 702 of the APA. Stewart's opinion for the majority held that, although environmental well-being is shared generally, the

---

58. In the amended suit, the Sierra Club alleged that its members used the forest area in question and would be affected by its development. See L. Carter, Administrative Law and Politics 218 (1983).
59. Floyd, Civil Rights Class Actions in the 1980's, 1984 B.Y.U.L. Rev. 1, 59 (1984).
60. 409 U.S. 205 (1972).
61. S. Breyer and R. Stewart, Administrative Law and Regulatory Policy 951 n.160 (1979); Connelly, Congressional Authority to Expand the Class of Persons with Standing to Seek Judicial Review of Agency Action, 39 Admin. L. Rev. 139, 145 (1987).
62. 412 U.S. 679 (1973).

widespread nature of the injury did not preclude standing for the individual claim. Stewart distinguished *SCRAP* from *Sierra Club* because of the presence of a specific injury on the part of the *SCRAP* litigants. This injury-in-fact "prevented the judicial process from becoming no more than a vehicle for the vindication of the value interests of concerned bystanders."[63]

In terms of the conceptual type of administrative representation, *SCRAP* clearly confirms the conceptualization. However, we should recognize that even as this decision was announced, interest group representation in administrative proceedings was taking a backseat to efficiency in the administrative process. By the mid-1970s, the political agenda was to retract broad judicial discretion over agency determinations.[64] Even as the Burger Court was debating the limits of relaxed standing, it reversed itself regarding the procedural rigidity in APA rule-making required by *Overton Park*.

In *United States v. Florida East Coast Railway*,[65] in 1973, the Court relaxed rule-making standards, as well as the requirements for a comprehensive record of proceedings. Rehnquist's majority opinion held that the APA did not require that agency rule-making conform to formal, quasi-adjudicative procedures—giving agencies impetus to shift to informal procedures in developing administrative policy. *Florida* was a significant decision with regard to citizens' access to the administrative process, as the return to more informal rule-making procedures handicapped litigants seeking to challenge the factual bases for agency decisions. Without a comprehensive record of administrative proceedings, judicial review of agency rules was dependent on evidence the agency deemed relevant, and judicial scrutiny of agency determinations would be limited to a rational basis analysis.[66] Thus, the result of *Florida* was to curtail public accounting of administrative conduct through judicial review.

The adjudicative, hybrid rule-making procedures required by *Overton Park* had been especially beneficial to environmental groups because participation in agency proceedings, and extensive opportunities for judicial review of agency actions, had allowed delay of nu-

---

63. 412 U.S. at 687.
64. G. Bryner, Bureaucratic Discretion 15, 41ff. (1987); P. Cooper, Public Law and Public Administration 266–68 (1988).
65. 410 U.S. 224 (1973).
66. S. Breyer and R. Stewart, Administrative Law and Regulatory Policy 492 (1979).

clear energy projects. In 1978, in *Vermont Yankee Nuclear Power Corp. v. Natural Resources Defense Council*,[67] the Burger Court seemed to reach the limits of its patience with obstructionist environmentalists.[68] A unanimous Court held that the APA established the maximum rule-making requirements imposed on agency decision making. Agencies were free to grant additional procedural rights in the exercise of administrative discretion, but reviewing courts were not to impose extra procedural requirements on agencies.[69] The Court implicitly rejected the notion of exclusive reliance on judicial review to ensure that agency decisions adequately address the social impacts of administrative choices.

Vermont Yankee illustrated that partisan policy disputes often underlay the judicial debate over formal rules. Courts were sensitive to the absence of strong social sentiment favoring environmental regulation—in stark contrast to public demand for restraint of trade or regulation of food and drugs.[70] To a certain degree, courts must weigh interests in administrative litigation, and the Burger Court's interest-balancing approach in *Vermont Yankee* was no exception. But the Burger Court's restraintist position in its last environmental cases clearly furthered congressional encouragement of the nuclear power industry. The National Environmental Policy Act of 1969 (NEPA) had directed federal agencies to prepare impact statements on actions significantly affecting the human environment.[71] However, in two 1980s cases concerning impact statements, the Court ruled that NEPA procedures could not be used to resolve policy in the courts under the guise of assessing risks associated with nuclear power.[72] In *Stryker's Bay Neighborhood Council v. Karlen*[73] in 1980 and *Metropolitan Edison Co. v. People Against Nuclear Energy*[74] in 1983, the Court construed NEPA as a merely formalistic obstacle to agency action.

The Court's approach in *Vermont Yankee* and the impact statement

---

67. 435 U.S. 519 (1978).
68. Marcel, Federal Environmental Litigation, 62 Or. L. Rev. 403, 435 (1983).
69. 435 U.S. at 524. Justice Rehnquist wrote the opinion of the Court.
70. Marcel, Federal Environmental Litigation, 62 Or. L. Rev. 403, 458 (1983).
71. 42 U.S.C. §4332(2)(c).
72. See Note, Supreme Court as Guardian of the Environment, 22 Duq. L. Rev. 479, 489 (1984).
73. 444 U.S. 223 (1980).
74. 103 S. Ct. 1556 (1983). This case concerned the adequacy of impact statements after the Three Mile Island incident.

cases deferred to governmental agencies, in that the decisions made no strong pronouncements in favor of groups' access to administrative proceedings. In other words, the pluralist balance in the political process was implicitly deemed sufficient to satisfy interest representation in administrative law. This attitude carried over to the Burger Court's construction of congressionally granted standing to sue, as evidenced by the Court's literal interpretation of standing provisions articulated in various agency statutes. Not only did injury have to directly accrue to the litigating party, but even given injury-in-fact, a litigant's standing could be denied if the relevant statute did not explicitly create a right of action for certain parties.

Several decisions in the early 1980s demonstrate this conservative approach to statutory standing provisions. In *Middlesex County Sewerage Authority v. National Sea Clammers Association*,[75] in 1981, the Court rescinded damages to commercial fishers under federal water pollution statutes because private enforcement actions were precluded by statute. Similarly, in *Bread PAC v. Federal Election Commission*,[76] in 1982, a unanimous Court rejected a suit under the Federal Election Campaign Act because the plaintiff was not one of the named classes entitled to certain expedited proceedings. Two years later, in *Block v. Community Nutrition Institute*,[77] the Court denied standing to consumer litigants seeking judicial review of milk market orders made pursuant to the Agricultural Marketing Agreement Act. Denial was based on an AMAA provision limiting complainants to milk handlers and producers. All three cases demonstrate that the Burger Court would not permit an action if the relevant statute failed to specifically provide for standing by a certain class of litigants.[78] All three decisions thus contradict the conceptual type of administrative representation, as least in terms of representation through litigation.

An exception to this retreat from the pluralization of administrative law was the 1982 decision of *Havens Realty v. Coleman*.[79] *Havens* concerned a class action brought under the Fair Housing Act, seeking injunctive relief against a realty company's "racial steering" housing policies. The litigants included "testers," their sponsoring organiza-

---

75. 453 U.S. 1 (1981).
76. 455 U.S. 577 (1982).
77. 104 S. Ct. 2450 (1984).
78. 104 S. Ct. at 2454.
79. 455 U.S. 363 (1982).

tion HOME, and neighborhood residents. A unanimous Court found actionable injury on the part of the first two groups of plaintiffs; the opinion seemed to suggest that the act barred courts from raising prudential barriers to standing.[80] Unlike the other standing decisions of the 1980s, *Havens* was consistent with the conceptualization of administrative representation. Further, its "presumption of reviewability"[81] appeared at odds with the Court's preclusion of judicial action in cases such as *Block* or *Bread PAC*. The decision also seemed to conflict with a later statutory civil rights action, in which the Court noted that traditional principles of preclusion should be applied to "the burgeoning use of administrative adjudication in the twentieth century."[82]

One can draw several inferences from the Burger Court's record on statutory standing questions. On the one hand, the Court's mixed record on representation through litigation paralleled changing attitudes toward the pluralization of the administrative process. Arguably, the Court followed the election returns by beginning to construe statutory rights of action more narrowly in the 1980s. Thus, as the concept of public representation in administrative proceedings fell out of political fashion, the Court construed agency statutes accordingly. However, one could also interpret the mixed record as evidence of the Burger Court's refinement of the idea of interest representation in administrative law. The movement from decisions like *Camp* to decisions like *Block* might constitute evidence of increasing judicial concern for plaintiff representativity, as well as increasing judicial deference to congressional judgment about appropriate litigants. Seen from this perspective, the later decisions do not retract public access to administrative proceedings, so much as they clarify that access should be a matter of representing specific (and/or statutorily specified) interests.

---

80. 455 U.S. at 373, 379. See Connelly, Congressional Authority to Expand the Class of Persons with Standing to Seek Judicial Review of Agency Rulemaking, 39 Admin. L. Rev. 139, 164 (1987).

It is important to note that in *Havens* the Court rejected the "third-party" standing of individual neighborhood plaintiffs because of insufficient proof of injury. Thus, the decision should be taken as moderately pro-interest representation in administrative law.

81. See S. Breyer and R. Stewart, Administrative Law and Regulatory Policy 896ff. (1979).

82. See *University of Tennessee v. Elliot*, 106 S. Ct. 3220, 3226 (1986), cited in Schwartz, Administrative Law Cases during 1986, 39 Admin. L. Rev. 117, 127 (1987).

It is difficult to assert definitively either interpretation of the statutory rulings on standing to challenge agency action. Perhaps this is to be expected, since the Burger Court presided over a period of changing attitudes about administrative accountability. But before we can draw conclusions about the decisions' conformity with the model of administrative representation, we must examine the Court's approach to "public actions." Public actions involve standing to seek judicial scrutiny of governmental conduct beyond agency conduct covered by specific statutes. Often, public actions involve taxpayer or public interest suits against some expenditure made by the federal government. The standing of public action litigants is based on Article III of the Constitution, which, arguably, allows for more judicial discretion and more judicial latitude to use standing to produce a certain policy result. The next section reviews the Burger Court's record on Article III standing, and its view of litigational representation absent a statutory mandate.

Representation through Litigation II: Public Actions

Absent statutory authorization, the Burger Court was reluctant to imply rights of action directly from the Constitution—reluctant, but not intractable. Nevertheless, the Burger Court's restrictive precedents on Article III standing promise to have a far-reaching impact on litigation in lower federal courts[83] because they reversed the Warren Court's open-door policy on public actions.

The 1968 *Flast* decision had held that a taxpayer could not employ the federal courts as a forum to air "generalized grievances" about the conduct of government; rather, in a public action, the taxpayer plaintiff had to assert a violation of a specific constitutional limitation on Article I taxing and spending powers. If the plaintiff demonstrated that the challenged enactment caused him concrete injury as a taxpayer, his appeal for judicial review was legitimate. The Burger Court retreated fairly consistently from *Flast*'s toleration of public interest litigation and from an expansive reading of standing in public action suits. However, as one scholar has commented, "The strength of the representational logic in the present doctrine of stand-

---

83. Maveety, Standing in the Pews: Access to Court in Church-State Litigation (paper presented to the Southern Political Science Association, Atlanta, Ga.) (Nov. 3–5, 1988).

ing shows itself nowhere more forcefully than in the Supreme Court's recent attempts to scotch it."[84]

A survey of the Burger Court's approach to citizen/taxpayer suits indicates that litigant representativity was even more narrowly defined than in the APA context. In two cases in 1974, the Court made clear that public action litigation did not mean that the public-at-large was an appropriate litigator. *United States v. Richardson*[85] denied taxpayers standing to challenge the confidentiality of CIA expenditures. The *Richardson* plaintiffs alleged a violation of section 9 of Article I, requiring a statement of account for expenditures of public money. Burger's majority opinion found the injury asserted to be common to all members of the public and, as such, a generalized complaint prohibited under the *Flast* guidelines. Burger stressed the "absence of any particular individual or class to litigate the claim";[86] to the five-judge majority, this made the subject a political question.[87] Powell's concurrence identified the dire consequences of granting standing in *Richardson*. "Allowing unrestricted taxpayer or citizen standing," he warned, "would significantly alter the allocation of power at the national level, with a shift away from a democratic form of government."[88]

The second 1974 case, *Schlesinger v. Reservists to Stop the War*,[89] involved a challenge to the membership of congressmen in the Armed Forces Reserve. The plaintiffs were members of the antiwar Reservists Committee, who based their standing claim on their status as citizens, taxpayers, and current or former reserve members. As in *Richardson,* the Court found that the action reflected a generalized grievance common to all citizens; further, the Court found no "logical nexus" between taxpayer status and the claim asserted.[90] The majority noted that the challenge in *Reservists* was not to Congress's taxing and spending power, but to the executive's permitting congressmen

---

84. Orren, Standing to Sue: Interest Group Conflict in the Federal Courts, 70 Am. Pol. Sci. Rev. 723, 736 (1976).
85. 418 U.S. 166 (1974).
86. 418 U.S. at 176–77, 179.
87. Four justices were unwilling to sound the death knell of taxpayer-initiated public interest lawsuits. Stewart's dissent likened the situation to that in *SCRAP:* "[S]tanding is not to be denied simply because many people suffer the same injury."
88. 418 U.S. at 188.
89. 418 U.S. 208 (1974).
90. 418 U.S. at 225–28.

to retain their reserve status.[91] Similar to Powell's concurrence in *Richardson,* Burger's majority opinion in *Reservists* sounded a hypothetical note of alarm: "The proposition that all constitutional provisions are enforceable by any citizen simply because citizens are the ultimate beneficiaries of those provisions has no boundaries."[92] Rather than settling the public action issue, the close decisions in *Richardson* and *Reservists* reveal that a nexus lies in the eye of the beholder. In terms of administrative accountability or litigational representation, both decisions contradict the conceptualization of administrative representation.

Another type of public action, which implies the notion of representation more directly, involves what are called "third-party intervenors." Such plaintiffs seek standing to challenge governmental conduct in order to vindicate the constitutional rights of third parties, as well as their own interests. Various prudential rules permit the assertion of third parties' rights: a substantial relationship may exist between the plaintiff and the third parties, or the third parties may be unable to assert their own rights.[93] Thus, third-party intervention also implies a "nexus" relationship—between the plaintiff's interests and those of third parties not present in the suit. With respect to these types of suits, the Burger Court's record was mixed. In an extremely complex example of standing litigation, *Warth v. Seldin,*[94] in 1975, the Court rejected a public action based on plaintiffs' taxpayer status, associational standing,[95] and third-party intervention.

The *Warth* case was addressed in Chapter 3, since it concerned a local zoning decision relevant to the conceptualization of territorial representation. However, *Warth* is also pertinent to representation through litigation—mainly for its restriction of judicial avenues for public challenges to governmental action. The restrictive zoning policies of the city of Penfield, New York, prevented the construction of

---

91. Stewart filed a concurrence; three justices—Douglas, Brennan, and Marshall—dissented from the ruling.

92. 418 U.S. at 227.

93. G. Gunther, ed., Constitutional Law 1574ff. (11th ed. 1985). See generally Note, Standing to Assert Constitutional *Jus Tertii,* 88 Harv. L. Rev. 423 (1974).

94. 422 U.S. 490 (1975).

95. An association has representational standing when its members have standing to sue in their own right, when the interests it seeks to protect are germane to the organization's purpose, and when neither the claim nor the relief requires participation of individual members in the suit. See NAACP v. Alabama, 357 U.S. 449 (1958).

homes affordable to persons with low to moderate incomes. The alleged effects of the zoning were a tax increase in neighboring Rochester to fund the area's required low-income housing, as well as the exclusion of prospective low-income and minority home buyers from Penfield. In a lengthy recitation, Powell's majority opinion rejected the standing of all three categories of plaintiffs complaining about these effects. Powell's reasoning centered largely on the absence of a nexus between the plaintiffs' interests and their asserted role as third-party intervenors.

Briefly, the Court held that neither Rochester taxpayers, nor minority persons who had looked for housing in Penfield, had constitutional interests of their own to assert. Neither group had suffered injury-in-fact, for the plaintiffs had failed to satisfy Article III's "causation" requirement.[96] The claims of both the taxpayer and minority plaintiffs were really assertions of harm to third parties, that is, persons of low to moderate income actively excluded by Penfield. The plaintiffs actually asserting third parties' rights were the various housing organizations; but in raising the "putative rights of third parties," the associational plaintiffs had demonstrated "none of the exceptions that allow such [third party] claims."[97] Interestingly, *Warth* occasioned one of the first impassioned remonstrances from a dissenter, who argued that the Court's rejection of standing "[could] be explained only by an indefensible hostility to the claim on the merits."[98] Leaving aside the veracity of this accusation, *Warth* certainly made public actions a more difficult undertaking. The decision elevated plaintiff "representativity" to ludicrous heights, and can only be seen as contradicting our conceptual type.

In the 1976 decision in *Singleton v. Wulff*,[99] the Court was somewhat more lenient in granting standing. Blackmun's majority opinion recognized the standing of physicians to challenge the terms of Missouri's abortion statute—standing that included asserting the interests of impecunious women seeking abortions.[100] The Court also held that physicians were the proper party to challenge state interference with abortion decisions; the justices implied that without the partici-

---

96. 422 U.S. at 507, 510.
97. 422 U.S. at 514.
98. 422 U.S. at 420 (Brennan, J., dissenting).
99. 428 U.S. 106 (1976).
100. 428 U.S. at 112–13.

pation of physicians in the suit, patients' rights would necessarily be diluted.[101] *Singleton* permitted the third-party intervention as an additional jurisdictional avenue for public actions; as such, the decision is consistent with the conceptual type of administrative representation.

Despite the Court's liberal attitude toward constitutional standing guidelines in *Singleton,* the Court dismissed third-party intervention in a second case in 1976. In *Simon v. Eastern Kentucky Welfare Rights Organization,*[102] an organization representing indigents challenged an IRS classification of certain hospitals as "charities" for tax purposes. The plaintiff organization complained that since many of the hospitals so classified did not readily accept indigent patients, the IRS was encouraging policies harmful to poor persons' interests. The Court did not even reach the question of whether a third party could challenge IRS treatment of another; the organization had failed to establish actual injury to its own interests or to those of its indigent clients. Powell's opinion for the Court found the harm alleged to be speculative only and to fall short of Article III's injury-in-fact requirement.[103] More consistent with the ruling in *Warth* than in *Singleton, Simon* is best seen as contradictory of the conceptual type of administrative representation.

Singleton was not the only decision granting standing in a public action. The 1978 decision of *Duke Power Co. v. Carolina Environmental Study Group*[104] illustrated a fairly generous view of the nexus relationship between plaintiffs' interests and the action challenged. In *Duke Power,* citizen and public interest group plaintiffs challenged the constitutionality of a federal statute that limited the liability of power companies for nuclear accidents.[105] The injury alleged by the *Duke* plaintiffs consisted of environmental and monetary risks associated with the development of nuclear power, as well as a restriction of their common law remedies for industry accidents. To establish a

---

101. The four justices who joined the broad third-party intervenor decision were Blackmun, Brennan, White, and Marshall. See G. Gunther, ed., Constitutional Law 1576 (11th ed. 1985).

102. 426 U.S. 26 (1976).

103. 426 U.S. at 41. Brennan wrote an opinion concurring in part, and objecting to the Court's view of injury in fact. See 426 U.S. at 55ff.

104. 438 U.S. 59 (1978).

105. The Price-Anderson Act, 42 U.S.C. §2210 et seq. The Act was upheld against the merits of the appellees' due process claim. 438 U.S. at 82–94.

causal link between the challenged statute and the development of Duke Power, the plaintiffs asserted that the liability limitation facilitated plant construction. Burger—the author of the restrictive *Richardson* and *Reservists* rulings—wrote the majority opinion granting plaintiffs' standing to challenge the terms of the statute.

Some commentators have suggested that *Duke Power* adopted guidelines for constitutional standing less restrictive than those for statutory challenges to administrative action.[106] More accurately, the Court scrupulously distinguished the *Duke* situation from earlier public action precedents. For example, the prudential limitations on standing in *Reservists* and *Warth* were not relevant, because the harm in *Duke Power* was not a generalized grievance.[107] Further, the Court clarified that the rules for taxpayer standing—specifically, the nexus between plaintiff status and the type of legislative enactment challenged—were not relevant to other sorts of public actions.[108] *Duke Power* perhaps invites the claim that "the law of standing [is] in a state of hopeless confusion that invites ad hoc manipulation of doctrine."[109] In terms of our conceptualization of administrative representation, however, the decision is consistent with a conception of litigation as a form of political access.

Following this mixed record came the Burger Court's most important precedent on Article III standing: the 1982 decision of *Valley Forge v. Americans United for the Separation of Church and State*.[110] *Valley Forge* has been interpreted as a quiet repudiation of *Flast*'s view of public actions, but, quiet or not, it has already had a significant impact on the actions of the Rehnquist Court.[111]

The plaintiffs in *Valley Forge* were challenging the disbursement of surplus federal property by HEW, authorized under the Federal Property and Administrative Services Act of 1949. Some of this property had been transferred to Valley Forge Christian College, a sectar-

---

106. S. Breyer and R. Stewart, Administrative Law and Regulatory Policy 959 (1979).
107. 438 U.S. at 72–75.
108. 438 U.S. at 78–79.
109. See Brennan's partial concurrence in Simon v. EKWRO, 426 U.S. 26 (1976). See also Tushnet, The New Law of Standing: A Plea for Abandonment, 62 Cornell L. Rev. 663 (1977).
110. 454 U.S. 464 (1982).
111. See Maveety, Standing in the Pews: Access to Litigation on Church-State Issues (paper presented to the Southern Political Science Association, Atlanta, Ga.) (Nov. 3–5, 1988).

ian educational institution. Asserting standing on behalf of concerned citizens and taxpayers, Americans United for the Separation of Church and State argued that the transfer violated the establishment clause of the First Amendment. Although the appellate court had found the claim of taxpayer standing to be dubious,[112] it sustained the plaintiffs' standing as citizens. Such standing turned on the injury to the citizen's right to a government of separation between church and state. Rehnquist's opinion for the majority repudiated the lower court's broad tolerance for citizen-initiated actions, and, perhaps to avoid the liberal *Duke Power* precedent, recast the action as a taxpayers suit. He then ruled that the plaintiffs' taxpayer status was inapposite, because the challenged action was made pursuant to Congress's power under the property clause of Article IV, not the taxing and spending power. Further, applying *Flast*'s "nexus test" for taxpayer standing, Rehnquist found the plaintiffs' claim to be merely the "generalized interest of all citizens in constitutional governance."[113]

Four justices dissented from the Court's failure to find "distinct, palpable, and actionable injury" on the part of the *Valley Forge* plaintiffs. In an angry dissent, Brennan recast the dispute in the case as an establishment clause battle. Similar to his charge in *Warth*, Brennan argued that the majority was venting its hostility to the Farmers' understanding of the establishment clause by "slam[ming] the courthouse door against plaintiffs who are entitled to full consideration of their claims on the merits."[114] This reading of the Burger Court's political use of standing doctrine "as a disguised method of deciding cases on the merits" has been echoed by several commentators.[115] Legal commentators have also supported Brennan's assertion that, in taxpayer suits, the Court should focus on the fact of questionable congressional expenditures, not on an expenditure's authorization under Article I, section 8.[116]

---

112. The reason being that the real interest of Americans United was not the saving of tax dollars, but the securing of "constitutional governance." See 454 U.S. 464, 470 (1982).

113. 454 U.S. at 479–80, 482–83.

114. 454 U.S. at 513. Brennan was joined in dissent by Marshall and Blackmun. Stevens wrote a separate dissent.

115. Nichol, Standing on the Constitution: A comment on *Valley Forge,* 61 N.C.L. Rev. 798 (1983); Note, Abusing Standing: Furthering the Conservative Agenda, 29 Wm. and Mary L. Rev. 387, 388 (1988). See also Rathjen and Spaeth, Denial of Access and Ideological Preferences, 36 W. Pol. Q. 71 (1983).

116. See 454 U.S. at 511–12. Note, Taxpayers' Suits: Standing Barriers and Pecuniary Restraints, 59 Temp. L.Q. 951, 961 (1986).

Clearly, the thrust of the *Valley Forge* opinion was to deflect controversies about governmental conduct from the judiciary to the political branches. Assertions of "personal rights" to have the government act in accordance with one's view of the Constitution could not "satisfy the requirements of Article III without draining those requirements of meaning."[117] The Court's seeming recognition of a need to prevent litigation from actually becoming a form of group representation animated many of its rulings on public actions. Rehnquist's stance in *Valley Forge* was similar to the Court's view in *Richardson* and *Reservists*. Like those decisions, *Valley Forge* must be interpreted as contradicting the conceptual type of administrative representation.

The repercussions of *Valley Forge* were felt almost immediately in the subsequent decision of *Allen v. Wright*,[118] in 1984. *Allen* concerned a challenge by parents of black public school students to the IRS continuation of tax exempt status for certain private, racially exclusive schools. The parents argued that this exemption constituted tangible financial aid to the schools and indirectly harmed their children's public school education. The argument of the *Allen* plaintiffs was reminiscent of the arguments raised in *Valley Forge* and in *Simon*, the case involving a challenge to certain hospitals' IRS classification as charitable institutions. Not surprisingly, the Court's opinion in *Allen* combined elements of these previous decisions.

O'Connor's majority opinion held that the plaintiffs had suffered no judicially cognizable or personalized injury as a result of the tax exemption because none of the plaintiffs' children had actually applied to the all-white schools. As in *Valley Forge,* their complaint constituted a generalized interest in a personal belief about constitutional governance. As for the private school exemption's financial effect on public schools, the causation requirement of Article III was not satisfied.[119] The *Allen* ruling again inspired an outcry from Brennan. He argued in dissent that "once again, the Court use[d] standing to slam the courthouse door, this time relying on the incantation of separation of powers."[120] *Allen* seemed to confirm the Court's earlier

---

117. 454 U.S. at 483.
118. 468 U.S. 737 (1984).
119. 468 U.S. 753–56, 757–58.
120. 468 U.S. at 766. Brennan cited in support of his position various scholarly writings on the Burger Court's approach to standing, among them L. Tribe, Constitutional Law §3–21 (1978).

observation: "The assumption that if the respondents have no standing to sue, no one would have standing, is *not* a reason to find standing."[121] *Allen* confirmed a view of public actions that contradicts the conceptualization of administrative and litigational representation.

The Burger Court's last decision on Article III standing did not disturb the trend of *Valley Forge* and *Allen,* but does call into question the accusations about certain justices' political maneuvering. In *Diamond v. Charles,* in 1986, the Court unanimously dismissed the standing of a physician to challenge Illinois' abortion law. *Diamond* was an odd case, because the plaintiff physician was appealing an injunction restricting various new regulations that Illinois had attempted to place on abortions. Illinois, however, was not challenging the injunction. Only the state, Blackmun held for the Court, had the "personal stake" to litigate to defend the validity of its statutes.[122] As for the physician's own stake in the issue, his "conscientious objection" to less regulation of abortion did not constitute actual and actionable injury under Article III.[123]

Diamond is most convincingly categorized as contradictory to the conceptualization of administrative representation because it limited the category of persons who could challenge governmental administration. The decision is an interesting postscript, however, to the public action issue: it suggests that the Burger Court's hostility to "litigational representation" was not an obvious surrogate for conservative policy-making.

Groups in the Administrative Forum

Clearly, the Burger years diminished judicial sponsorship of group litigation in the administrative process. More generally, the Court retreated from the earlier liberalization of standing to challenge governmental action. This retreat was more pronounced with respect to "public actions" than challenges to agency decision making. Of course, we should also note the Court's presumption against a "private right of initiation"—standing to challenge agency inaction or

---

121. Schlesinger v. Reservists, 418 U.S. at 227, cited in Valley Forge v. Americans United, 454 U.S. at 489.
122. 106 S. Ct. 1699, 1703–4 (1986).
123. 106 S. Ct. at 1705–6.

nonenforcement of rules.[124] In other words, the Burger Court was hardly activist in its view toward relaxation of statutory standing or Article III "case or controversy" provisions. Many of the Burger Court's decisions seemed to assume that the question of popular representation in governmental administration was primarily a political one; "public action" in the administrative process again meant action through the traditional forum of political representation in the legislature.[125]

Unfortunately, asserting that access was a "political question" did not rectify the problem of administrative accountability. The problem of administrative representation was in many ways analogous to the *Reynolds* situation. The judicial role in supervising political representation often requires activist inroads against legislative torpor. If litigants' access to judicial review of agency action is to be realized as effective representation, judicial intervention is necessary. Yet if we review the administrative decisions in terms of our conceptualization of affirmative representation through litigation, the Burger Court does not seem to have made many activist inroads. Its record of support for private rights of action was mixed, with its later decisions tending to construe statutory standing provisions rather narrowly. Likewise, the preponderance of its public action decisions restricted public interest plaintiffs' access to the judiciary, *Singleton* and *Duke Power* being the only exceptions. Given these findings, it would be hard to maintain that the Burger Court was not repudiating a form of group representation that would broaden administrative accountability.

On the other hand, the administrative representation decisions could be construed as reformative in indirect ways. The decisions were reactions to the expressive function performed by citizen group litigation; thus, even unsuccessful group legal action offered organi-

---

124. Heckler v. Chaney, 470 U.S. 821 (1985) (challenge to FDA's failure to scrutinize lethal injection executions denied). See Brisbin, The Politics of Private Rights of Action (paper presented to the Southern Political Science Association, Atlanta, Ga.) (Nov. 3–5, 1988). See also Sunstein, Review of Agency Inaction after *Heckler v. Chaney*, 52 Chi. L. Rev. 653 (1985).

125. The Burger Court increasingly treated administrative procedure, particularly standing issues, as a separation of powers question. The pre-*Flast* conception of standing excluded courts from "prescribing how the other two branches should function in order to serve the interests of the majority itself." See Scalia, The Doctrine of Standing as an Element of Separation of Powers, in Views from the Bench 200, 208 (M. Cannon and D. O'Brien eds. 1985).

zations greater publicity and could facilitate fund-raising and member support.[126] Further, as the Burger Court acknowledged, the claims of interest group litigants influence the debate over agencies' policy-making; citizen legal actions were effective, for example, in delaying certain environmental policies. The Court's curtailing available review procedures perhaps concedes how effective citizen litigation can be.[127] The judicial recognition of group litigation as a political tactic also bore fruit—in a more positive way—in civil rights class actions, because the Court viewed such class actions as a representational device.[128]

The verdict on the correspondence between the Burger Court's decisions and the conceptual type of administrative representation seems to turn on this issue of plaintiff representativity. The Court generally found litigation as representation to be more amenable to special interests than to broad public interest claims. Of course, the Court was not entirely insensitive to public actions as assertions of group rights, as the justices did not altogether reject the *Flast* ruling. What the decisions of the Burger Court do seem to confirm is the slow death of the pluralization of the administrative process. Thus, the Court's circumscribed conception of public action was a way of burying the pluralist vision of administration as merely group political struggle.[129] However, the Burger Court's decisions do not move toward apolitical, scientific governmental administration, but rather toward a more limited definition of group litigation as group political action. The Burger Court's administrative law decisions, rather than advocating the "debilitating complexity"[130] of the 1960s interest-rep-

---

126. Perritt, Negotiated Rule Making before Federal Agencies, 74 Geo. L.J. 1625, 1641 (1986).

127. See the discussion of *Vermont Yankee, supra* at 205ff.

128. Hutchinson, Class Actions: Joinder or Representative Device? 1983 Sup. Ct. Rev. 459, 503.

129. See M. Shapiro, Who Guards the Guardians? 136–37 (1988); Stewart, The Discontents of Legalism: Interest Group Relations in Administrative Regulation, 1985 Wis. L. Rev. 655.

130. This term, describing the highly judicialized administrative procedures of the 1960s and early 1970s, comes from Harrington, Regulatory Reform, 10 Law and Poly. 293, 298 (1988). She argues that the move away from accountability through litigation to nonadversarial negotiation "reconstitutes the public philosophy of interest group liberalism in a theory of political legitimacy associated with a minimalist state." Id. at 309. According to this view, the Burger Court's restriction of access to litigation constitutes an ideological position as well as a representation policy.

resentation model, illustrate an important part of the Burger Court's group-balancing approach to representation rights: fitting the right group interests with the right representation procedures. The conceptual type of administrative representation allows us to see that, at least with respect to plaintiffs' standing to challenge governmental action, the Burger Court left a record of concern for the *process* of political access to administrative proceedings. Thus, the Court's fairly restrictive view of a "representative" plaintiff was a way of protecting the viability of litigational representation, by preserving the notion of judicial resolution as a genuine, concrete solution—not a symbolic act of protest.

Though the administrative representation cases are not about elections or politics in the usual sense,[131] their concern for the integrity of the political process is common to the Burger Court's representation decisions more generally. Yet unlike some of the representation decisions we have discussed, the full impact of the Burger Court's opinions on interest group litigation does not await post-census reapportionment. Rather, the impact of the Burger Court's administrative law decisions, and our assessment of the uniqueness of the Court's doctrinal vision, depends on lower federal courts' compliance with these precedents.[132] While it is too soon to make any definitive judgments about judicial impact, it is clear that, with respect to standing to seek judicial review of agency actions, the Burger Court cannot be described as having merely continued the doctrines of its predecessor.

---

131. Although to many political scientists who study access to litigation, judicial "gatekeeping" devices such as standing are inherently political. See Rathjen and Spaeth, Access to Federal Courts: An Analysis of Burger Court Policy Making, 23 Am. J. Pol. Sci. 360 (1979); Taggart and DeZee, Substantive Access Doctrines in the U.S. Supreme Court: A Comparative Analysis of the Warren and Burger Courts, 38 W. Pol. Q. 84 (1985).

132. On the study of judicial impact, see Johnson, Law, Politics, and Judicial Decision Making: Lower Federal Court Uses of Supreme Court Decisions, 21 Law and Soc. Rev. 325 (1987); Songer, Alternative Approaches to the Study of Judicial Impact, 16 Am. Pol. Q. 425 (1988).

CHAPTER 8

Group Rights: Political Vigilance and Political Conflict

A recent study of group litigation behavior offered this appraisal of the judicial process:

> Judicial politics may not be significantly different from the legislative and executive processes, which are widely understood to be characterized by the presence of competing group interests.[1]

This statement, which acknowledges that interest groups compete for access to the courts in much the same way as they do for access to "political" forums, sheds some light on the phenomena we have been discussing: litigation on behalf of group representation rights. The purpose of this study has been to illustrate that group political access was the focus of representation law during the Burger years. Its approach was twofold. First, the study sought to demonstrate that the Burger Court made a unique and distinctive jurisprudential contribution and was not simply an atheoretical judicial interregnum. Second, and relatedly, the study sought to explicate and clarify the current status of representation law as a result of the Burger Court's work; my argument has been that constitutional representation policy has become more compatible with the reality of how political institutions operate and interact. That reality is one of group political action. Thus, the Burger Court's distinctive contribution to representation policy was to validate group-based representation claims across a range of political institutions and bring constitutional doctrine into harmony with pluralist politics.

Verification of these assertions requires an evaluation of the overall coherence of the Burger Court's vision of political representation.

---

1. L. Epstein, Conservatives in Court 156 (1985).

First, we must assess the role of group political access in contemporary representation policy. As this study has shown, group political access was both the subject and the object of litigation;[2] therefore, "litigational representation" was an act of political vigilance, as well as a means of establishing substantive representation rights. Did the Court's decisions endorse litigational representation in both senses, and, if so, did this endorsement contribute to a coherent vision of group representation? Second, we must assess the descriptive value of the study's taxonomy with respect to the Burger Court's record on representation issues. Was the Court's "group-balancing" approach actually a rank-ordering of the five conceptualizations of group representation, and, if so, how would this affect the explanatory utility of the taxonomy? We will assess each conceptual type's degree of support in the Court's decisions, and then use this information to evaluate the coherence and precedential importance of the representation law of the Burger years.

One of the questions with which we began this inquiry was whether the Burger Court's decisions realized the goal of "fair and effective representation." This question entails consideration of the importance of group political action for meaningful representation. We can begin to address this issue by recalling Harlan's dissent in *Reynolds v. Sims*. He warned that excessive judicial interference in the political process would "erode the vitality" of the democratic system and result in a "complacent" body politic.[3] In his prophecy of a complacent citizenry having no active interest in its representation rights, Harlan misread the future impact of *Reynolds*. The passive reliance on judicial remedies that Harlan feared did not come to pass. Instead, the successful solicitation of judicial scrutiny of representative structures encouraged a modern, pluralist version of political vigilance.

This pluralist version of citizen vigilance was litigation as the articulation of group political interests. Litigation becomes an act of political vigilance when its objective is to awaken governmental atten-

---

2. This statement is not meant to imply any comprehensive or systematic study of litigant types or litigation strategy. Rather, I am simply recognizing that any study of representation law must acknowledge that litigation itself can be a form of political expression or a group lobbying tactic. On groups' use of litigation other than to achieve substantive outcomes, see T. O'Neill, Bakke and the Politics of Equality 8, 19 (1985).

3. 377 U.S. at 589 (1964). See also W. Elliot, The Rise of Guardian Democracy 237–64 (1974).

tion to the need for political access for a group interest. Clearly this was the purpose of many of the representation claims brought to the Court—not only those concerning administrative agencies, but also plaintiffs' challenges to dilutionary electoral systems. Thus, group political access—in the form of litigation on behalf of group rights—has been important in making representation rights meaningful to a broader class of political actors. From the pluralist perspective, increased judicial supervision of the political process has also meant more opportunities for such litigational vigilance; legal victories securing group political influence precipitate related claims for judicial scrutiny of other political institutions.

Did the Burger Court view litigation as an expression of political vigilance, as a popular check on governmental institutions? While the Court became more strict on access to court in certain situations,[4] it also entertained various groups' equal protection and freedom of association claims. In terms of its receptivity to group political action as the subject of litigation, the Burger Court gave little indication of preference for Harlanesque citizen vigilance. Rather, as a result of the Burger years, litigation as a method of plural representation is firmly established, if not expanded in application. Through the acceptance of litigation as a representative act, the Burger Court's decisions did further "fair and effective" representation.

For litigation as political vigilance—as a means of scrutinizing representative government—to be instrumentally meaningful, it must also secure substantive rewards. As review of the case data indicated, the active solicitation of judicial remedies resulted in a doctrinal explosion in representation case law, as an increasing number of representative practices were subject to rights-based claims. The Burger Court's contribution to the case law was its recognition that group political rights, in addition to individual political rights, were a legitimate object of litigation. As both an expressive and an instrumental activity, then, litigational representation contributed to fair and effec-

---

4. A recent quantitative study of the Supreme Court's use of access doctrines found "little evidence to support the contention that the Burger Court has been more restrictive than the Warren Court with respect to expanding accessibility to the Supreme Court," although "the Burger Court has been somewhat more willing to lessen proper party standards, and has clearly decided a greater percentage of cases to both enlarge and restrict access." Taggart and DeZee, Substantive Access Doctrines in the U.S. Supreme Court: A Comparative Analysis of the Warren and Burger Courts, 38 W. Pol. Q. 84, 90–91 (1985).

tive representation, by asserting that group political access was an important part of the constitutional meaning of representation.

The notion of litigation as popular vigilance for modern pluralist politics did not necessarily entail that its collective outcome would be a coherent theoretical vision of group representation. An inescapable fact is that several conceptions of group representation operated simultaneously in the case law. As reflected by the conceptual types, no one approach to group representation dominated the Court's decisions. Rather, the justices were adept at balancing group-rights claims—at times using them as checks on one another.

Did this judicial juggling of group-rights claims mean that the Court was without a coherent vision, or that the taxonomy of group representation employed in this study was flawed? This leads us to a second evaluative question, concerning the descriptive utility of the conceptualizations of group representation and their degree of support in the Court's decisions. The five exogeneously constructed conceptualizations of group representation were drawn from prevailing conceptions of representation in American history, democratic theory, and contemporary politics. This taxonomy was used to label categories of decisions and compared relevant decisions' correspondence with each conceptual type. The results of these comparisons revealed a predominance of certain conceptualizations in the Court's decisions on group representation rights.

We can rank the five conceptualizations in terms of the decisions' degree of support for them. This ranking is somewhat inferential, and more useful as a review of the results under each of the five conceptual types than as a definitive ranking of the legitimacy of various group rights. In general, the descriptive correspondence between the conceptualizations of group representation and the case data varied. With respect to the first conceptual type, territorial representation, the Court's local government decisions constituted weak confirmation. However, the decisions were notable for their lack of a theoretical justification for "the geographic community" as a distinct, representable interest. In the case of the second conceptual type, corporatist representation, the decisions on special district government and political action by economic interests demonstrated strong consistency. However, the small number of cases in this sample makes generalizations about the importance of the conceptualization difficult. The third conceptual type, demographic representation, introduced the notion of "compensatory majoritarian competition," a relatively recent value in electoral districting. The decisions, involving race- and partisan-based districting as matters of statutory and constitutional law, were consistent with this conceptual type. However, both the conceptualization's sources and the Court's opinions offered fairly confused standards for assessing relative political influence and competitiveness of district elections. The fourth conceptual type presented a dualistic tradition of partisan representation; the party decisions echoed and reinforced this dualism. The Court's party decisions were those that most closely followed a theoretical conceptualization, and these decisions confirmed the descriptive utility of the conceptual type of partisan representation. Finally, the conceptual type of administrative representation indicated that the Burger Court conceived of administrative procedure and accountability as properly a part of the political process. Nevertheless, in terms of substantive outcomes, the administrative representation decisions were the least consistent with the conceptualization that purported to describe them.

With this information, we can rank-order the conceptual types in terms of their importance to and influence on the Court's decisions on group representation rights. The highest degree of consistency was seen between the partisan, corporatist, and territorial conceptualizations and the relevant decisions. At an intermediate level of consistency was the demographic conceptualization of representation. Because the latter dealt with cutting-edge issues of districting fairness, the ambiguity within these decisions suggests that the Burger Court's successor inherits a particularly confused doctrinal guide for the post-census reapportionment struggles. The lowest degree of consistency applied to the administrative conceptualization, which was generated from the interest representation model of administrative law. The standing decisions, including both agency-related complaints and public actions, seemed to illustrate the Burger Court's hesitancy about the appropriateness of pluralist conflict as a means to representation in administrative decision making.

While this ranking reveals something about the group interests most favored in the Court's decisions, the simultaneity of the conceptual types remains a striking aspect of the Burger Court's record. Was this simultaneity simply haphazard? Arguably, it was the product of consistent judicial disagreement about the legitimacy of representation for specific group interests: there were recognizable and durable voting blocs[5] in support of certain conceptualizations of group representation. For example, there was a "geographic bloc"—consisting of Rehnquist, Burger, Powell, Stewart, and later O'Connor—who supported the representation of geographic communities of interest. Another recognizable voting bloc, and a bloc that tended to oppose the territorial conceptualization, were the proponents of demographic districting policies for racial and political interests. The "demographic bloc" consisted of Brennan, Marshall, White, and Stevens. Blackmun and, notably, Powell also voted with this bloc, but not uniformly. Powell's concern was chiefly group-based districting to benefit parties; arguably, his vote in *Bandemer* expressed his position on partisan representation, rather than concern for demographic districting per se. While the four core supporters of the demographic conceptual type all acknowledged a group interest in voting, they expressed different reasons for doing so. Brennan and Marshall saw the aggregate voting right as furthering the participational goal of one person, one vote for minorities; White and Stevens viewed the idea of group-based districting as a legitimate constraint on the excesses of equipopulism. At times, the split among the justices paralleled tensions within conceptualizations of representation—for example, identifiable blocs formed with respect to the dualistic tradition of partisan representation. Douglas, Brennan, Marshall, and later Stevens tended to favor the claims of party members over party establishment controls. Conversely, Powell, Rehnquist, Burger, Stewart, and later O'Connor tended to favor the organization's dominance of party affairs, as well as to support traditional two-party competition. The "group-balancing approach" applied to the behavior of the justices themselves, as well as to the Court's decisions on representation; indeed, the very pluralism of the Burger Court was at least partly responsible for the group-balancing approach to representation questions.

Though it is worthwhile to comment on whether some justices

---

5. This is not to imply that any systematic study of bloc voting patterns or attitude scaling of individual justices has been done. On the use of such cumulative scaling techniques to examine voting behavior of judges, see Schubert, A Psychological Analysis of the 1960 Term of the Supreme Court, 56 Am. Pol. Sci. Rev. 90 (1962); Danielski, Values as Variables in Judicial Decision-Making, 19 Vand. L. Rev. 721 (1966); Spaeth, Idiosyncratic Factors in Decision Making, in Courts, Law and Judicial Processes 387 (S. Ulmer ed. 1981).

seemed predisposed to certain conceptualizations of group representation, more important than the voting blocs' composition is the inference one draws from the presence of such blocs. The simultaneous operation of the conceptual types of group representation was not haphazard; simultaneity, as well as any ranking of the conceptualizations, resulted from consistent patterns of judicial sponsorship for certain groups' access. But did the pluralism and interest balancing within the Court itself imply that its collective vision of political representation was a distorted, incoherent one?

We can partly answer this question by elaborating on how the conceptualizations are related to one another, and what preference for some conceptions of group representation might indicate. Clearly, none of our conceptual types of group representation provide sufficient political access for the cacophony of interests in American society. Indeed, the simultaneous operation of the five conceptualizations throughout American history suggests that plural interests require diverse, and often clashing, representative forums. This taxonomy of group representation thus articulates a politics of conflict—the conflict throughout American political history over how to implement and, at the same time, restrain democratic government. The interrelationship of the conceptual types lies in their collective vision of how group-based political disagreements should be accommodated: through complementary yet competing procedures whose purpose is, not to resolve, but to preserve conflict as the check on majoritarianism. Obviously, this "adversarial" vision of political representation is unlike the populist sentiment behind one person, one vote—a principle that deemphasized group political rivalry. One person, one vote celebrated the legitimacy of numerical majorities of individuals whose interests did not need to be aggregated in terms of plural group identity. As such, the equipopulist logic was antipluralist.

By contrast, the Burger Court's decisions envisaged representation as a series of overlapping procedures for plural political access. The rulings stressed the importance of assessing the "electoral context"[6] to evaluate whether groups' political access was competitive. The electoral context and, thus, political influence were broadly defined to

---

6. A Thernstrom, Whose Votes Count? 194 (1987). Thernstrom connects the emphasis on the electoral environment with the rulings on the Voting Rights Act.

include voting and district setting, as well as associational opportunities and legal action in the administrative forum. Representation rights were premised on pervasive group conflict across these electoral contexts; as such, the Burger record was the theoretical antipathy of Warren Court populism.[7] The coherence of the Burger Court's vision of political representation acknowledges that pluralism implies a politics of group conflict and, further, that representation law should protect outlets for its expression.

The idea that pluralism defines politics in terms of group conflict is hardly earth-shattering news to political scientists, but it was a concept alien to pre–Burger Court representation case law. The Warren Court's decisions pursued the laudable goals of individual political equality and majoritarian policy-making; both, of course, are foundational to pluralistic competition. However, in pursuit of these goals, the Warren decisions threatened to enshrine numerical majoritarianism as the solution for group-based political conflict. Although even the late Warren Court began to see this solution as unworkable, the task of retooling one person, one vote majoritarianism fell to the Burger Court. It did so by condoning nonarithmetic methods of interest articulation; majoritarianism was still a value, but representation law increasingly viewed "the majority" as one of many plural interests to be balanced.[8] During the Burger years, representation rights thus came to imply procedural opportunities for groups' expression of conflict.

Thus, the conflictual vision of politics that underlies and unites the exogenous conceptualizations of representation also helps to explain the distinctiveness of the Burger Court's doctrinal legacy. The Court's decisions were consistent with classical pluralism's support for institu-

---

7. Cf. Baker, Whatever Happened to the Reapportionment Revolution in the United States? in Electoral Laws and Their Political Consequences 257 (B. Grofman and A. Lijphart eds. 1986). Baker argues that the post-*Reynolds* record lacked any "fresh dialogue" about the "concept of representative government in a complex modern society." Instead, sober exploration of representation took place only sporadically, as problems arose. Id. at 267. Baker views the Burger Court as unwillingly bound to the equipopulous logic of the Warren precedents and, therefore, unable to make a mark of its own. Id. at 275–76.

8. For example, in the corporatist representation decisions, a "majority" interest was sacrificed in favor of the access rights of an economic group—even when those access rights appeared to violate one person, one vote.

tions that accommodate or arbitrate group conflicts.[9] The decisions revived one traditional method of conflict-as-check: federalism as local self-rule. In addition, new definitions of "competitive" group conflict were present in the corporatist and demographic representation decisions. The importance of the conflictual vision of politics is also seen in the partisan representation decisions. In that context, judicial disagreement about the utility of certain kinds of party conflict arguably led to the bifurcated view of partisan group rights. Interestingly, when conflictual politics were deemed unrelated to political competition, group access rights were not forthcoming. The obvious example here is the Court's record on citizen standing to challenge administrative action, where the Court retreated from an interest-representation model of administrative government. Why group conflict should be inappropriate in the administrative context was never adequately explained by the Court, perhaps suggesting that the Court could not completely accept that administrative access was a question of representation. Whether these standing precedents will affect the future use of litigational representation is a doctrinal quandary the Burger Court left to its successor.

What, then, is the likely impact of the Burger Court's balancing of group interest claims? As a preliminary observation, we see the Rehnquist Court already retreating from certain precedents. For example, in *Federal Election Commission v. Massachusetts Citizens for Life*,[10] in 1987, the Court chose not to broaden corporatist representation and drew distinctions between the political rights of expressive and commercial corporations.[11] Further, the Court also declined an opportunity to apply the *Bandemer* precedent on partisan districting to a California districting challenge,[12] and opted not to permit special representation for local subdivisions that conflicted with one person, one vote.[13] Of course, the Rehnquist Court has also continued certain representation policies: consideration of racial factors in municipal annexations, concern for party freedom of association in the opera-

---

9. For a general definition of the pluralist theory of government, see J. Shafritz, The Dictionary of American Politics 407 (1988).

10. 107 S. Ct. 616 (1987).

11. The political role of nonprofit business-oriented corporations—specifically, corporate expenditures in state candidate elections—was further curtailed in Austin v. Michigan Chamber of Commerce, 110 S. Ct. 1391 (1990).

12. Jurisdiction was denied in Badham v. Eu, 108 S. Ct. 1993 (1988).

13. Board of Estimate v. Morris, 109 S. Ct. 1433 (1989).

tion of primary elections, and extension of the populist party tradition of condemning patronage employment.[14]

Whether the Rehnquist Court carries on a jurisprudence of group interests depends in part on its need to balance and mitigate internal court conflict; this need becomes less pressing as justices with pronounced conservative philosophies come to dominate the Court. The conservative ideology represented by Ronald Reagan's judicial appointments emphasizes individual freedom and responsibility—not an ideology especially conducive to group entitlement claims. If the Rehnquist Court does begin to propound its own version of constitutional individualism, then the Burger Court's group-balancing approach to political representation will seem all the more distinctive.

In sum, the Burger Court's representation decisions reversed one person, one vote's weakening of the theoretical basis of pluralism.[15] Thus, the Court's vision of group representation was coherent, to the degree that the political philosophy of pluralism is coherent. Significantly, the portion of the *Reynolds* precedent that lives on through the Burger Court's work is the pluralist guarantee of fair and effective representation. The latter is not a constitutional right,[16] but became an important mediating principle for group access claims largely because of the Burger Court's influence. While the epitaph "the pluralist Court" or "the Great Balancer"[17] inspires little emotional fanfare, it implies a certain sagaciousness: the Burger Court's judicious reminder was that pluralism is a value hard to satisfy and, at times, conceptually unsatisfying.

---

14. City of Pleasant Grove v. U.S., 107 S. Ct. 794 (1987); Tashjian v. Republican Party of Connecticut, 107 S. Ct. 544 (1986); Rutan v. Republican Party of Illinois, 58 U.S.L.W. 4872 (June 19, 1990); on partisan representation, see also Eu v. San Francisco County Democratic Central Committee, 109 S. Ct. 1013 (1989).

15. See R. Dixon, Democratic Representation 475ff. (1968). But cf. Baker, Whatever Happened to the Reapportionment Revolution in the United States? in Electoral Laws and Their Political Consequences 257 (B. Grofman and A. Lijphart eds. 1986).

16. See Lowenstein, *Bandemer's* Gap: Gerrymandering and Equal Protection of the Laws (paper presented to the American Political Science Association, Chicago, Ill.) (Sept., 1987).

17. The Burger Court's predilection for interest balancing extended beyond representation issues; its First Amendment jurisprudence is replete with three-part and four-part balancing tests. See generally Blasi, The Rootless Activism of the Burger Court, in The Burger Court 198 (V. Blasi ed. 1983); Dorsen and Gora, The Burger Court and Freedom of Speech, in The Burger Court 28 (V. Blasi ed. 1983); Emerson, Freedom of the Press in the Burger Court, in The Burger Court 1 (V. Blasi ed. 1983); Emerson, First Amendment Doctrine and the Burger Court, 68 Calif. L. Rev. 422 (1980); Redlich, The Separation of Church and State: The Burger Court's Tortuous Journey, in The Burger Years 56 (H. Schwartz ed. 1987).

Appendixes

APPENDIX A

Table of Justices, the Warren and Burger Courts

The Warren Court (1953–69)

At the time of *Baker v. Carr* (1962)
Warren, C. J.
Black
Frankfurter
Brennan
Douglas
Clark
Whittaker
Stewart
Harlan

At the time of *Reynolds v. Sims* (1964)
Warren, C. J.
Black
Goldberg
Brennan
Douglas
Clark
White
Stewart
Harlan

Final term, at the time of *Kirkpatrick v. Preisler* (1969)
Warren, C. J.
Black
Fortas
Brennan
Douglas
Marshall
White

For the purpose of partially identifying "natural courts," the Justices of the Warren and Burger Courts are grouped by reference to the dates of significant districting cases.

234 / *Representation Rights and the Burger Years*

    Stewart
    Harlan

The Burger Court (1969–86)

    At the time of *Whitcomb v. Chavis* (1971)
    Burger, C. J.
    Black
    Blackmun
    Brennan
    Douglas
    Marshall
    White
    Stewart
    Harlan

    At the time of *Mahan v. Howell* (1973)
    Burger, C. J.
    Powell
    Blackmun
    Brennan
    Douglas
    Marshall
    White
    Stewart
    Rehnquist

    At the time of *UJO v. Carey* (1977)
    Burger, C. J.
    Powell
    Blackmun
    Brennan
    Stevens
    Marshall
    White
    Stewart
    Rehnquist

    Final term, at the time of *Davis v. Bandemer* (1986)
    Burger, C. J.
    Powell
    Blackmun
    Brennan
    Stevens
    Marshall
    White
    O'Connor
    Rehnquist

APPENDIX B

Table of Cases, Listed Chronologically

(Page numbers of discussions of cases in text follow case citations.)

Luther v. Borden, 7 How. 1 (1849)
Schechter Poultry Corp. v. U.S., 295 U.S. 495 (1935): 75
U.S. v. Butler, 297 U.S. 1 (1936): 75
National Labor Relations Board v. Jones-Laughlin Steel Co., 301 U.S. 1 (1937)
U.S. v. Carolene Products Co., 304 U.S. 144 (1938)
Smith v. Allwright, 321 U.S. 649 (1944): 154, 155
Colegrove v. Green, 328 U.S. 549 (1946): 21
Terry v. Adams, 345 U.S. 461 (1953)
Sweezy v. New Hampshire, 354 U.S. 234 (1957)
NAACP v. Alabama, 357 U.S. 449 (1958): 155, 173, 187
Gomillion v. Lightfoot, 364 U.S. 339 (1960): 102, 113
Baker v. Carr, 369 U.S. 186 (1962): 22, 24, 30, 101, 135, 138
NAACP v. Button, 371 U.S. 415 (1963): 194
Gray v. Sanders, 372 U.S. 368 (1963): 25, 35
Wesberry v. Sanders, 376 U.S. 1 (1964): 25, 36
Wright v. Rockefeller, 376 U.S. 52 (1964): 26, 27, 30, 110, 111
Reynolds v. Sims, 377 U.S. 533 (1964): 1, 13, 20, 21, 23, 27, 28, 29, 30, 31, 35, 37, 44, 67, 82, 85, 101, 187, 217, 222, 230
Davis v. Mann, 377 U.S. 678 (1964)
Lucas v. Colorado General Assembly, 377 U.S. 713 (1964): 23, 27, 28, 51, 139
Fortson v. Dorsey, 379 U.S. 433 (1965)
Carrington v. Rash, 380 U.S. 89 (1965)
Harman v. Forssenius, 380 U.S. 528 (1965): 44
United Church of Christ v. Federal Communications Commission, 359 F.2d 994 (D.C. Cir. 1966): 195
South Carolina v. Katzenbach, 383 U.S. 301 (1966)
Harper v. Virginia Board of Elections, 383 U.S. 663 (1966): 44–45
Burns v. Richardson, 384 U.S. 73 (1966)
Fortson v. Morris, 385 U.S. 231 (1966)
Kilgarlin v. Hill, 386 U.S. 120 (1967)
Moody v. Flowers, 387 U.S. 97 (1967)
Sailors v. Board of Education, 387 U.S. 105 (1967)
Dusch v. Davis, 387 U.S. 112 (1967)
Avery v. Midland County, 390 U.S. 474 (1968): 29, 30, 43, 80, 83
Flast v. Cohen, 392 U.S. 83 (1968): 196, 200, 208, 214, 218
Williams v. Rhodes, 393 U.S. 23 (1968): 155, 168, 169
Hunter v. Erikson, 393 U.S. 385 (1969): 52, 55

Allen v. State Board of Elections, 393 U.S. 544 (1969): 31–34, 113, 114, 115
Hadnott v. Amos, 394 U.S. 358 (1969): 155
Kirkpatrick v. Preisler, 394 U.S. 526 (1969): 30, 31
Wells v. Rockefeller, 394 U.S. 542 (1969): 31
Kramer v. Union School District, 395 U.S. 621 (1969): 45, 46
Cipriano v. City of Houma, 395 U.S. 701 (1969): 45, 46
Hadley v. Junior College District, 397 U.S. 50 (1970): 80
Association of Data Processing Service Organizations v. Camp, 397 U.S. 150 (1970): 200–201, 202
Goldberg v. Kelly, 397 U.S. 254 (1970)
City of Phoenix v. Kolodzieski, 399 U.S. 204 (1970): 46, 79
Perkins v. Matthews, 400 U.S. 379 (1971)
Citizens to Preserve Overton Park v. Volpe, 401 U.S. 402 (1971): 201–2, 204
Swann v. Charlotte-Mecklenburg Board of Education, 402 U.S. 1 (1971): 50
James v. Valtierra, 402 U.S. 137 (1971): 52, 53, 54
National Labor Relations Board v. Natural Gas and Utility District, 402 U.S. 600 (1971): 80, 81, 83
Gordon v. Lance, 403 U.S. 1 (1971): 53, 54
Whitcomb v. Chavis, 403 U.S. 124 (1971): 34, 35, 36, 126, 127, 128, 138, 141
Abate v. Mundt, 403 U.S. 182 (1971): 46, 47, 49
Jenness v. Fortson, 403 U.S. 431 (1971): 169
Cousins v. City of Chicago, 466 F.2d 830 (1972)
Bullock v. Carter, 405 U.S. 134 (1972)

Dunn v. Blumstein, 405 U.S. 330 (1972): 47
Sierra Club v. Morton, 405 U.S. 727 (1972): 202–3, 204
Rizzo v. North City Area-Wide Council, 406 U.S. 963 (1972): 193
Pipefitters Local Union v. U.S., 407 U.S. 385 (1972): 88
Wright v. Council of the City of Emporia, 407 U.S. 451 (1972)
O'Brien v. Brown, 409 U.S. 1 (1972): 160, 161, 162, 166
Trafficante v. Metropolitan Life Insurance Company, 409 U.S. 205 (1972): 203
U.S. v. Florida East Coast Railway, 410 U.S. 224 (1973): 204
Mahan v. Howell, 410 U.S. 315 (1973): 36, 39, 49
Marston v. Lewis, 410 U.S. 679 (1973)
Burns v. Fortson, 410 U.S. 686 (1973)
Salyer Land Co. v. Tulare Lake Basin Water District, 410 U.S. 719 (1973): 81, 82, 83, 84, 85, 86, 94, 95
Associated Enterprises v. Toltec Watershed Improvement District, 410 U.S. 743 (1973): 82
Rosario v. Rockefeller, 410 U.S. 752 (1973): 161, 162
San Antonio Independent School District v. Rodriguez, 411 U.S. 1 (1973)
Georgia v. U.S., 411 U.S. 526 (1973): 115, 140
City of Burbank v. Lockheed, 411 U.S. 624 (1973)
U.S. v. SCRAP, 412 U.S. 679 (1973): 203–4
Gaffney v. Cummings, 412 U.S. 735 (1973): 36, 37, 132, 133, 141
White v. Regester, 412 U.S. 755 (1973): 37, 127, 128, 141
White v. Weiser, 412 U.S. 783 (1973): 132–33, 141
Miller v. California, 413 U.S. 15 (1973)

Broadrick v. Oklahoma, 413 U.S. 601 (1973): 178, 179
Kusper v. Pontikes, 414 U.S. 51 (1973): 161, 162, 163, 165, 166, 167
Communist Party v. Whitcomb, 414 U.S. 441 (1974): 170
Lubin v. Panish, 415 U.S. 707 (1974)
Storer v. Brown, 415 U.S. 724 (1974): 169, 171
American Party of Texas v. White, 415 U.S. 767 (1974)
Village of Belle Terre v. Boraas, 416 U.S. 1 (1974): 57, 58
U.S. v. Richardson, 418 U.S. 166 (1974): 209–10, 213, 215
Schlesinger v. Reservists to Stop the War, 418 U.S. 208 (1974): 209–10, 213, 215
Milliken v. Bradley, 418 U.S. 717 (1974)
Cousins v. Wigoda, 419 U.S. 477 (1975): 162, 163, 166
Chapman v. Meier, 420 U.S. 1 (1975)
Hill v. Stone, 420 U.S. 289 (1975): 47, 48
Austin v. New Hampshire, 420 U.S. 656 (1975)
City of Richmond v. U.S., 422 U.S. 358 (1975): 116, 140
Warth v. Seldin, 422 U.S. 490 (1975): 58, 210–11, 213, 214
Buckley v. Valeo, 424 U.S. 1 (1976): 94–95, 173, 174, 175, 176, 186
Mathews v. Eldridge, 424 U.S. 319 (1976)
Beer v. U.S., 425 U.S. 130 (1976): 116, 123, 140
Hill v. Gautreaux, 425 U.S. 284 (1976)
Simon v. Eastern Kentucky Welfare Rights Organization, 426 U.S. 26 (1976): 212, 215
Pennsylvania v. New Jersey, 426 U.S. 660 (1976)
City of Eastlake v. Forest City Enterprises, 426 U.S. 668 (1976): 54

Hughes v. Alexandria Scrap Corp., 426 U.S. 794 (1976)
Young v. American Mini Theaters, 427 U.S. 50 (1976)
New Orleans v. Dukes, 427 U.S. 297 (1976)
Elrod v. Burns, 427 U.S. 347 (1976): 179, 180, 181, 183, 186
Singleton v. Wulff, 428 U.S. 106 (1976): 211–12, 217
Arlington Heights v. Metropolitan Housing Corporation, 429 U.S. 252 (1977): 60
Steelworkers v. Usery, 429 U.S. 305 (1977)
Concerned Citizens v. Pine Creek District, 429 U.S. 651 (1977): 83–84
United Jewish Organization v. Carey, 430 U.S. 144 (1977): 128–31, 141
Lockport v. Citizens for Community Action, 430 U.S. 259 (1977): 54, 55
Chappelle v. Greater Baton Rouge Airport District, 431 U.S. 159 (1977): 84
Connor v. Finch, 431 U.S. 407 (1977)
Moore v. City of East Cleveland, 431 U.S. 494 (1977): 58, 59
Mandel v. Bradley, 432 U.S. 173 (1977)
Arlington County Board v. Richards, 434 U.S. 5 (1977)
Vermont Yankee Nuclear Power Corp. v. Natural Resources Defense Council, 435 U.S. 519 (1978): 205
First National Bank of Boston v. Bellotti, 435 U.S. 765 (1978): 91, 92, 93, 94
Duke Power Co. v. Carolina Environmental Study Group, 438 U.S. 59 (1978): 212–13, 214, 217
Penn Central Transportation Co. v. New York City, 438 U.S. 104 (1978): 60
Holt Civic Club v. Tuscaloosa, 439 U.S. 60 (1978): 48, 49, 58, 65, 66
Marchioro v. Chaney, 442 U.S. 191 (1979): 163, 164, 166

Stryker's Bay Neighborhood Council v. Karlen, 444 U.S. 223 (1980): 205
Schaumberg v. Citizens for a Better Environment, 444 U.S. 620 (1980)
Branti v. Finkel, 445 U.S. 507 (1980): 180, 181, 182, 183, 186
Mobile v. Bolden, 446 U.S. 1 (1980): 118, 119, 123, 126, 140
City of Rome v. U.S., 446 U.S. 156 (1980): 117, 118, 140
Agins v. City of Tiburon, 447 U.S. 255 (1980): 60
Consolidated Edison v. Public Service Commission, 447 U.S. 530 (1980): 92–93, 94
Democratic Party v. LaFollette, 450 U.S. 107 (1981): 164, 165, 166, 167, 176
City of Memphis v. Greene, 451 U.S. 100 (1981): 61
Ball v. James, 451 U.S. 355 (1981): 84, 85, 86, 94, 95
Middlesex County Sewerage Authority v. National Sea Clammers Associations, 435 U.S. 1 (1981): 206
California Medical Association v. Federal Election Commission, 453 U.S. 182 (1981)
Federal Election Commission v. Democratic Senatorial Campaign Committee, 454 U.S. 27 (1981)
Citizens Against Rent Control v. City of Berkeley, 454 U.S. 290 (1981)
Valley Forge Christian College v. Americans United for the Separation of Church and State, 454 U.S. 464 (1982): 213–16
Havens Realty v. Coleman, 455 U.S. 363 (1982): 206, 207
Hoffman Estates v. Flipside, 455 U.S. 487 (1982)
Bread PAC v. Federal Election Commission, 455 U.S. 577 (1982): 206, 207
Zobel v. Williams, 457 U.S. 55 (1982): 62, 63, 64
Washington v. Seattle School District, 458 U.S. 457 (1982): 56

Federal Election Commission v. National Right to Work Committee, 459 U.S. 550 (1982)
Rodriguez v. Popular Democratic Party, 102 S.Ct. 2194 (1982)
Rogers v. Herman Lodge, 102 S.Ct. 3272 (1982): 120
Clements v. Fashing, 102 S.Ct. 2836 (1982): 170
City of Port Arthur v. U.S., 103 S.Ct. 530 (1983): 121, 122, 140
Brown v. Socialist Workers '74 Campaign Committee, 103 S.Ct. 416 (1983)
City of Lockhart v. U.S., 103 S.Ct. 998 (1983): 122, 140
White v. Massachusetts Council of Construction Employees, 103 S.Ct. 1042 (1983): 63, 64
Bellotti v. Connolly, 103 S.Ct. 1510 (1983): 166
Metropolitan Edison Co. v. People Against Nuclear Energy, 103 S.Ct. 1556 (1983): 205
Anderson v. Celebrezze, 460 U.S. 780 (1983): 171, 176–77
Karcher v. Daggett, 462 U.S. 725 (1983): 133
Brown v. Thompson, 103 S.Ct. 2691 (1983)
Gingles v. Edmisten, 590 F.Supp 345 (EDNC 1984)
Allen v. Wright, 468 U.S. 737 (1984): 215–16
United Building and Construction Trades Council v. City of Camden, 104 S.Ct. 1020 (1984): 63, 64
City Council of Los Angeles v. Taxpayers for Vincent, 104 S.Ct. 2118 (1984): 60
Block v. Community Nutrition Institute, 104 S.Ct. 2450 (1984): 206, 207
Federal Election Commission v. National Conservative Political Action Committee, 105 S.Ct. 1479 (1985): 175, 177, 186

Diamond v. Charles, 106 S.Ct. 1699 (1986): 216
Thornburg v. Gingles, 106 S.Ct. 2752 (1986): 122, 123, 131, 140
Davis v. Bandemer, 106 S.Ct. 2797 (1986): 134, 135, 136, 137, 138, 141, 226, 229
Tashjian v. Republican Party of Connecticut, 106 S.Ct. 1257 (1986) (aff'd on appeal);107 S.Ct. 544 (1987): 167, 171
Federal Election Commission v. Massachusetts Citizens for Life, 107 S.Ct 616 (1987): 229
City of Pleasant Grove v. U.S., 107 S.Ct. 794 (1987)
Badham v. Eu, 108 S.Ct. 1993 (1988)
Eu v. San Francisco County Democratic Central Committee, 109 S.Ct. 1013 (1989): 167, 171
Board of Estimate v. Morris, 109 S.Ct. 1433 (1989)
Rutan v. Republican Party of Illinois, 58 U.S.L.W. 4872 (1990)

Bibliography

Adamany, David. "Legitimacy, Realigning Elections and the Supreme Court." 1973 Wis. L. Rev. 790 (1973).

Adamany, David. "Political Parties in the 1980's." In Money and Politics in the U.S. 74 (M. Malbin ed. 1984).

Advisory Commission on Intergovernmental Relations. Citizen Participation in the American Federal System (1979).

Alexander, H., and Haggerty, B. PACs and Parties: Relationships and Interrelationships (1984).

Alfange, Dean. "Gerrymandering and the Constitution: Into the Thorns of the Political Thicket at Last." 1986 S.Ct. Rev. 175 (1986).

Althoff, P., and Grieg, W. "The U.S. Supreme Court on Rights and/or Participation: The 'Deviant' Voting Cases." 13 J. Contemp. L. 31 (1987).

Auerbach, Carl. "Commentary." In Reapportionment in the 70's 78 (N. Polsby ed. 1971).

Backstrom, Charles. "Problems of Implementing Redistricting." In Representation and Redistricting Issues 43 (B. Grofman et al. eds. 1982).

Backstrom, C., et al. "Partisan Gerrymanders in post-*Bandemer* Era." 4 Con. Com. 310 (1987).

Backstrom, C., and Robins, L. "What's Next in Gerrymandering?" Paper delivered to the American Political Science Association, Washington, D.C., September 1988.

Baker, Gordon. "Judicial Determination of Political Gerrymandering: A 'Totality of Circumstances' Approach." 3 J. L. Pol. 1 (1986).

Baker, Gordon. "Whatever Happened to the Reapportionment Revolution in the U.S.?" In Electoral Laws and their Political Consequences (B. Grofman and A. Lijphart eds. 1986).

Balinsky, Michel, and Young, H. P. Fair Representation (1982).

Barber, Benjamin. Strong Democracy (1984).

Basehart, Harry. "The Nature of Representation." 69 Nat'l Civic Rev. 546 (1980).

Baum, Lawrence. "Comparing the Policy Positions of Supreme Court Justices from Different Periods." 42 W. Pol. Q. 509 (1989).

Beitz, Charles. "Equal Opportunity in Political Representation." In Equal Opportunity 155 (N. Bowie ed. 1988).

Beitz, Charles. Political Equality (1989).

242 / *Bibliography*

BeVier, Lillian. "Justice Powell and the First Amendment's 'Societal Function.'" 68 Va. L. Rev. 177 (1982).
Bickel, Alexander. The Supreme Court and the Idea of Progress (1970).
Birch, A. H. Representation (1971).
Blacksher, James. "Drawing Singlemember Districts to Comply with the Voting Rights Amendments of 1982." 17 Urb. Lawyer 347 (1985).
Blacksher, James, and Menefee, Larry. "At-large Elections and One Person, One Vote." In Minority Vote Dilution 203 (C. Davidson ed. 1984).
Blasi, Vincent. "The Rootless Activism of the Burger Court." In The Burger Court 198 (V. Blasi ed. 1983).
Bogdanor, Vernon. What is Proportional Representation? (1984).
Boles, Janet, and Dean, Dorothy. "Communities of Interest in Legislative Districting." 58 State Govt. 101 (1985).
Bollens, John. Special District Government in the United States (1957).
Brams, Steven. "Approval Voting." In Representation and Redistricting Issues 137 (B. Grofman, A. Lijphart, et al. eds. 1982).
Brisbin, Richard. "Federal Courts and the Changing Role of Political Parties." 5 N. U. Ill. L. Rev. 31 (1984).
Brown, Stuart M. "Black on Representation: A Question." 10 Nomos 147 (1968).
Burt, Robert. "The Burger Court and the Family." In The Burger Court 92 (V. Blasi ed. 1983).
Burt, Robert. "The Constitution of the Family." 1979 S. Ct. Rev. 329.
Busteed, M. A. Geography and Voting Behavior (1975).
Butler, Katherine. "Constitutional and Statutory Challenges to Electoral Structures." 42 La. L. Rev. 875 (1982).
Butler, Katherine. "Denial or Abridgement of the Right to Vote: What Does It Mean?" In The Voting Rights Act 44 (L. Foster ed. 1985).
Cain, Bruce. "Perspectives on Davis v. Bandemer." In Toward Fair and Effective Representation: Political Gerrymandering and the Courts (B. Grofman ed. 1990.
Cain, Bruce. "Predicting Partisan Redistricting Disputes." 12 Legis. Stud. Q. 265 (1987).
Cain, Bruce. The Reapportionment Puzzle (1984).
Cain, Bruce. "Simple vs. Complex Criteria for Partisan Gerrymandering." 33 U.C.L.A. L. Rev. 213 (1985).
Campbell, A., et al. The American Voter (1960).
Carr, Craig, and Scott, Gary. "The Constitutionality of State Primary Systems: An Associational Rights Analysis." 10 J. Contemp. L. 83 (1984).
Casper, Jonathan D. "The Supreme Court and National Policy Making," Am. Pol. Sci. Rev. 50 (1976).
Chermerinsky, Erwin. "Rethinking State Action." 80 Nw. U.L. Rev. 503 (1985).
Clabby, Robert. "The Supreme Court and State Regulation of Political Parties." (M.A. Thesis, The Johns Hopkins University, Baltimore, Md., 1976).

Claude, Richard. The Supreme Court and the Electoral Process (1970).
Common Cause. Toward a System of Fair and Effective Representation (1977).
Cox, A. "Federalism and Individual Rights." 73 Nw. U. L. Rev. 1 (1978).
Cox, A. "Forward: Freedom of Expression in the Burger Court," Harv. L. Rev. 1 (1980).
Crotty, W., and Jacobson, G. American Parties in Decline (1980).
Dahl, Robert. Dilemmas of Pluralist Democracy (1982).
Dahl, Robert. "Federalism and the Democratic Process." 25 Nomos 95 (1983).
Dahl, Robert. Pluralist Democracy in the U.S. (1967).
Danielski, David. "Values as Variables in Judicial Decision Making." 19 Vand. L. Rev. 721 (1966).
Davidson, Chandler. "Minority Vote Dilution: An Overview." In Minority Vote Dilution 1 (C. Davidson ed. 1984).
Denniston, Lyle. "The Burger Court and the Press." In The Burger Years 23 (H. Schwartz ed. 1987).
Derfner, Armand. "The Voting Rights Act Amendments of 1982." In Minority Vote Dilution 145 (C. Davidson ed. 1984).
Diggs, B. J. "Practical Representation." 10 Nomos 28 (1968).
Dixon, Robert. "The Court, the People, and 'One Man, One Vote.'" In Reapportionment in the 70s, 7 (N. Polsby ed. 1971).
Dixon, Robert. Democratic Representation (1968).
Dixon, Robert. "Fair Criteria and Procedures for Establishing Legislative Districts." In Representation and Redistricting Issues 7 (B. Grofman et al. eds. 1982).
Dixon, Robert. "The Warren Court Crusade for the Holy Grail of One Man, One Vote." 1969 S. Ct. Rev. 219 (1969).
Dorenberg, Donald. "Collective Rights and Standing." 73 Cal. L. Rev. 52 (1985).
Dorsen, Norman, and Gora, Joel. "The Burger Court and Freedom of Speech." In The Burger Court 28 (V. Blasi ed. 1983).
Dry, Murray. "The Case Against Ratification: Anti-Federalist Constitutional Thought." In The Framing and Ratification of the Constitution 271 (L. Levy and D. Mahoney eds. 1987).
Durchslag, Melvyn. "*Salyer, Ball* and *Holt:* Reappraising the Right to Vote in Terms of Political 'Interest' and Vote Dilution." 33 Case W. Res. L. Rev. 1 (1982).
Edelman, Martin. Democratic Theories and the Constitution (1984).
Edelman, Murray. The Symbolic Uses of Politics (1967).
Eismeier, Theodore, and Pollock, Phillip. "Political Action Committees: Varieties of Organization and Strategy." In Money and Politics in the United States 122 (M. Malbin ed. 1984).
Elliot, W. Y. The Rise of Guardian Democracy (1974).
Ely, John Hart. Democracy and Distrust (1980).
Emerson, Thomas. "First Amendment Doctrine and the Burger Court." 68 Cal. L. Rev. 422 (1980).

Emerson, Thomas. "Freedom of Press under the Burger Court." In The Burger Court (V. Blasi ed. 1983).
Engstrom, Richard. "Post Census Representational Districting." 7 S. U.L. Rev. 173 (1981).
Engstrom, Richard. "Racial Vote Dilution: The Concept and the Court." In The Voting Rights Act 13 (L. Foster ed. 1985).
Engstrom, Richard, et al. "Cumulative Voting as a Remedy for Minority Vote Dilution: The Case of Alamogordo, New Mexico." 5 J. of L. and Pol. (1988).
Epstein, Lee. Conservatives in Court (1985).
Epstein, Lee, and Hadley, Charles. "On the Treatment of Political Parties in the U.S. Supreme Court, 1900–1986." 52 J. of Pol. 413 (1990).
Epstein, Leon. Political Parties in the American Mold (1986).
Etzioni, Amitai. Capital Corruption (1984).
Farber, Daniel A. "Corporate Speech and First Amendment Theory." 74 Nw. U.L. Rev. 372 (1979).
Fiss, Owen. "Free Speech and Social Structure." In Equal Opportunity 175 (N. Bowie ed. 1988).
Fiss, Owen. "Groups and the Equal Protection Clause." 5 Phil. and Pub. Affairs 107 (1976).
Floyd, C. Douglas. "Civil Rights Class Actions in the 1980's." 1984 B.Y.U.L. Rev. 1 (1984).
Flynn, John. "The Jurisprudence of Corporate Personhood." In Corporations and Society 131 (W. Samuels and A. Miller eds. 1987).
Foster, Lorn. "Political Symbols and the Enactment of the 1982 Voting Rights Act." In The Voting Rights Act 85 (L. Foster ed. 1985).
Frug, Gerald. "The City as a Legal Concept." 93 Harv. L. Rev. 1059 (1980).
Gelfand, David. "The Burger Court and the New Federalism." 21 B.C.L. Rev. 763 (1980).
Gelfand, David. "The Constitutional Position of American Local Government." 14 Hast. Const. L.Q. 635 (1987).
Gelfand, David. "Voting Rights and the Democratic Process." 17 Urb. Law. 333 (1985).
Gitelson, Alan. American Political Parties: Stability and Change (1984).
Golden, Larry, and Hayler, Barbara. "The Politics of Judicial Elections: Minority Representation and the Voting Rights Act Challenges in Chicago, Ill." Paper presented to the Law and Society Association, Berkeley, Calif., May 31–June 3, 1990.
Goldman, Sheldon. "Reaganizing the Judiciary: The First Term Appointments." 68 Judicature 313 (1985).
Gottschall, Jonathan. "Reagan's Appointments to the US Courts of Appeal: The Continuation of a Judicial Revolution." 70 Judicature 50 (1986).
Grofman, Bernard. "Alternatives to Singlemember Plurality Districts." In Representation and Redistricting Issues 107 (B. Grofman, A. Lijphart, et al. eds. 1982).

Grofman, Bernard. "Bandemer and Thornburg: Toward a Coherent Theory of Fair and Effective Representation." In Toward Fair and Effective Representation: Political Gerrymandering and the Courts (B. Grofman ed. 1990).
Grofman, Bernard. "Criteria for Districting." 33 U.C.L.A. L. Rev. 77 (1985).
Grofman, Bernard. "For Singlemember Districts Random Is Not Equal." In Representation and Redistricting Issues 55 (B. Grofman et al. eds. 1982).
Grofman, Bernard. "Toward a Coherent Theory of Gerrymandering." In Toward Fair and Effective Representation: Political Gerrymandering and the Courts (B. Grofman ed. forthcoming).
Grofman, Bernard, and Handley, Lisa. "Why Are There So Few Black or Hispanic Congressmen?" Paper delivered to the American Political Science Association, Chicago, Ill., 1987.
Grofman, Bernard, and Lijphart, Arend, eds. Electoral Laws and Their Consequences (1986).
Grofman, Bernard, Migalski, Michael, and Noviello, Nicholas. "The Totality of Circumstances Test." 7 Law and Pol'y. 199 (1985).
Gudgin, G., and Taylor, P. J. Seats, Votes, and the Spatial Organisation of Elections (1979).
Gunn, Priscilla. "Initiatives and Referendums." 22 Urb. L. Ann. 154 (1981).
Gunther, Gerald, ed. Constitutional Law (11th ed. 1985).
Hanock, Paul, and Tredway, Lora. "The Bail Out Standard of the Voting Rights Act." 17 Urb. Law. 379 (1985).
Hardy, Leroy C. "Considering the Gerrymander." 4 Pepperdine L. Rev. 243 (1977).
Hardy, L., and Heslop, A. Reapportionment Politics: The History of Redistricting in the States (1981).
Harrington, Christine. "Regulatory Reform: Creating Gaps and Making Markets." 10 Law and Poly. 293 (1988).
Hart, H. M., and Wechsler, H. Federal Courts (2d ed. 1973).
Hawkins, Robert. Self-Government by District (1976).
Hensley, Thomas, and Rhoads, James. "Studying the Studies: An Assessment of Judicial Politics Research in Four Major Political Science Journals, 1960–1987." Paper presented to the Southern Political Science Association, Atlanta, Ga., November 3–5, 1988.
Herrnson, Paul. Party Campaigning in the 1980's (1988).
Hoover, K. The Elements of Social Scientific Thinking (1988).
Horwitz, Morton. "*Santa Clara* Revisited: The Development of Corporate Theory." In Corporations and Society 13 (W. Samuels and A. Miller eds. 1987).
Jacobs, Paul W., and O'Rourke, Timothy G. "Racial Polarization in Vote Dilution Cases Under Section 2 of the Voting Rights Act." 3 J. L. & Pol. 295 (1986).
Jacobson, Gary. "Money in the 1980 and 1982 Congressional Elections." In Money and Politics in the U.S. 38 (M. Malbin ed. 1984).

Johnson, Charles. "Law, Politics, and Judicial Decisionmaking: Lower Federal Court Uses of Supreme Court Decisions." 21 Law and Soc. Rev. 325 (1987).
Johnson, Janet, and Josyln, Richard. Political Science Research Methods (1986).
Kamienki, S. Party Identification, Political Behavior and the American Electorate (1988).
Kasperson, Roger. Participation, Decentralization and Advocacy Planning (1974).
Kayden, Xandra. "The Nationalization of the Party System." In Parties, Interest Groups and Campaign Finance Laws 257 (M. Malbin ed. 1980).
Kelso, William. American Democratic Theory (1978).
Koblyka, Joseph. "Leadership on the Supreme Court: Chief Justice Burger and the Establishment Clause." 42 Western Pol. Q. 545 (1989).
Kolker, Michael. "National League of Cities, the Tenth Amendment and the Conditional Spending Power." 21 Urb. L. Ann. 217 (1981).
Kousser, J. Morgan. "The Undermining of the First Reconstruction: Lessons for the Second." In Minority Vote Dilution 27 (C. Davidson ed. 1984).
Krislov, S. "The Amicus Curiae Brief: From Friendship to Advocacy." 71 Yale L.J. 694 (1963).
Kweit, M., and Kweit, R. Implementing Citizen Participation in a Bureaucratic Society (1981).
Ladd, C. Everett. "Party Reform and the Public Interest." In Elections American Style 222 (A. Reichley ed. 1987).
Ladd, C. Everett. "Party Reform Since 1968." In The American Constitutional System Under Strong and Weak Parties 85 (P. Bonomi ed. 1981).
Ladd, C., and Hadley, C. Transformation of the American Party System (1978).
Lane, Robert. "Individualism and the Market Society." 25 Nomos 374 (1983).
Latus, Margaret. "Assessing Ideological PACs: from Outrage to Understanding." In Money and Politics in the United States 142 (M. Malbin ed. 1984).
Lawson, Kay. "How State Laws Undermine Parties." In Elections American Style 240 (A. Reichley ed. 1987).
Lee, W. "The Supreme Court and the Right to Receive Expression." 1987 S. Ct. Rev. 303 (1987).
Levi, Julian. "Application of Municipal Bond Ordinances to Special Purpose Districts." 12 Urb. L. Ann. 86 (1976).
Levinson, Sanford. "Gerrymandering and the Brooding Omnipresence of Proportional Representation." 33 U.C.L.A. L. Rev. 260 (1985).
Lijphart, Arend. Democracies (1984).
Linowes, R., and Allensworth, D. The Politics of Land-use Law (1976).
Lourich, Nicholas P., Jr., and Sheldon, Charles H. "The Racial Factor in Non-Partisan Judicial Elections." 41 W. Pol. Q. 807 (1988).
Low, P., and Jeffries, J., eds. Civil Rights Actions (1988).
Lowenstein, Daniel. "Bandemer's Gap: Gerrymandering and the Equal Protection Clause." Paper delivered to the American Political Science Association, Chicago, Ill., September 1987.

Lowenstein, Daniel. "Constitutional Rights of Major Political Parties." Paper delivered to the American Political Science Association, Washington, D.C., September 1988.
Lowenstein, D., and Steinberg, J. "Districting in the Public Interest." 33 U.C.L.A. L. Rev. 1 (1985).
Lowi, Theodore. The End of Liberalism (1976).
Lutz, Donald. "The First American Constitutions." In The Framing and Ratification of the Constitution 69 (L. Levy and D. Mahoney eds. 1987).
McClesky, Clifton. "Parties at the Bar: Equal Protection, Freedom of Association and the Rights of Political Organizations." 46 J. Pol. 346 (1984).
McConnell, Grant. Private Power and American Democracy (1966).
McDonald, Michael, and Engstrom, Richard. "Detecting Gerrymanders." In Toward Fair and Effective Representation: Political Gerrymandering and the Courts (B. Grofman ed. 1990).
McFarland, Andrew. "Public Interest Lobbies vs. Minority Factions." In Interest Group Politics 324 (A. Cigler and B. Loomis eds. 1981).
Magleby, David. Direct Legislation (1984).
Maisel, L. Parties and Elections in America (1987).
Malbin, Michael. "Congress During the Convention and Ratification." In The Framing and Ratification of the Constitution 185 (L. Levy and D. Mahoney eds. 1987).
Maltz, Earl. "Powell, Equal Protection and the Pure Classification Problem." 40 Ohio St. L.J. 941 (1979).
Mansbridge, Jane. Beyond Adversary Democracy (1980).
Mashaw, Jerry. Due Process in the Administrative State (1985).
Mashaw, Jerry. "Rights in the Federal Administrative State." 92 Y.L.J. 1129 (1983).
Matasar, A. Corporate PACs and Federal Campaign Financing Laws (1986).
Maveety, Nancy. "The Burger Court and Group Access to the Political Process." Paper delivered to the American Political Science Association, Chicago, Ill., 1987.
Maveety, Nancy. "Standing in the Pews: Access to Court in Church-State Litigation." Paper delivered to the Southern Political Science Association, Atlanta, Ga., 1988.
Merton, Robert. Social Structure (1964).
Michaelman, Frank. "Political Markets and Community Self-Determination: Competing Judicial Models of Local Government Legitimacy." 53 Ind. L.J. 145 (1977–78).
Michaelman, Frank. "Conceptions of Democracy in American Constitutional Argument: Voting Rights." 41 Fla. L. Rev. 443 (1989).
Miller, Arthur. "Corporations and Our Two Constitutions." In Corporations and Society 241 (W. Samuels and A. Miller eds. 1987).
Miller, Arthur. The Supreme Court and American Capitalism (1968).
Miller, Warren. "Party Preference and Attitudes on Political Issues." 47 Am. Pol. Sci. Rev. 50 (1953).

Moeller, John. "The Federal Courts Involvement in the Reform of Political Parties." 1987 W. Pol. Q. 717 (1987).
Mollenkopf, John. The Contested City (1983).
Moreland, Lois. White Racism and the Law (1970).
Morgan, Edmund. Inventing the People (1988).
Mosher, Frederick. Democracy and the Public Service (1968).
Neighbor, Howard. "Toward a Model of Reapportionment." 71 Nat'l Civic Rev. 188 (1982).
Neighbor, Howard. "The Voting Rights Act: Old and New." 72 Nat'l Civic Rev. 481 (1983).
Nie, N., Verba, S., and Petrocik, J. The Changing American Voter (1979).
Niemi, Richard. "The Effects of Districting on Tradeoffs among Party Competition, Electoral Responsiveness and Seats-Votes Relationships." In Representation and Redistricting Issues 35 (B. Grofman et al. eds. 1982).
Niemi, Richard G., Powell, Lynda W., and Bicknell, Patricia L. "The Effect of Community-Congressional Districting Congruity on Knowledge of Congressional Candidates." 11 Legis. Stud. Q. 187 (1986).
Nordlinger, Eric. "Representation, Stability, and Decisional Effectiveness." 10 Nomos 108 (1968).
Note. "Campaign Hyperbole." 2 J. L. Pol. 405 (1985).
Note. "The Constitutional Imperative of Proportional Representation." 94 Yale L.J. 163 (1984).
Note. "Corporate Speech on Political Issues." 1985 U. Ill. L. Rev. 445 (1985).
Note. "Cousins and LaFollette: an Anomoly Created by a Choice Between Freedom of Association and the Right to Vote." 80 Nw. U.L. Rev. 666 (1985).
Note. "The Dilemmas of Federalism." 71 Nat'l Civic Rev. 500 (1982).
Note. "Geometry and Geography: Racial Gerrymandering and the Voting Rights Act." 94 Yale L.J. 189 (1984).
Note. "Gerrymandering: It's Time to Face the Issues." 71 Nat'l Civic Rev. 172 (1982).
Note. "Getting Results under Section 5 of the Voting Rights Act." 94 Yale L.J. 139 (1984).
Note. "Group Representation and Race-Conscious Apportionment." 91 Harv. L. Rev. 1847 (1978).
Note. "Interest Groups in American Public Law." 38 Stan. L. Rev. 29 (1985).
Note. "Primary Elections and the Collective Right to Freedom of Association." 94 Yale L.J. 117 (1984).
Note. "Taking Federalism Seriously." 90 Yale L.J. 1694 (1981).
Note. "United Jewish Organization and the Need to Recognize Aggregate Voting Rights." 87 Yale L.J. 571 (1978).
O'Connor, Karen, and Epstein, Lee. "The Rise of Conservative Interest Group Litigation." 45 J. of Pol. 479 (1983).
O'Kelley, Charles R., Jr. "The Constitutional Rights of Corporations Revisited." 67 Geo. L.J. 1347 (1979).

O'Neill, Timothy. Bakke and the Politics of Equality (1985).
O'Rourke, Timothy G. The Impact of Reapportionment (1980).
Orren, G. "Changing Styles of American Party Politics." In The Future of American Political Parties 4 (Joel Fleishman ed. 1982).
Owen, Guillermo, and Grofman, Bernard. "Optimal Partisan Gerrymandering." Pol. Geog. Q. (forthcoming).
Packer, Mark. "Tracking the Court through a Political Thicket." 22 Urb. L. Ann. 227 (1982).
Parker, Frank. "Racial Gerrymandering and Legislative Reapportionment." In Minority Vote Dilution 85 (C. Davidson ed. 1984).
Parker, Frank. "The 'Results' Test of Section 2 of the Voting Rights Act: Abandoning the Intent Standard." 69 Va. L. Rev. 715 (1983).
Peck, Miller, et al. "Davis v. Bandemer-Political Gerrymandering Challenged on Equal Protection Grounds." 17 Urb. L. 945 (1985).
Pennock, J. R. Democratic Political Theory (1979).
Pennock, J. R. "Political Representation: An Overview." 10 Nomos 3 (1968).
Pitkin, Hanna. "Commentary: the Paradox of Representation." 10 Nomos 38 (1968).
Pitkin, Hanna. The Concept of Representation (1967).
Piven, F., and Cloward, R. Why Americans Don't Vote (1988).
Polakoff, K. Political Parties in American History (1981).
Polsby, Nelson. The Consequences of Party Reform (1983).
Population Reference Bureau. Election Demographics (1988).
Ranney, Austin. "Comment." In The American Constitutional System Under Strong and Weak Parties 68 (P. Bonomi ed. 1981).
Ranney, Austin. Curing the Mischief of Factions (1975).
Ranney, Austin. The Doctrine of Responsible Party Government (1962).
Rathjen, Gregory, and Spaeth, Harold. "Access to Federal Courts: An Analysis of Burger Court Policymaking." 23 Am. J. of Pol. Sci. 360 (1979).
Rathjen, Gregory, and Spaeth, Harold. "Denial of Access and Ideological Preferences." 36 W. Pol. Q. 71 (1983).
Redlich, Norman. "The Separation of Church and State: The Burger Court's Tortuous Journey." In The Burger Years 56 (H. Schwartz ed. 1987).
Richardson, Elliot L. "Introduction." 6 Publius 5 (1976).
Riker, William. "Democracy and Representation: A Reconciliation of *Ball v. James* and *Reynolds v. Sims*." 1 S.Ct. Econ. Rev. 39 (1982).
Rohr, John. To Run a Constitution (1986).
Rome, Edwin, and Roberts, William. Corporate and Commercial Free Speech (1985).
Sabato, Larry. "Real and Imagined Corruption in Campaign Financing." In Elections American Style 155 (A. Reichley ed. 1987).
Samuels, Warren. "The Idea of the Corporation as a Person." In Corporations and Society 113 (W. Samuels and A. Miller eds. 1987).
Scarrow, Howard. "The Impact of Reapportionment on Party Representation." In Representation and Redistricting Issues of the 1980's 67 (B. Grofman and A. Lijphart eds. 1982).

Schaffer, William. "Partisan Loyalty and the Perceptions of Party, Candidates and Issues." 25 W. Pol. Q. 424 (1972).
Schattschneider, E. E. Party Government (1977).
Schlesinger, A., Jr. "The Crisis of the American Party System." In Political Parties and the Modern State 71 (R. McCormick ed. 1984).
Schneider, Carl E. "Free Speech and Corporate Freedom." 59 S. Cal. L. Rev. 1227 (1986).
Schubert, Glendon. "A Psychological Analysis of the 1960 Term of the Supreme Court." 56 Am. Pol. Sci. Rev. 90 (1962).
Shafritz, Jay. Dictionary of American Politics (1988).
Shapiro, Martin. "Fathers and Sons: The Court, the Commentators and the Search for Values." In The Burger Court 218 (V. Blasi ed. 1983).
Shapiro, Martin. "Gerrymandering, Unfairness and the Supreme Court." 33 U.C.L.A. L. Rev. 227 (1985).
Shapiro, Martin. Law and Politics on the Supreme Court (1964).
Simon, Todd. "Defining Commercial Speech." 20 New Eng. L. Rev. 215 (1984–85).
Sobolweski, Marek. "Electors and Representatives: A Contribution to the Theory of Representation." 10 Nomos 95 (1968).
Songer, Donald. "Alternative Approaches to the Study of Judicial Impact." 16 Am. Pol. Q. 425 (1988).
Sorauf, Frank. Money in American Elections (1988).
Sorauf, Frank. Party Politics in America (1984).
Spaeth, Harold. "Ideosyncratic Factors in Decision Making." In Courts, Law and Judicial Processes 387 (S. Ulmer ed. 1981).
Spitz, Elaine. Majority Rule (1984).
Stephens, Marcy. "Provisions for Apportionment." 72 Nat'l Civic Rev. 174 (1982).
Stewart, Richard. "Problems of Federalism in National Environmental Policy." 86 Yale L.J. 1196 (1977).
Still, Edward. "Alternatives to Singlemember Districts." In Minority Vote Dilution 249 (C. Davidson ed. 1984).
Still, Edward. "Political Equality and Election Systems." 91 Ethics 385 (1981).
Stokes, Donald. "Political Parties in the Normative Theory of Representation." 10 Nomos 150 (1968).
Sundquist, James. "Strengthening the National Parties." In Elections American Style 195 (A. Reichley ed. 1987).
Taggart, William, and DeZee, Matthew. "Substantive Access Doctrines in the U.S. Supreme Court: A Comparative Analysis of the Warren and Burger Courts." 38 W. Pol. Q. 84 (1985).
Taylor, P. J., and Johnston, R. J. The Geography of Elections (1979).
Thelan, David P. "Two Traditions of Progressive Reform." In The American Constitution Under Strong and Weak Parties 37 (P. Bonomi ed. 1981).
Thernstrom, Abigail. "The Odd Evolution of the Voting Rights Act." 55 Pub. Interest 49 (1979).
Thernstrom, Abigail. Whose Votes Count? (1987).

Tribe, Lawrence. Constitutional Law (1978).
Tushnet, Mark. "Corporations and Free Speech." In The Politics of Law 253 (D. Kairys ed. 1982).
Vining, Joseph. Legal Identity (1978).
Vose, C. "Litigation as a Form of Pressure Group Activity." 319 Annals 20 (1958).
Wahlke, J., and Eulau, H., et al. Legislative Behavior (1962).
Wekkin, Gary. "National-State Party Relations." 99 Pol. Sci. Q. 45 (1984).
Wells, David. "Affirmative Action Gerrymandering." 67 Nat'l Civic Rev. 10 (1978).
Wells, David. "How to Inhibit Gerrymandering." 71 Nat'l Civic Rev. 183 (1982).
Whelan, Frederick. "Democratic Theory and the Boundary Problem." 25 Nomos 3 (1983).
Wright, Deil S. Understanding Intergovernmental Relations (1982).
Zagarri, Rosemary. The Politics of Size (1986).
Zimmerman, Joseph. "Substate Regional Governance." 67 Nat'l Civic Rev. 272 (1978).
Zisk, Betty. Money, Media and the Grass Roots (1987).

Index

Administrative accountability, 16, 189–91, 193–98, 208, 210, 217, 225
  and litigational representation, 16, 190–91, 194, 199–200, 202, 206–8, 210, 216–19, 222–25, 229
Administrative Procedures Act, 15, 192, 200–202, 204–5, 209
  section 702, 192, 202–3
Agency rulemaking procedures, 192–93, 195, 197–98, 200–202, 204–5
Aggregate voting right, 107–8, 123, 125, 135, 142, 147, 157 n.38, 171, 226
At-large elections, 31, 35, 42, 102, 112, 114, 118, 120, 123–24, 141
  and multimember districts, 34–35, 37, 46, 115, 117 n.74, 125–27
  and municipal annexations, 112, 116–17, 121
  and racial vote dilution, 32, 34, 37, 102, 115, 118, 122, 126

"Benefits and burdens" of citizenship, 44–46, 48, 53, 55, 60–61, 79–81, 84
Black, Justice Hugo, 32 n.62, 45, 52–53, 80, 168
Blackmun, Justice Harry, 34 n.68, 53 n.59, 56, 57 n.78, 64, 85 n.74, 162 n.49, 180, 211, 212 n.101, 214 n.114, 216, 226
Brennan, Justice William, 24, 30, 48–49, 53 n.59, 54 n.65, 58, 81–82, 85 n.74, 91 n.97, 117, 122–23, 129 n.116, 130, 162, 169 n.76, 170, 175 n.98, 178–80, 182, 210 n.91, 212 nn.101, 103, 213 n.109, 214–15, 226
Burger, Chief Justice Warren, 4, 34 n.68, 53–54, 62, 92 n.100, 123 n.99, 129 n.116, 163 n.55, 170, 180 n.111, 195, 209–10, 213, 226
Burger years
  doctrinal legacy of, 2, 4, 36, 167, 199, 228, 230
  significance of, 2 n.4, 4–5, 19, 34, 38, 216, 221, 228–30

Campaign financing, 157, 167–68, 171–73, 184
Civil Rights Act, 194 n.23, 203
Civil service (restricted partisanship therein) 178, 184
Collective freedom of association (partisan), 154, 156–57, 160, 162–66, 167 n.69, 168 n.73, 171–72, 174–76, 180, 182–84, 187, 229
Communitarian politics, 42, 52, 67
"Compensatory majoritarianism," 98, 104–6, 108–9, 111–12, 116, 122–25, 130–31, 133, 138, 140, 143, 145, 147, 225

253

"Corporate pluralism," 70 n.3
Corporate political rights, 14, 55, 72, 77, 79, 86–93, 95, 175, 229
Corporatism, definitions of, 69–71, 73–76, 78, 83, 86
Corporatist antecedents in American politics
  corporate "citizenship," 77, 79, 94
  New Deal policies, 72, 74, 191
  special district governments, 14, 72, 75–76, 79, 94

Demographic districting, 14–15, 98, 100, 103, 105–7, 111, 123, 125, 128, 130, 226
  partisan-based, 14–15, 108–9, 131–33, 139, 144, 225, 229
  race-based, 15, 23, 106, 109–10, 115, 126, 129, 139, 144, 225
Districting criteria, formal, 100, 103–5, 110
  community of interest, 23, 37, 100, 104–5
  compactness, 30, 100, 104–5, 122, 142
  contiguity, 105, 106 n.34, 107
  equipopulous (population-based), 12–13, 30–31, 104–5, 132
  respect for subdivision boundaries, 35, 38, 100, 104–5
Dixon, Robert, 33
Douglas, Justice William, 26–27, 29 n.50, 30, 57, 82, 110, 169 n.76, 178, 201, 210 n.91, 226
Dualistic tradition of political parties, 15, 148–49, 152–54, 158, 168, 176, 183, 185–86, 225–26
  hierarchical, 149–50, 158–61, 163, 166–67, 169, 171, 174, 176–81, 184–86
  legal heritage from, 148, 154–55, 184–85
  populist, 149, 151–52, 158, 165, 168–70, 174, 176–82, 184–86, 230

Economic interests, representation of, 69–70, 72, 76–79, 81–82, 86, 88–89, 91–95, 224, 228 n.8
Economic protectionism, 61–64, 66
Electoral representation
  and accountability, 6, 8–9, 141, 174–75
  and political competition, 94, 97–103, 105, 108–11, 115, 121–22, 124–25, 128–30, 133, 138, 159, 170, 173, 225
"Equally effective" vote, 33, 35, 66, 125, 127
Equally weighted vote (numerically equal vote), 20, 23, 24 n.23, 25, 27, 31–33, 38, 114, 125, 190
  and equal political influence, 43, 49, 51–52, 55

"Fair and effective" representation, 3, 17, 27, 31, 37, 187, 222–24, 230
Federal Election Campaign Act, 88, 206
  1974 amendments, 88, 173
Federalism, 62, 65, 66, 163 n.55, 229
Fifteenth Amendment, 112–13, 129, 155 n.32
First Amendment
  establishment clause, 214
  freedom of speech, 72, 77, 88 n.86, 89–91, 94, 173, 178, 182
  right of association, 2 n.3, 59 n.83, 155–56, 162, 166, 169–70, 176, 179–81, 223
Fortas, Justice Abe, 30, 31 n.56, 34 n.68, 83, 85
Fourteenth Amendment, 118, 119 n.81, 129, 132, 155 n.32
  equal protection clause
    application of, 29, 31, 44 n.18, 52–53, 56, 62, 111, 113, 124, 131, 134–35, 136 n.148, 155, 168–69, 170 n.77, 223
    and justiciability, 22, 24, 135–36, 138
Frankfurter, Justice Felix, 24

Geographic-based districting, 20–22, 26–27
  and communities of interest, 12, 21, 24, 26, 39
  and subdivision lines, 20, 26, 36, 39
Geographic boundaries
  and geographic communities of interest, 13, 21, 23, 38, 43–44, 46, 48–49, 54, 56, 58, 65–66, 68–69, 224, 226
Gerrymander, 3, 20–21, 26, 28, 35, 39, 101–4, 111, 124–25, 133–34, 136–38, 140, 142
  "affirmative action," 107
  reverse, 129
Goldberg, Justice Arthur, 26
"Guardian" democracy, 27

Harlan, Justice John, 24, 26–27, 30–32, 35, 45, 80, 222

"Interest representation" model of administrative law, 195–97, 198 n.42, 201, 206–7, 218–19, 225, 229

Litigational political vigilance, 222–23
Local self-rule, 42, 48, 50–52, 55–56, 64–65, 118 n.76, 159, 229
  as defining "quality of community life," 40, 43, 49–51, 57–61, 63, 65–66
  as defining "stake in the community," 40, 43–44, 47–49, 60, 62, 65

Marshall, Justice Thurgood, 46, 48, 53 n.59, 82, 85 n.74, 91 n.97, 117–18, 129 n.116, 167 n.69, 169 n.76, 170–71, 175 n.98, 178, 210 n.91, 212 n.101, 214 n.114, 226
Minor parties and independent candidacies, 149, 151, 154 n.23, 157, 167–71, 173–74, 176
  and ballot access restrictions, 155, 157, 167–71, 174, 184, 186

"Natural" courts, 4
Nonretrogression standard, 116–17, 122–23, 140

O'Connor, Justice Sandra Day, 63 n.100, 64 n.106, 123 n.99, 137, 166 n.67, 170, 171 n.82, 215, 226
"One person, one vote," 1, 3–4, 7, 11–12, 14, 19–20, 23, 25–28, 32–33, 35–37, 43, 51, 53, 65, 67–69, 71–72, 79, 82, 86, 95, 97, 126, 139, 144–45, 163 n.55, 169 n.76, 226–30
  and local governments, 29–30, 43, 45–46, 80–81

Partisan electoral competition, 108, 131, 134, 157, 167, 169–72, 174 n.95, 182–184, 187, 226
Partisan gerrymandering, 27, 31, 36, 108, 134 n.138, 135–37, 141, 182–83
Partisan representation
  electoral, 149, 153, 157, 162, 167–68, 171–73, 175–77, 180, 184
  governmental, 149, 156–57, 176–77, 181–82, 184
  and interparty democracy, 149, 157, 168, 169 n.76, 170, 174, 176, 179, 182
  and intraparty democracy, 149, 151, 157, 161, 167
Party functions, 148–49, 153, 156–58, 172, 179, 181, 183, 185–87
  organizational, 148, 156–57, 160–61, 163, 165–66, 171, 176–77
Patronage practices, 156–57, 177, 179–82, 184, 186
Plaintiff "representativity," 199, 203, 209, 211, 218–19

256 / Index

Political action committees (PACs), 88–89, 94, 153–54, 157, 168, 172–77, 184, 186
Political question doctrine, 22, 24 n.20, 102, 161, 209
Poll tax, 44–45, 101
Powell, Justice Lewis, 56 n.72, 58, 84 n.67, 91–93, 118, 121 n.91, 122, 123 n.99, 129 n.116, 135, 137, 163 n.55, 165, 170, 171 n.82, 180–81, 209–12, 226
Presidential Election Campaign Fund Act, 175
Primary elections, 151, 154–56, 159, 161, 163–64, 165 n.65, 167, 184
and delegate selection, 152, 156, 159–62, 164, 184, 186
Private attorney general, 194
Private right of action, 193, 199, 206–8, 216–17
Public actions, 195–96, 199–200, 202, 208–13, 215–18, 225
Public interest, concept of, 40, 53 n.59, 61, 66, 73–74, 77, 83 n.64, 85, 103, 191, 195, 198, 217–18

Racial gerrymandering, 26, 110, 126, 128, 130, 140
and "cracking," 106
and "packing," 26, 106, 110
Racial group interests, representation of, 52, 56, 57 n.78, 59, 61, 106, 129
Referendum, 42, 51–56, 65–66, 76, 90
Rehnquist, Justice William, 36, 48, 63, 81, 84 nn.67, 68, 92, 123 n.99, 129 n.116, 137 n.155, 162 n.49, 163 n.55, 166 n.67, 170, 171 n.82, 174–75, 180 n.111, 204, 205 n.69, 214, 226
Rehnquist Court, 2, 166–67, 171, 182, 213, 229–30

Representation, definitions of
as "acting for," 5–6, 16
"adversarial," 227–29
as aggregation of interests, 20–21, 86, 227
as allocation of power, 7
as "filtering," 99–100
functional, 73–74, 82
litigational. See Litigational political vigilance
plural, 98, 110, 138, 142–44, 190, 223, 225
as proportional influence, 25, 37, 99, 105–6, 106 nn.31, 34, 107, 114, 120, 123, 128, 130, 132, 136–37, 143–45
as "standing for" (descriptive) 5–6, 14, 70, 99, 107
symbolic, 10, 70
virtual, 70, 131
Residency requirements, 44, 47, 49
"Responsible party government," 15, 147–49, 150 n.8, 156, 158, 160 n.44, 176, 183–84, 186

Size and democracy, 41–43, 99
Spatial theory of elections, 7, 12, 39, 41, 101, 142
Special district elections, 30 n.52, 72, 80–82, 86, 224
and land-based representation, 76–77, 81, 83–85, 95, 98
special purpose elections, 45, 79–80, 85
Standing to sue, 58, 190–92, 195–96, 199, 208–10, 216, 217 n.125, 219, 225, 229
Article III requirements, 196, 199–200, 202, 208–9, 211–14, 216
statutory definitions, 194, 199–201, 203, 206–8, 217
Stevens, Justice John, 48 n.39, 54 n.65, 58 n.83, 61, 84 n.67, 93, 119, 129 n.116, 133–35, 166 n.67, 171, 175 n.98, 179 n.108,

180–81, 182 n.120, 214 n.114, 226
Stewart, Justice Potter, 28, 31, 49 n.43, 51, 55, 59 n.83, 84, 85 n.72, 115, 117–19, 129 n.116, 139, 162, 163 n.55, 164–65, 178, 180, 202–3, 209 n.87, 210 n.91, 226
Suffrage restrictions, 43, 45–47, 49, 60, 62, 79

Taxonomy of representation
 heuristic/hermeneutic purpose of, 8–10, 16, 224, 227
 methodology of, 7–8, 10–11, 224–25
Tenth Amendment. *See* Federalism
"Totality of circumstances" test, 118 n.79, 120, 122–23, 126, 128

Vote dilution
 partisan, 126, 131, 134, 136, 138, 140, 142–43
 racial, 32–33, 101–2, 114–16, 124, 126, 128 n.113, 140–43
Voting Rights Act, 32, 111–14, 117, 119, 123–25, 128, 140–41
 section 5, 31–32, 112–18, 121–22, 129
 section 2, 112, 118, 120–22, 140
 and the intent standard, 113, 118–19
 and the "results test," 119–20, 122–23, 140–41

Warren, Chief Justice Earl, 26–27, 29–30, 34 n.68, 114, 139, 168 n.73
Warren Court
 doctrinal legacy of, 1–2, 13, 32, 43–45, 51, 101, 110, 113–14, 126, 155–56, 168, 187, 196, 199
 populist emphasis of, 3, 11–12, 19, 22–23, 28, 30, 33, 37, 66, 126, 208, 223 n.4, 228
White, Justice Byron, 31, 35, 37, 46, 52, 57 n.78, 85 n.74, 91, 116, 117 n.74, 120, 126, 129, 131–33, 135–36, 138–39, 169–70, 171 n.82, 175 n.98, 212 n.101, 226
"White primary," 101, 154–55, 157 n.39, 159

"Zone of interests" test, 201–2
Zoning, 56–61, 65–66, 77 n.37, 210–11